Writing in the Business Professions

Writing in the Business Professions

Edited by
Myra Kogen

Advisory Editors:
Virginia A. Book
Donald H. Cunningham
Robert D. Gieselman
Nell Ann Pickett

National Council of Teachers of English
1111 Kenyon Road, Urbana, Illinois 61801

The Association for Business Communication
University of Illinois at Urbana-Champaign
608 South Wright Street, Urbana, Illinois 61801

Executive Director, The Association for Business Communication: Robert D. Gieselman

Staff Editors: Sheila A. Ryan, David Hamburg

Book Design: Interior, Tom Kovacs for TGK Design; cover, Michael J. Getz

NCTE Stock Number 59001

Library of Congress Cataloging-in-Publication Data

Writing in the business professions / edited by Myra Kogen.
   p.   cm.
Includes bibliographies.
ISBN 0-8141-5900-1
1. Business writing. 2. English language—Business English.
3. Business writing—Study and teaching. I. Kogen, Myra, 1941-
HF5718.3.W75   1989
808'.066651—dc19   88-34615
                                                                CIP

Contents

III Teaching Professional Writing

IV Surveying Professional Writing Programs

Writing in the Business Professions

Introduction

Myra Kogen
Brooklyn College, CUNY

This book on writing in the business professions is part of a general wave of interest in an exciting new discipline usually called professional writing or business communication. Actually, this discipline is not new; it has been around since early in the century. However, recent shifts in academic interest have caused it to expand very rapidly. Now that business programs are attracting so many students, their influence is being felt throughout the curriculum. Undergraduate and graduate courses in business communication have mushroomed. New texts are continually being published. Faculty assigned to teach these courses, some for the first time, want to know more about research and methodology in the field.

All this activity has resulted in a great deal of enthusiasm, but has also raised some serious questions. On the one hand, many people are beginning to see that the discipline of professional writing can contribute much to our understanding of writing and communication in general; articles on business communication are appearing regularly in many journals. On the other hand, there has been some confusion and controversy. Some have said that the discipline's boundaries seem unclear, both in terms of subject matter and in terms of where programs are housed in the university. Others have questioned whether research in the new field is rigorous and scholarly enough.

Actually, these are not new issues; they have been with the profession from its inception and may stem directly from the intrinsic nature of business communication and its customary situation within the workplace and academia.

The Origins of Business Communication

The first course in business writing was taught at the University of Illinois in 1902, and the first college text appeared in 1916.[1] Similar courses quickly developed at other colleges, most as adjuncts to newly forming schools of commerce, where it was felt that future business leaders needed to be trained in effective writing. The courses themselves seem to have been extremely practical, emphasizing style and form in sales correspondence and report writing. Many of the most popular axioms of the field, such as the "you" attitude, concise, conversational style, and the division of business letters into types, began very early with these first courses. The Association of College Teachers of Business Writing (later called the American Business Communication Association and, recently, The Association of Business Communication) was formed in 1935 by college professors who felt that they needed an organization more relevant to their concerns than the American Marketing Association. Its *Bulletin,* first published shortly thereafter, continued to emphasize report and letter writing as well as effective teaching and curriculum planning.[2]

Interestingly, though the early courses were designed as correlates to business programs, they were frequently situated in liberal arts departments, often in English or rhetoric. There seems to have been some sense, almost from the beginning, that writing, even commercial writing, belonged in the humanities. Thus, liberal arts faculty were often drafted to teach these courses, even though many of them had no formal training in professional writing. As one early instructor, H. L. Creek, describes the situation:

> I settled down to teaching ordinary composition and literature classes at the University of Illinois. Unfortunately, somebody remembered that I had once been a stenographer, and suggested I was admirably fitted to teach classes in business letter writing. Not wishing to fail again, I took the classes. Since I knew nothing about business letters except a few things not to do, I had to learn a little more. I did this by reading the textbook — by a college professor, of course. And so I became an expert in business writing. . . . The students liked the business writing courses even as we taught them; and the heads of the English departments were glad to find anybody to do the work. I need not say that we were sometimes looked upon with a certain condescension by the "real scholars" in the Department.[3]

In these early experiences can be seen the seeds of issues that have characterized the discipline up to the present day. The subject matter of business writing was in a kind of limbo between business and the humanities. Courses were placed in a variety of homes (commerce, English, rhetoric), none of which seemed entirely appropriate or welcoming: The people who taught the courses had no formal training (there was none to be had) but were drafted from some other field (literature, business, speech, economics). These teachers, influenced by their previous training, had individual and characteristic ways of formulating curriculum and research, ways not necessarily shared or understood by others in the new field. And, overall, there was often the sense that colleagues in other fields had no way of understanding or valuing what business communication was all about.

The Discipline's Subject Matter

The field of business writing has always been intensely multidisciplinary, and this has accounted for its strength and adaptability as well as for many of its problems. The basic business writing course, undergraduate and graduate, is designed not for future writers but for those who will be writing in their roles as accountants, managers, social workers, lawyers, teachers, and so on. (In the past decade, a number of programs designed to train career writers have also been developed.) For most of these basic courses the early emphasis on practical skills has remained, with a concentration on writing as the central activity — usually from either a functional approach (model documents are categorized and studied) or a newer process approach (the composing of documents receives as much attention as end products) or an equally innovative context approach (rhetorical contexts are emphasized over letter types, usually through the use of cases).

In addition to these practical applications, courses also include important theoretical underpinnings often incorporated from other fields. For example, from psychology, sociology, and management have come theories of how communication operates within complex organizations; from speech have come ideas on communication channels and group dynamics; from reading, linguistics, and psychology have come important notions of how people absorb and integrate new material; from rhetoric and composition have come all sorts of ideas on how writers formulate and compose documents; and, most recently, from information theory have come theories on the ways in which information is transmitted in a technological society.

This multidisciplinary blend has sometimes resulted in certain conflicts and confusions. Faculty, meeting across disciplinary lines for the first time, have been known to experience each other's work as alien or even useless. For example, I remember that when I took my first look at *The Journal of Business Communication,* I felt that I had entered into foreign territory. The articles were in a form that I, with my background in English, had never seen before. Indeed, the studies seemed more like research in the social sciences than in composition or literature.

There has been some disagreement through the years over what is of true value as far as subject matter and research are concerned. Scholars with backgrounds in composition, in communication, in business and technology sometimes have difficulty in agreeing on what is meaningful and important. Conflicts are also created by the pull between those who value business communication's traditional emphasis on practical skills and those who wish to bring the field more in line with the kind of intellectual examination characteristic of modern academic scholarship. There has, in recent years, been considerable feeling that research in business communication often lacks intellectual force and rigor.[4] There has been criticism, especially, of the many surveys that characterize scholarship in the field.[5]

Along with all this, however, important changes are occurring in composition, business, communication, and the social sciences that are bringing all these fields closer together. For example, although past research in composition has often been intuitive and analytic, composition scholars are now learning the value of scientific methodology; similarly, whereas research in the social sciences has traditionally been objective and scientific, social scientists are now acknowledging the value of discovery and intuition. Unavoidably, as the field of business communication becomes more important, it will inevitably become more traditionally academic in its interests and accomplishments (if for no other reason than that status and academic respectability will demand it).[6]

The Boundaries of the Discipline

Because the subject matter of communication in the world of work is traditionally shared by a number of fields, there have been doubts about whether a bona fide discipline of business communication actually exists. There are, of course, undergraduate and graduate courses called "business communication," and even whole programs in business communication in many colleges. There are also courses in organizational communication (usually in business divisions or in speech), technical writing (in engineering or other technical divisions, or in English) and, recently, managerial communication (in business or English), in addition to courses in legal writing, medical writing, scientific writing, and so on. Some of these courses are characteristically more concerned with theory while others are more concerned with practice, but all share a particular point of view: namely, that professional communication, communication undertaken in the service of business or government or industry or the professions, is as worthy of analysis and study as is, say, expository writing, or journalism or literature.

As to whether all these various courses and programs make up one discipline or several disciplines, or, in fact, no discipline at all, there has been no final agreement. On the one hand, certain scholars argue that professional writing, having no rhetorical method of its own, is not a discipline but simply a subfield of composition. On the other hand, some have argued that professional writing is indeed a discipline since it focuses on characteristic themes and concerns and exhibits all the usual features of a discipline: namely, courses and texts, academic research, professional organizations, and scholarly journals. Others believe that professional writing is actually made up of two disciplines: business writing, which is represented by organizations such as The Association for Business Communication and journals such as *The Journal of Business Communication* and *The Bulletin of the Association for Business Communication,* and technical writing, which is represented by organizations such as the Society for Technical Communication and the Association of Teachers of Technical Writing and journals such as the *Journal of Technical Writing and Communication* and *The Technical Writing Teacher.*

The elements of what constitutes an academic discipline are subtle and complex. Although we like to believe that such things are determined by internal logic, custom and use are often more important. For example, a debate took place several years ago at a university where I was working, about whether a business communication course could be considered a liberal arts course (a debate, which because of its political implications, was being widely reflected in the literature).[7] After much arguing, it became clear that it would be as impossible to get liberal arts credit for business communication as it would be to take such credit away from courses that traditionally had it but deserved it less. In other words, in academia as in other organizations, past practice and convention are often more important than logic.

Does a discipline of professional writing exist apart from the discipline of composition? It is apparent that those working in the field believe that it does. This is probably as persuasive a justification as can be made by most disciplines that break away to form their own homes (as logical, say, as the separation of political science from history or computer science from mathematics). Whether business writing and technical writing are two disciplines or two aspects of one discipline has yet to be decided. Certainly it makes sense to envision them as one discipline since they are obviously so closely related.[8] However, the tendency until now has been as much toward separation as toward togetherness, with separate historical traditions confirmed by separate courses, texts, associations, and journals. Although many give lip service to the concept of one discipline, published articles in either one of these fields often ignore relevant research in the other field; major bibliographies often conceive of the two fields as distinctive;[9] and, perhaps most important, employers have been known to consider those experienced in one field unqualified to teach in the other.

The Purposes of This Book

This book is part of the effort to conceptualize and define the field of business communication in relation to the changes that have been occurring in academia in the past twenty years. Its purpose is to retain what is valuable from the past (the traditions, the willingness to stretch toward ideas from other disciplines) and also to move forward toward the values and methods of the future. This book is part of an expanding effort to test former ideas and givens in the field in light of what we have discovered about language and writing, especially through research in modern composition and rhetoric, but also through research in business, communication, linguistics, and the social sciences. Part of its intent is to aid business communication in becoming a respectable academic discipline, with all the strengths and weaknesses that this implies.

In this book the term *business communication* is being interpreted very broadly to encompass all aspects of professional writing, including organizational communication, managerial communication, legal and other career writing, and even technical writing. The word *business* in the title is also being used very broadly to signify any working situation, whether corporate, governmental, professional, or industrial. Although perhaps controversial, it seems particularly important to include academia within these contexts because academicians, in particular, are often unaware that professional writing is part of what they do.

The book is divided into four sections, all involved with both theoretical and practical concerns. Advisory editors Virginia Book,

Donald Cunningham, Robert Gieselman, and Nell Ann Pickett have aided in the planning and processing of these sections. The articles in the first section, "Process in Professional Writing," attempt to define the special circumstances and characteristics of professional writing. Linda Flower, drawing upon her research in cognitive psychology, describes the complex ways in which professional writers create documents. Jack Selzer, by looking closely at how business prose is organized, adds to our knowledge of the characteristics of professional writing and also challenges some long-held assumptions. Edward P. J. Corbett, by placing professional writing within the tradition of classical rhetoric, describes the particular importance of the relationship between writer and audience. Barbara Couture and Jone Rymer describe what their study, the Professional Writing Project, reveals about collaborative writing in the workplace.

The articles in the second section, "Writing in Corporations, Government, the Law, and Academia," describe the particular characteristics and conventions of writing in several major fields. Janice Redish, using research undertaken at the Document Design Center, analyzes why professional writing in government and other large organizations is often unreadable. Linda Driskill discusses how context and culture affect corporate communication. George Gopen describes the state of legal writing: its peculiarities, strengths, and constraints. And Dan Dieterich, using his work with faculty and administrators, shows how academic writing exhibits all the features, good and bad, of other types of professional writing.

The articles in the third section of the book, "Teaching Professional Writing," suggest how new theories and methods affect pedagogy. John DiGaetani, in describing the case method used at Harvard, analyzes how case studies can improve the teaching of professional writing. David Lauerman shows how the use of a new kind of field research aided in the creation of a business communication course that reflects the complexities of actual writing situations. Brian Gallagher evaluates the ways in which business communication texts define the professional writing curriculum. And C. H. Knoblauch, asserting that textbooks, research, and courses have often ignored the realities of the workplace, draws some important implications for teaching.

The fourth section, "Surveying Professional Writing Programs," describes how business communication is currently categorized and defined by colleges and universities. Mary Munter delineates what is actually being taught in courses in business and management communication. And John Brereton shows how professional writing programs, properly constituted, can meet the growing needs of English departments and students.

On the whole, then, *Writing in the Business Professions* attempts to describe a growing and changing discipline — its research, theory, and pedagogy — for an expanding pool of academicians who are becoming involved in its courses and scholarship. Such a description, it would seem, is particularly important at a time when the profession is seeking to understand and agree upon its station and its aims.

Notes

1. This description of the origins of business communication is based on Fran W. Weeks, "The Teaching of Business Writing at the Collegiate Level, 1900–1920," in *Studies in the History of Business Writing*, ed. George H. Douglas and Herbert W. Hildebrandt (Urbana, Ill.: The Association for Business Communication, 1985), 201–215.

2. For more information on the founding of the American Business Communication Association see Clyde W. Wilkinson, "ABWA and ABCA: The Growth of an Organization," *The ABCA Bulletin* 47 (December 1984): 24–28.

3. H. L. Creek, "How I Became an Expert in Business English," *The ABWA Bulletin* 17 (October 1952): 5–7. Also quoted by Fran Weeks in *Studies in the History of Business Writing*.

4. For more on these matters see Philip V. Lewis, "ABCA Research Respectability and Credibility," *The Journal of Business Communication* 20 (Fall 1983): 5–12; and in the same issue, "Improving the Publications of ABCA: A Panel Discussion," 13–27. See also Carter A. Daniel, "Remembering Our Charter: Business Communication at the Crossroads," *The Journal of Business Communication* 20 (Summer 1983): 3–11; and "Responses to Carter A. Daniel's Article," *The Journal of Business Communication* 21 (Summer 1984): 17–32.

5. One major reason for the proliferation of surveys, I think, is that people in such a fluid discipline feel the need to know what is being taught, how it is being taught, where it is being taught, and so on. See, for example, Larry Smeltzer, "An Analysis of Communication Course Content for MBA Students," *The ABCA Bulletin* 47 (September 1984): 28–33; Carol David, "Report on Standards for a Business Communication Composition Course: Results of a Survey," *The ABCA Bulletin* 45 (March 1982): 21–29; and Jean Dorrell and Betty Johnson, "A Comparative Analysis of Topics Covered in Twenty College-Level Communication Textbooks," *The ABCA Bulletin* 45 (September 1982): 11–16.

6. Two fine collections with excellent scholarly articles are Paul V. Anderson, R. John Brockmann, and Carolyn Miller, *New Essays in Technical and Scientific Communication: Research, Theory, Practice* (Farmingdale, N.Y.: Baywood, 1983); and Lee Odell and Dixie Goswami, *Writing in Nonacademic Settings* (New York: Guilford Press, 1985).

7. For discussions of this important issue see Elizabeth Harris, "In Defense of the Liberal-Arts Approach to Technical Writing," *College English* 44 (1982): 628–36; Arthur L. Ford, "Technical Writing and the Liberal Arts School," *Journal of Technical Writing and Communication* 9 (1979): 173–83; and Carolyn R. Miller, "A Humanistic Rationale for Technical Writing," *College English* 40 (1979): 610–17.

8. See the recently published *Iowa State Journal of Business and Technical Communication* for one journal that reflects this point of view.

9. See, for example, Mary Ann Bowman and Joan D. Stamas, *Written Communication in Business: A Selective Bibliography, 1967–1977,* (Urbana, Ill.: The Association for Business Communication, 1980); and Sarojini Balachandran, *Technical Writing: A Bibliography* (Urbana and Washington: The Association for Business Communication and the Society for Technical Communication, 1977).

I Process
in Professional Writing

1 Rhetorical Problem Solving: Cognition and Professional Writing

Linda Flower
Carnegie-Mellon University

What Does a Professional Need to Know?

When my father went to college in Chicago during the 1930s, business writing was taught as the art of writing elegant and persuasive sales letters. But as he and modern surveys observed, much of that work is now carried on over the phone. The sales letter, like the five-paragraph theme in freshman composition, looks a bit antiquated and seems to have lost its claim as the archetypal business writing task, the task we assume will "transfer" to all others. The field of business seems too large to reduce to a single genre. Even the ubiquitous "memo" is more a format than a rhetorical genre. And compared to the old-time sales letter, which required the mastery of popular psychology, rhetorical moves, and vivid style, the memo is an impoverished genre at that. But if these standard genres are an inadequate basis for a course of instruction, what then should we teach to novice business and professional writers? What is the knowledge most worth having?

What Should We Teach and Can We Do So?

The question, "What should a business and professional writing course teach?" is often raised quite suddenly for English teachers who may have spent little time thinking about this subject in graduate school. A dean or department head suddenly realizes that "we need to offer a business writing course, and you are the best person to design it." Even ten years ago this task might have been easier, if one had been happy with the standard style and format approach to business writing. But the writing-across-the-curriculum movement has further expanded our vision of what writing outside the English class involves and of the way writing is stubbornly embedded in a rhetorical situation and

3

a larger discourse community. Our clientele in business writing courses represents (future) professionals and business people for whom writing is a way to succeed at their work. It seems a little short-sighted to require an engineer to master the "complaint letter answer" (a task one sees in many textbooks) or to ask the future accountant to perfect a process description of a gear train assembly. The task of teaching professionals (in business, engineering, design, computer science, accounting, and so on) raises a fundamental question: *Can we teach the knowledge that these writers really need?*

A look at the current debate on this question suggests that there are at least four rival answers:

1. One familiar answer is that we can't and, indeed, shouldn't try. English classes should return to teaching the canon, or should at least stay with personal and/or academic writing, and leave professional writing to the disciplines and on-the-job learning where it belongs. For different reasons, this position is also held in professional writing circles by people who are acutely aware of the job-specific know-how and interpersonal savvy that often make business communications work. Learning to communicate in business, they observe, comes from learning the ropes — and that knowledge isn't found in classes or books.

2. A second answer assumes, more optimistically, that we can do something useful; but because good writing is ultimately a matter of talent or experience, all we can really teach are the forms and conventions of discourse. Hence, we find courses that are the analogs of traditional freshman English, focused on grammar, style, and forms. The literary and personal essay, for example, is replaced with the memo, the process description, and the claim letter.

3. A third, more ambitious answer claims that we *can* teach the knowledge worth having, but, in the spirit of the writing-across-the-curriculum movement, it must be highly discipline-specific. Students must learn to think and write in the idiom of their discipline or at least must learn to handle the discourse conventions of their field.[1] There have been some exemplary programs under the writing-across-the-curriculum banner, and many schools have a tradition of a few upper-level, team-taught courses that combine disciplinary projects and writing. On a larger scale, this approach is sometimes difficult for people trained in English to take with confidence, and there is some tendency to end up teaching formulas: to concentrate on the formats of the discipline rather than on its underlying intellectual maneuvers.

4. A fourth answer asserts that some of the most worthwhile knowledge rests within our own discipline and that we can teach rhetorical knowledge and principles of rhetorical problem solving that transfer across different writing tasks. This approach acknowledges the importance of discourse conventions but concentrates on broader rhetorical strategies for analyzing the audience, planning, revising, and managing one's time and writing process.

This is obviously not a new debate. The positions are familiar from the debate on freshman composition that Richard Young described in "Arts, Crafts, Gifts and Knacks."[2] According to Young, the "current-traditional paradigm" in writing instruction (reflected in answers 1 and 2 here) is an outgrowth of neoromantic assumptions that writing is a talent, a gift that cannot be taught. Since that assumption might leave a great many English teachers unemployed, the current-traditional paradigm does not throw in the towel altogether, but sensibly shifts its attention to what it feels can be taught: mechanics and style. In essence, freshman composition as an institution found a way to hold on to its neoromantic assumptions, but manages to avoid the consequences of answer 1 and still keep teaching.

Answers 3 and 4 are trying to play a different game. To take those positions, one must assume there is a coherent intellectual base to composition teaching — something beyond knack, talent, and experience. Writing instruction can teach the art of writing in the classical sense of an art because it is based on a substantive body of knowledge about rhetorical principles and strategies, about underlying discourse conventions (beyond format), and about one's own writing process. Rhetorical and discourse knowledge is typically harder to learn than mechanics, format, and style; it stretches the mind, just as physics, economics, and programming do.

The debate separating answers 3 and 4 is whether this knowledge needs to be taught in a discipline-specific context in order to be useful. Clearly you must learn to "think like a physicist" in order to do physics (learning formulas will only get you through an exam). But is "writing like a physicist" a special art (assuming you can think like one to get your work done)? Or can future bankers, graphic designers, and administrators be taught more general rhetorical strategies which *they* adapt to new situations after college and to the specific conventions and typical strategies of their discourse community? In other words, how general can our art be and still be practical?

These are difficult questions to answer. Yet, it is hard to design a coherent course without taking some sort of stand, since these different answers dictate important decisions: how you spend teaching time (focusing on practice or actively teaching strategies and conventions); what model texts you choose (selecting examples or format or exemplars of rhetorical problems); and what criteria you use (requiring the mastery of correctness, of a plain style, of conventions, or of rhetorical effectiveness).

Although my personal bias clearly rests with answers 3 and 4, we must, indeed, value each of these different sorts of knowledge, whether it is business savvy, imagination, or rhetorical awareness. To educate is to make a decision about the knowledge students need most. And that suggests that we might do well to look at the writers themselves.

The Knowledge Behind Performance

The debate in English studies has focused on what to teach and how to design courses. In cognitive psychology and in educational research, a debate closely parallel to this one is being conducted about knowledge and performance. Modern cognitive psychology has tended to focus its attention on the nature of knowledge itself and the process of using it: What do experts know? What do novices in an area typically know and need to learn? How is the knowledge of both groups organized? What knowledge and/or process seems best to account for differences in performance? A cognitive perspective might frame the question this way: "What knowledge does a writer call upon to create a rhetorically effective writing plan, to write like an expert in his or her profession?" The research we will look at suggests three plausible answers:

1. Experts rely on their knowledge of schemas.
2. Experts rely on the structure of their topic knowledge.
3. Experts rely on the constructive process of rhetorical problem solving.

How Do Writers Construct "Expert" Writing Plans?

1. The first answer to our question is the one implicitly supplied by any traditional business writing text: Expert writers can draw on ready-made plans supplied by genre, conventions, or schemas for the texts they are writing. Current research on how people use genre knowledge to comprehend stories helps explain how this process might work. For example, children learn elementary story grammar by the time they are three or four years old. They use their knowledge (which predicts that anything called a "story" will have an actor, an action, a goal, conflict, and resolution, etc.) to produce their own "gram-

matical," if bizarre, stories. If you have a mental schema about what to expect at a birthday party[3] or a script for eating at a restaurant,[4] your recall of the event will not only be richer and faster, it will be more accurate (as long as the event conforms to your schema). As this research shows, knowledge of conventions and schemas has generative power; it allows people to reconstruct information that should be there (even if it wasn't). Having such slots waiting to be filled will be an obvious advantage to the writer. For example, Schumacher, Klare, and Scott's studies of professional journalists writing obituaries (a schema in which journalism students are drilled) found that planning time for these genre experts was reduced to short bursts of apparently local, what-to-say-next planning.[5] The bottom line, we were told, is that no matter how famous you become, a good journalist will be able to write your obit for *The New York Times* in twenty minutes flat.

The power of genre knowledge is impressive. The military has come to rely heavily on this approach to planning in developing what are called Fully Proceduralized Instructions. This genre calls for the writer to specify every object and every step that occurs in the performance of some technical task. Likewise, traditional technical writing instruction has often viewed itself as a teacher of formulas and conventions.

However, this research leaves us with an important question: If the task is to produce a significant piece of writing, how much of the planner's work is done by these skeletons provided by conventions? If the task is the writing of Fully Proceduralized Instructions, a child's narrative, or even a news story (who, what, when, where, why), these conventions appear to do a great deal of the work for the writer. But for many adult texts, with their more complex goals and greater information load, these skeletal plans offer the writer only an abstract frame and limited information about the contents of an optimal plan. Discourse conventions and schemas are valuable, but limited, guides when the writer must construct an expert plan.

2. A second answer to our question, "How do writers construct plans?" is that they draw on extensive topic knowledge. Topic knowledge carries very important information about how to conceive, categorize, and talk about a topic. For example, one landmark study on the role of topic knowledge asked people with high topic knowledge and people with low topic knowledge about baseball to read and recall an account of a particular game.[6] People with low knowledge didn't know what details to attend to (e.g., they remembered players' names but not the key plays), and they didn't recognize the implications of major events (e.g., that certain hits were important because they advanced base runners). The baseball cognoscenti, on the other hand,

could select what details to remember and would then reconstruct an entire play by drawing inferences from those salient facts.

This study suggests that writers with high topic knowledge might have some of the following advantages in developing a writing plan: First, they could *select* the important information from the "noise." They could then *keep* this relevant information in short-term memory (or focal attention) while they observed, read, or thought about the topic. Finally, they could *relate* observed actions to the goal behind those actions (e.g., they would be able to infer why something happened). These advantages, it appears, affect not only the focus and organization of ideas on paper, but the processes of thinking and writing as well.

There is, however, another side of this picture. Topic knowledge can offer a ready-made plan for organizing discourse, but what if that plan does not fit the assignment well? Langer found that high school history students whose knowledge of a topic had a loose, associative structure did well on "write about" assignments.[7] But on exam questions or assignments that asked them to apply their knowledge, this associative structure was a handicap compared to the hierarchically organized knowledge other students were shown to possess. Students with the loose, associative body of ideas either did poorly on these assignments or simply ignored them and produced a "write about" essay anyway. Note that in the Langer study the structure one already possessed dictated the structure of the text — even when it was inappropriate. Clearly, the next step in writing like an expert is learning to restructure one's knowledge when the task calls for such cognitive effort.

Business and professional writing is full of situations in which topic knowledge is simply not enough to produce good writing. For example, subject matter experts in technical fields are notoriously poor at explaining their knowledge to novices. High-tech companies often entrust their instructional writing to people who know the equipment, only to find that they can't write about it.

Why does topic knowledge fail? One reason may be that these writers are unwilling or unable to simulate the response of a reader other than themselves. In one study, Bond asked lawyers to revise an impenetrable piece of federal regulation prose so it could be understood by lay readers.[8] (As one lawyer said of this piece, "The sentences are long enough to choke a horse.") However, some of the lawyer readers simply could not detect any problems with the text — even when we politely asked them to try again. They could not or would not imagine the interpretive process and response of their readers.

Another reason topic knowledge may fail to produce a good plan is that the structure of the writer's knowledge may not approximate the structure of the reader's knowledge, or that structure which the reader needs.[9] Kern diagnosed this misfit as one of the major problems with writing for the military.[10] The manuals they studied offered the trainee topic-based information, such as a description of the various parts of a tank and a discussion of the nature of combustion. The trainee, however, needed a performance-based discussion organized around the actions he was expected to perform. The performance-based revision of the tank passage, for instance, told the gunner and the driver what each needed to do (locating all the relevant information for each reader in a single spot instead of letting it trickle out as the text explored the tank). And the quasitechnical passage on combustion was replaced with a graphically arresting statement that came to the real point of the passage: Don't put oily rags in cans.

The manuals Kern surveyed were not necessarily poorly written in a formal sense; they were poorly designed for readers. The writers' topic knowledge of the technology was not enough to produce a good writing plan. My own work with business writers may help explain the source of the problem. The reports supervisors often complain about and the drafts written by my business students were often organized as narratives focused on the discovery process of the writer or as a descriptive memory dump of what the writer knew or observed.[11] I labeled this strategy as "writer-based" prose for two reasons. One was that it was not organized around what the reader needed, which was usually a concise analysis organized around a problem, an issue, or a decision the reader needed to make. However, this writer-based prose was not an accident. It reflected the organization of knowledge in the writer's thinking or memory and it represented a very efficient way for the writer to retrieve information. A writer-based recitation of topic knowledge can serve the writer well, as long as it is a strategy for invention, not a plan for the text. When topic knowledge isn't an adequate blueprint for a reader-based text (and this seems to be the case more often than not), expert writers must turn to our third source of expert plans: the construction of a plan.

When topic and genre knowledge aren't adequate, writers rise to rhetorical problem solving: it is a more expensive, effortful cognitive process, but it is also more powerful and flexible. In turning to constructive planning, writers generate a network of goals — they explore the problem before them; they develop goals and subgoals; they notice constraints or conflicts in their tentative plan; and they replan and rethink goals as they work on the problem.

If writers in general, then, draw on these three kinds of knowledge, what does the task of writing in the business profession require? What knowledge, if we could teach it, would have the most visible effect on our students' performance?

Rising To the Occasion: The Role of Rhetorical Problem Solving

Some writing tasks can be handled by either topic knowledge or knowledge of conventions and schemas. Those tasks may even account for fifty percent of the writing a person does; after all, practice and experience should confer some benefits. However, in my experience both as a consultant and as a professional who writes, there are at least two situations that this knowledge doesn't handle. One is the process of learning to do a new task. I now have a schema for writing letters of recommendation that does at least some of the work for me. I know some conventions for establishing credibility and objectivity; I have a set of goals I normally try to accomplish, such as tying my comments to the strengths I know the candidate is trying to argue for, too. But my first such letter, not to mention the second and third, forced me to turn in some anxiety to first principles, to worry over what should be in such a letter, to infer the rhetorical moves behind the examples I had seen, and to test my plan and prose by trying to role-play a reader. Learners often have to build from the ground up when they meet a new task. Since we cannot hope to teach our students the conventions for the enormous variety of minor genres they will meet, they need to have some first principles to build upon when they encounter new tasks.

A second situation that requires rhetorical problem solving is the task that may come only once a week or once a year, but is the significant piece of writing which has to work (not just sit in a file to confirm a phone call) and by which the writer is often judged. These significant writing tasks fall to new trainees and old hands alike. It is this writing that causes writers the most difficulty (and anxiety), and it is this writing that the managers as audience are most likely to read, to care about, and to complain about. Under these circumstances the quality of one's business writing makes a difference. To make it clear that these instances of significant writing are not mere special cases, here are some typical examples from my experience in which the writing task called for rhetorical problem solving:

1. For many bank trainees, even those with MBAs, a typical entry-level position is in the credit department where the trainee's main job is to *write* a credit analysis. The trainee sifts through a mound of

information and, then, unsure of what to select or eager to show the evidence of industrious homework, writes a twelve-page descriptive essay on the prospective client. The credit managers (who also evaluate this new trainee) are regularly annoyed by this: In order to carry out their job, they want a three-page analysis — focused on the relevant information — that can support a decision. The managers read this analysis in order to act, but the writers fail to respond to this rhetorical situation.

2. The company I was working for had just reorganized its department into independent profit centers, so all of the managers had to write budget justifications and projections for the year to come. The company accountants who had to compile this information couldn't get the managers to comply; it was starting to look like a standoff. In a seminar on writing in the company, which included both the accountants and a number of the managers, we happened to look at the memo that had requested all this information from the managers, as an example of current writing. It became suddenly clear that the accountants had ignored their readers, many of whom simply did not know how to make such a projection, didn't know what records to keep, and didn't know what information the accountants really needed. And they weren't going to ask. For the company accountants to solve their own financial planning (i.e., getting information), they had to design their memo so that the readers could solve their own problem of how to respond. The original memo was accurate and conventionally appropriate, but was a rhetorical failure for at least a third of the readers in that room.

3. In college, graphic designers develop both creative and technical abilities. They learn to solve design problems for commercial clients who want a distinctive product image or for subway systems that need signs that work. But the surprise for many designers, with their trained "eye" for what works, is that their clients don't always have such an "eye," and the designer must depend on words to propose a plan that will win a contract, or to justify an innovative design. Writing can be a necessary professional skill that supports and interprets a visual design. Unfortunately, technical skill as a designer is not adequate preparation for the verbal, rhetorical task of showing a client how this design solves his practical problems.

4. Engineers I met at a major research and development center spent most of their time in the lab or at the computer, and their technical reports reflected this. They wrote conventional technical reports of the sort published in journals: concise and technically

detailed. As the manager said, the writers were most happy when they could plot three results on the same graph, though this tended to make the graph unreadable to outsiders. The problem: This R. & D. Center had to earn its way. It was evaluated by the extent to which engineers in the field found these reports useful and adopted the lab's recommendations. And most of these concise, conventional, but unreadable reports were gathering dust out in field office shelves around the country. To make matters worse, although this manager was critical of his staff, he was also rather unwilling to share his sense of what the field offices needed with the engineers — that knowledge was a part of his power as the liaison. So to succeed in that office and escape his red pen, writers had to figure out a great deal about these reports for themselves.

5. In a sense, the rhetorical problem in the previous example turns up with any technical report. The reports I write with my colleagues as a result of a research grant may have a distribution list of one hundred people. Some of those people are also doing writing research (and are easy folks to write to); some are interested in the problem, but from a variety of backgrounds (English, psychology, linguistics) or for different reasons (teaching, modeling cognitive process, designing computer-aided instruction programs); and some readers, connected with the National Science Foundation, for instance, come with even broader and harder-to-predict concerns. Yet writing effectively for multiple audiences is a basic problem many professionals who write face every day. In this situation, neither topic knowledge nor schemas are adequate without rhetorical problem solving.

6. Fifteen or twenty years ago, most computer documentation was written for a small circle of experts who had the know-how and willingness to learn a new system through experimenting with it. Programmers didn't have to be writers. But as first-time users are starting to flood the market, the computer industry is finding that the quality of its documentation can have a big impact on sales. Good writing means the manual can pass a particularly rigorous test — it can *work* for the user. Similarly, because the army, navy, and air force constitute one of the nation's largest postsecondary educators, they must design instructional texts and maintenance manuals that will let enlisted men and women use and maintain the high technology equipment of aircraft, submarines, and computers. Explaining new technology has become both a profession (for those who see themselves as technical "writers") and a part of one's professional work (for those who see themselves as "technologists"). If the vigorous job market for

such professional writers and the popular opinion of the quality of current technical instructional writing is any indication, this is not a skill subject-matter experts just naturally acquire.

7. Finally, to bring the demand for rhetorical problem solving closer to home, we only need look at the budget justifications, long-term reports, and year-end statements that our own deans and department heads make as college or university administrators, or at the yearly progress reports and the tenure and promotion statements that we as faculty make. Like the trainees on their first job in the credit analysis office, we as professionals depend on writing to work for us, and we may put in considerable effort getting it to do so.

Designing Rhetorically Sophisticated Courses in Professional Writing

In this discussion so far, we have looked at the debate over what we should teach, at research on the knowledge and cognitive processes of writers, and at some of the tasks they face. I would like to pull these strands — our teaching, the writer's knowledge and cognition, and the professional task — together to help answer the following questions: How might we design a cognitively sophisticated course in business and professional writing? How can we actively teach the knowledge (and thinking processes) our students will need for significant writing tasks? Let me suggest three guidelines in this enterprise and then look in more detail at what we might teach.

1. Recognize the Different Kinds of Knowledge Writers Need

Writers, I would suggest, need to operate with at least four levels of knowing. I choose the word "knowing" to suggest that a writer's knowledge goes beyond having statable "knowledge about" something. It includes procedural knowledge — knowing "how to" manage one's own thinking process. We often talk of such knowing as a capacity (e.g., to imagine a reader's response) or as an ability (e.g., to plan) or as a higher-level skill (e.g., in testing and evaluating a text).

The first level is topic knowledge, a necessary but not sufficient condition for writing. The second level is discourse knowledge. One needs to know the conventions of writing in general and of the discourse-specific moves one can make in a given genre or kind of discourse. The third is rhetorical problem solving, which involves a repertory of strategies for the task of writing itself — for exploring the rhetorical problem, for generating ideas, for adapting to the reader, and for understanding and monitoring one's own writing process. The fourth level, which I will return to at the end of this paper, is metaknowledge — knowing what you know. Because there are no simple rules for managing rhetorical problem solving, expert writers often depend on meta-awareness of their own strategies and options. This knowledge is what lets writers rise above individual tasks, review their options, and consider what they *might* do in the face of their new problem. It lets writers manage their own composing process.

Writers who work with the first level of knowledge have little recourse when they encounter a new task or need to adapt their knowledge to a reader's need. Writers who work primarily at the level of discourse conventions may indeed have a good deal of knowledge about writing, but may use that knowledge only when the context says to (e.g., revising is a strategy one uses in English class). Writers who are able to move to rhetorical problem solving have learned to explore that task itself and to use knowledge about topic, the genre, and about writing strategies to meet the goals they set. Finally, writers who can rise to meta-awareness of their knowledge and process not only expand their options in the face of any given problem, but also learn the most from experience and from our classes.

2. Teach for the Significant Tasks

I don't want to overstate the case for rhetorical problem solving. There is no point in assuming that it is always necessary, any more than we should assume that a clear, explicit, plain prose style is always best — even though we value it and write textbooks on how to achieve it. In fact, jargon and even vagueness, fustian, and indirection have their place in the real world. Part of the savvy that experience brings is knowing when not to say anything. Likewise, a fair amount of the writing people do is an everyday affair for which knowing the genre or having the right facts to relate offers a ready-made, quite acceptable plan.

On the other hand, we don't bother to teach padded, indirect prose; people seem to pick it up quite well by themselves. We teach those more difficult-to-learn skills that writers need for the more significant tasks. Rhetorical problem solving calls for knowledge and skill. In using the word "skill," I want to emphasize that we are talking about intellectual skills, about acts of cognition that are typically carried out with some effort and development through practice. Such knowledge can give a practical, yet substantive, intellectual base to a college-level course. And unlike savvy, it is also teachable. It helps students learn to control their own process of writing when topic knowledge or prior schemas won't carry them through.

3. Teach from Our Special Strength

When we include rhetorical problem solving in our curriculum we are teaching from our greatest strength. As English teachers we are obviously experts in writing — not in accounting or engineering or in the inside dynamics of sales offices, or in the discourse moves of middle management negotiation. Moreover, if our goal is serious substantive teaching, we could never deal in depth with the conventions of all those discourse communities even if we knew them.

The positive side of this issue is even more important. There is a long tradition in rhetoric underlying the teaching of composition. This perspective on writing as both discovery and communication informs current research in the writing process as well. Our teaching can (and I believe should) be based on a substantive body of discipline-specific knowledge.[12] This, in addition to our training in how language works and in being perceptive readers and interpreters of both expert and student texts, gives us a body of *knowledge* about rhetorical choices and a *language* for articulating those choices that is our distinctive disciplinary strength. Furthermore, if writing classes don't help students develop this combination of awareness and substantive knowledge about their own writing process, about the effects of language, and about dealing with rhetorical problems — if writing classes don't teach this — what other part of a university or on-the-job training will?

The Practice of Rhetorical Problem Solving

Knowing that our students will need to do rhetorical problem solving is one thing; teaching it is another. Once again we find ourselves making decisions about what aspects of this process are most worth teaching. The following case study of a small company in Kansas City lets us follow the problem-solving path a group of writers took through a real rhetorical problem. It illustrates three key points along the path at which writers typically rise to rhetorical problem solving: (1) in exploring the rhetorical problem (especially at the outset); (2) in creating a plan; and (3) in reviewing and testing both plans and text. After looking at how these three problem-solving processes operated in their real-world context, I would like to look more closely at each as a cognitive or intellectual process and ask the questions: What would the expert's path through this process look like? Would it differ from the path a less experienced writer or learner might take?

Exploring a Rhetorical Problem

In business and professions, problematic situations turn up with great regularity. However, people do not solve situations; they solve only that problem which they have defined for themselves, within that situation. In the case we will follow, the rhetorical situation was complex, but what mattered was how the writers explored and defined the problem they would then attempt to solve.

Twentieth Century Investors is a small but well-established mutual fund company that makes its money by investing the accumulated capital of many smaller investors in the stock and bond market. Investors in mutual funds, who range from individuals with nest eggs to companies and institutions investing their entire pension plans, get the price advantage of large purchases and the benefit of professional management to select and buy and sell stock as needed. But investing is not predictable, and in early 1984 the economy had not been stable. The stock market had taken a series of dives and Twentieth Century's earnings had gone with it. During the last six-month period, its largest fund, called GROWTH, had declined in value by 13.9 percent. Nevertheless, it was time for a Semiannual Report that is required by the Federal Securities Commission and mailed to all shareholders.

How might we represent the rhetorical problem this situation posed? Herbert Simon has described such a situation as a problem space, using as an example the problem of choosing a move in a chess game.[13] The theoretical problem space of any given problem contains all the goals and constraints one might consider, all the possible moves or actions one could take at that point, and all the possible solutions or outcomes one could achieve.

The problem space of most rhetorical problems is very large indeed. However, the space (i.e., the information) which counts is that which writers represent to themselves. Novices, it appears, often cut short the exploration process, and in doing so, define smaller problems than do experts. The task they give themselves is more manageable, but it may overlook possible solutions and it may ignore some crucial constraints. For example, we could imagine a problem space for the Twentieth Century Semiannual Report problem that contained little more than the assignment (Figure 1).

The assignment here, like those for school tasks, offers only a skimpy version of the problem. Writing, especially significant writing, goes on in a social context in which writers have goals and readers have certain needs and possible responses. One of the key actors in this particular rhetorical situation was the shareholder. During this period of economic

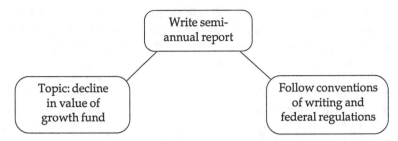

Fig. 1. A problem space defined by the assignment.

instability, shareholders were especially likely to be concerned about earnings, to read the report, and to use it to make decisions about future investments. Twentieth Century had, in fact, recently introduced two new funds to which it wanted to attract investors. But because they had been introduced in November, at the beginning of the current decline, they showed losses in value of 14.2 percent and 20.4 percent. The goals and expectations of the primary actors in this rhetorical situation did not appear to be in sync.

This rhetorical problem had another dimension. People who read investment reports belong to a discourse community that expects certain things. Nevertheless, there are some important differences within that community. Some readers are accountants with institutions that invested in the fund — people trained to read figures, analyze financial statements, and evaluate the long-term success of a fund. Others are small investors who read the synopsis at the front of the report and look for the bottom line — the percent of growth or loss over the current period. This was an important part of the problem because Twentieth Century estimated that nearly half its clients were small shareholders with investments of less than $25,000. And these shareholders had been indicating that they wanted more communication from the company. However, Twentieth Century was a small company and a "no-load" fund. This meant that it didn't charge the 8 percent fee on all purchases that the "load" funds did; it didn't maintain a large sales staff, and it didn't even have a public relations office. A big ad campaign to offset weak returns was not the way it did business.

When it came time to write the Semiannual Report, these goals, constraints, and features of the readers were all part of the rhetorical problem, as James Stowers, president of the company, and his investment team saw it. They had already given themselves a rich problem that went well beyond a formal task (writing a financial report) and beyond the apparent content they had to report. However, it was when one additional dimension was added to this problem space that the whole nature of the writing task changed.

Most people might have defined the rhetorical problem as one that deals with an awkward failure. Stowers and the investment team defined it, surprisingly, as how to deal with success. For twenty-seven years Twentieth Century had been a small no-load fund, chugging along with little or no marketing and low visibility, but maintaining a solid, steady performance. As the company put it, Kansas City is not the center of the fund industry. Moreover, it was strongly committed to an investment policy geared to long-term return — to keeping its assets fully invested and not trying to predict the short-term dips and jumps of the market. Then suddenly, in the next five years, this little company in Kansas City had blossomed into a highly competitive fund. It was on the front page of *Money* magazine and celebrated in *Forbes* and *Fortune*. As a result, many new investors, who had just become aware of mutual funds, had joined when the market was at a peak. They had become used to a steady diet of good news and returns.

But many did not understand how the market operates; they expected the fireworks to last. So the problem, as Stowers saw it, was how to deal with explosive growth and success. How do you deal with a fundamental conflict between the expectations of some of your investors and the realities of investing, especially given your philosophy of picking investments for their long-term potential rather than for their prospects for the next six months? The problem, as Twentieth Century saw it, involved fundamental conflicts between the company's and (some of) the readers' perceptions. This conflict, like the results it had to report and the federal regulations mandating how the company did it, was a part of the report writers' task — a part of the goals and constraints they had to work with.

The problem space (Figure 2) is, of course, only a partial record of the information, goals, and constraints these writers actually considered. But even this sketch makes one point clear: This rhetorical problem is a construction. A sense of the problem based merely on genre knowledge or content knowledge would never have produced this picture of the writers' task. In "considering their audience" for instance, these writers did not merely survey the obvious. For good or ill, they selected or imagined certain features of those readers that came into conflict with their own goals. Such rhetorical problems are made, not found. (We will study their solution later.)

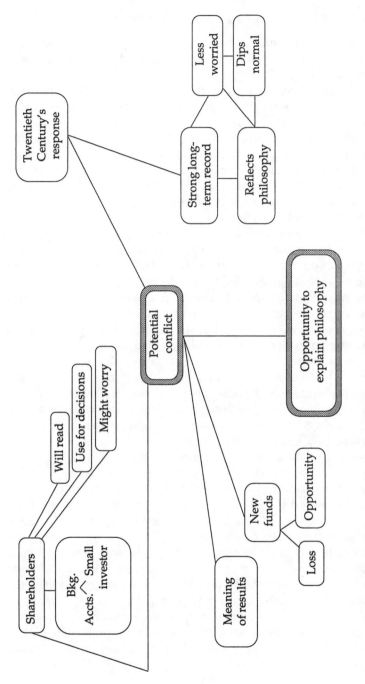

Fig. 2. A problem space constructed by exploring the rhetorical problem.

The Expert's Path in Exploring Rhetorical Problems

Once described, the problem sketched above may seem commonplace enough. The problem definition doesn't depend on expert topic or discourse knowledge. The expertise it illustrates lies in the act of going beyond the assignment to explore and construct a specifically rhetorical problem. Yet it appears that this process is one that inexperienced writers often fail to use and which we may need to teach. The reasons for this neglect are easy to see. In school writing the social, rhetorical context is often buried and the student is used to dealing with assignments, not problems. When the writer enters a new discourse community (whether it is our class or a job in banking) the writing strategies learned in school may persist. Many times the savvy and sophistication people develop in personal relations on the job fail to transfer to the task of writing. When the writer sits down to compose, his or her old assignment-driven strategies for producing text leave no room in the writing for rhetorical problem solving. Moreover, as researchers such as Lee Odell,[14] Jack Selzer (in this volume), and Caroline Miller[15] point out, this process is a substantial cognitive act that calls for inferences, hypotheses, and critical thinking. Constructing a rhetorical problem, like any high-level cognitive act, calls for a bit of work. Our textbooks, on the other hand, tend to suggest that general awareness of the reader and a spot of empathy will see you through.

What might an expert path through problem exploration look like? Complex processes don't have simple rules, and we have a lot to learn about how people manage such cognition. However, some provocative insights into how this process works come from studies of the paths experts take in different domains.

Voss and his colleagues,[16] for example, asked a number of social scientists, students, and chemists to place themselves in the following administrative position: "You are the new Soviet Minister of Agriculture. Agricultural production has been low for the past five years. How would you improve it?" The striking feature of the experts' process was the large proportion of time and attention devoted to developing a representation of the problem. Unlike the novices, who isolated a few possible causes and then began to list solutions, the experts searched out constraints in the problem, such as Soviet ideology, the outcome of past efforts, the effects of climate, and the amount of arable land. Moreover, in considering possible solutions, the experts continued to dig out the hidden constraints in the problem (e.g., you could increase fertilizer production, but there is only one railroad across Siberia to transport such goods to the farmers). This elaborated representation also helped the experts to classify the problem in a general way (as primarily technological, political, social, etc., although different experts made different decisions) and to consider solutions in light of this more abstract orientation.

Although topic knowledge was very important in this process, Voss et al. found that students who worked on this problem at both the beginning and at the end of a course in Soviet economic policy did no better on their second attempt. They had learned new information, it appeared, but not how to use that information; they had not learned *the cognitive process of exploring a problem as an expert would.*

In my own research with John R. Hayes, we found that experienced writers generated far more plans and goals during the writing process.[17] As they compose, writers construct what we have called a Working Goal Network which includes goals, subgoals, criteria, and tests. Although the sheer number of such elements is not the whole issue, in the space of an hour's work one of the experts generated 103 elements to a novice's 19. Although they wrote comparable amounts of text, they were responding to radically different, self-constructed problem spaces.

Another important part of invention and exploration is the search for relevant information outside one's own mind. For on-the-job writers this may also mean going outside one's own area of expertise and locating information. In a study of the search procedures people used on a new library computer catalog, Sullivan uncovered interesting differences in the search strategies of expert and novice searchers.[18] By analyzing the thinking-aloud protocols of people planning a computer search, Sullivan was able to track their mental search paths, goals, and decisions.

When asked to discover as many references as they could on the topic of "erotic art," the student searchers, like the novices in the Voss et al. and Flower and Hayes studies, ended up with an impoverished set of possibilities. They seemed to rely on trial and error and often chose the first plan that presented itself. The experts, like Voss's experts, ran mental simulations of plans they considered, imagining the outcomes of different approaches.

The experts, however, did not employ a single strategy: There is no algorithm for a good search on difficult problems. Sullivan found some experts who worked as Explorers. They started by building an imaginary pool of terms that would give them a large number of what librarians call "hits" or potential references (e.g., they would consider "ero" because it might pull in the French references to *erotism*). They would then mentally wander around in this accumulated information, looking for likely search paths. Other experts worked as Definers. They put a great deal of initial effort into thinking about the question and defining the best possible first term to use. They tried to narrow the search down as quickly as possible, to find an angle or a well-specified probe that would give them the references they wanted, yet would exclude all others (e.g., they would quickly eliminate the term "art" as a probe).

Both kinds of experts, however, showed the flexibility to change methods when difficult searches demanded it; that is, when they encountered a problem or thought of a new subgoal, they would switch to a strategy that might work.

These studies are only a beginning, but they point to some features of an expert exploration:

1. The methods of exploration experts use are adapted to the task at hand or to a given discourse. Librarians, social scientists, and writers use strategies tailor-made for their tasks. We would predict that a student who was good at exploring a problem in economics or accounting would not necessarily have learned how to explore the *rhetorical* problem of supporting an economic analysis or explaining an accounting decision.

2. In addition, experts themselves may differ in the methods they use to explore a complex problem. For significant tasks there is no simple formula, uniquely best method, or single "expert" process.

3. However, the expert paths we see across these tasks have a lot in common. The experts conduct a broader exploration of their problem; they look at more facets of the task, they set goals, and they test their exploration against their goals. Exploring a rhetorical problem appears to be a process that calls for some clearly definable expert strategies.

Creating a Plan

The investment team at Twentieth Century clearly succeeded in constructing a rich problem definition, one that recognized a wide array of important goals and constraints. However, having created a sophisticated representation of their problem, it is unlikely that a plan based merely on genre knowledge or on format schemas would solve the problem any more than would a plan based on presenting their topic knowledge. Rhetorical problems call for intelligent rhetorical planning. The process of creating a plan is the second point at which writers often rise to rhetorical problem solving.

The decisions made by the Twentieth Century staff illustrate two steps in such planning: The first is to create a high-level plan and the second is to generate ways to instantiate that plan in text. In planning their report the staff members had a number of standard options: ignore the problem and it will go away (as, in fact, they were confident it would), resort to generalities about the economy and the market in general, take a positive posture in negative times by celebrating past performances ("Fourteen years ago we . . ."), or shift the focus from performance altogether to other features of the fund, such as new services or new products. The top-level plan they chose was somewhat more radical. They decided to face the situation directly and use it as an occasion to explain their investment philosophy — the policy of investing for long-term capital gains and riding out these dips in the market. They decided, in effect, to educate their shareholders — to convince their readers to take the long view, to see this dip as part of the big picture, and even to consider increasing their investments now when stock prices were low.

Creating a top-level plan that is sensitive to the larger problem is a critical first step. Without it, no amount of correct, careful, or well-styled prose will succeed at solving the rhetorical problem. On the other hand, it is not always clear how to carry out such plans, even if they offer potentially brilliant solutions. Creating a plan also means creating a way to instantiate those global intentions. Instantiation is the process of generating a specific instance of a more global or abstract plan. For example, if we have a computer program that will format a bibliography, we instantiate the abstract set of instructions by typing in the specific authors, book titles, and publication data that allow the program to run. Global plans (or instructions) such as "educate the reader," allow so many possible instantiations that, however clever the plan, the writer's work has only begun. The writer must try to generate an instance of "educating the reader" that meets all the goals and criteria set up in his or her representation of the problem.[19]

In the excerpt from the final report (Figure 3) you can see how the staff at Twentieth Century chose to instantiate this plan. Its text plan revolved around a metaphor that James Stowers, the president, had used for years to explain his philosophy: When you invest for the long term, look for the tennis balls that bounce back when the market recovers — and avoid the chicken eggs. The second feature of the plan at this level was to create a new two-color graph, called a "mountain investment chart," which could graphically show the long-term success of the company's fund and make the quarterly results easier to understand. Both of those plans had to be instantiated at yet another level with specific content and organization, and eventually with actual words and designs. The "bounce back" metaphor, for instance, was

Investing with Twentieth Century

A   N   O   V   E   R   V   I   E   W

While you as a shareholder of Twentieth Century are concerned first of all with the actual results achieved on your behalf, you may also be interested with how those results are achieved. The following comments address four key aspects of the investment policies we pursue on behalf of Twentieth Century.

1. How we choose stocks
2. Characteristics of the Twentieth Century funds
3. How timing affects your investment results
4. The importance of investing for the long-term

How we choose stocks

Twentieth Century is guided by the conviction that *companies demonstrating an acceleration of earnings and revenue growth are likely to appreciate in market value.* Each day our investment team searches for publicly-traded companies with this accelerating growth, using extensive computer hardware and software designed especially for us. Companies that are accelerating are candidates for purchase. Companies that are not accelerating are avoided, or sold if already owned. This process of *active management* allows us to continuously monitor and update the portfolios of Twentieth Century to reflect the latest information available about the companies meeting our criteria.

Another important element of our investment policy is a *commitment to staying fully invested*—a policy that has worked well for us in the past. We do not speculate as to which direction the market is going since we don't know anyone who has consistently outguessed its sporadic moves. While our policy of staying fully invested can produce short-term disappointments, Twentieth Century's record

suggests this approach is really more of an opportunity than a risk for serious, long-term shareholders.

Characteristics of the Twentieth Century funds

Perhaps one of the first things you'll notice about your investment in Twentieth Century Investors is that *share prices change almost daily.* The funds do not have a constant value. This is because the common stocks we purchase for the funds represent ownership interests in various companies. As the progress of these companies ebbs and flows, so does the value of the funds' ownership in them. In addition, common stocks as a class of investments are influenced by the relative attractiveness of other investments such as bonds, certificates of deposit, and money market funds.

Shares of Twentieth Century Investors can fall as well as rise in price. Your investment is not immune to corrections in the stock market or disappointments in the companies selected for investment. However, our stock selection policies are designed to help contend with the uncontrollable meanderings of the stock market.

In simple terms, we believe some stocks are like tennis balls, and others are like chicken eggs. A falling market takes them both down. But when the market bottoms, tennis balls bounce back. So our goal is simple: find the tennis balls, and avoid the chicken eggs. As a result, Twentieth Century's funds have had the *ability to bounce back strongly in price when the stock market recovers.*

Another characteristic of the Twentieth Century common stock funds is that most of the return they provide is in the form of *capital appreciation*—that is, a higher share price. Their production of *dividend income*

Fig. 3. The Twentieth Century Investors report: the text.

is relatively low. The only consistent income provider of our common stock funds is Select Investors. Shareholders who want substantial current income are advised to consider Twentieth Century's U.S. Governments, a bond fund invested in government issues.

How timing affects your investment results

You may be surprised to learn that the single most important factor in your early success with Twentieth Century Investors is the date on which you make your original investment. For example, if you began at a time when the stock market was depressed you probably have had relatively good early investment experience and are quite happy. On the other hand, if you began at a time when the market was peaking, you may be disappointed by your early lack of progress.

The effect of the starting date on your investment results can be overcome by time and effective portfolio management. For example, suppose you had invested $10,000 in Select Investors on Sept. 13, 1978. Early results would have been disappointing because Select and the stock market declined in price shortly after the purchase. The original investment would have declined in value by 14% in eight months.

Thereafter, however, Select staged a strong recovery. Within another eight months, your holding would have bounced back (remember those tennis balls) to a value of $12,900 and by April 30, 1984, to a value of $29,400—almost three times the original investment. Had you redeemed your shares after the initial setback, you would have lost money and would not have had the opportunity to participate in the subsequent growth.

Because of this timing effect, we make the following suggestions:

1. Consider spreading out your investment over time in order to minimize the possibility of making an investment at a market peak.

2. Recognize that the value of your shares will fluctuate up and down.

3. Take advantage of lower prices— buy more shares and average down your cost.

4. Be prepared to give your investment the time necessary to provide its worth.

The importance of investing for the long-term

Twentieth Century recently celebrated its 25th birthday. One of our more important discoveries over the years is the fact that common stock investing is not a short-term proposition. The pursuit of investment excellence requires lots of patience and time—three to five years or more. Shorter periods are chancy because too many events can happen that are beyond the control of investment managers—oil embargos, wars, credit crunches, etc. The symbol of Twentieth Century Investors is an oak tree, signifying growth, strength and durability. We think the development of a successful long-term investment record is similar to the growth cycle of the oak—neither happens overnight. Yet, with proper care, pruning (as needed) and patience the potential of both the acorn and the well-selected investment can be realized. There are no substitutes for careful management and time.

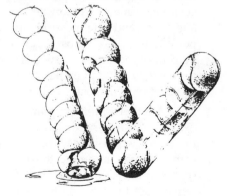

instantiated visually with a small time-lapse drawing of an egg and a ball falling side by side — one of which breaks while the other bounces up. The text in Figure 3 shows you how this idea was then carried over into prose and typography. Writing this report was a collaborative affair which involved not only top management — Stowers and the investment team — but also portfolio managers and an advertising company which contributed the visual instantiation of Stowers' metaphor. The process of instantiating plans then went on at many levels and involved a number of people trying to carry out a coherent, collaborative plan.

Creating a Plan: The Expert Path

What would an expert path through this planning process entail? In the Voss et al. study, we saw that novices leaped from exploration into solution making with great speed. Likewise, studies of novice writers frequently note the speed with which novices leap into producing text with little to no planning. However, the time spent in prewriting (or even in planning during the whole process) is not a reliable indicator of expertise. What matters is how writers use that time. Consider these differences:

1. In a study which compared the writing process of college students with their instructors', Hayes and I found that the students spent their time constructing what we might call plans *To Say*.[20] That is, they were searching for and organizing content material, things one could say in a text. Of the new ideas they generated in one hour, 70 percent were statements of content information that could go directly into the paper. The experienced writers, by contrast, were putting their effort into developing plans *To Do* something through writing. That is, they were spending time in rhetorical planning, considering their goals, their audience, and the possible implications of various choices. Their performance was almost a complete reversal of the novices': Only 31 percent of the experts' new ideas were devoted to simple content plans for what *To Say*, and 69 percent of their new ideas involved a rhetorical consideration of goals, audience, or form.

2. Another difference stands out in the focus and organization of expert and novice texts. Novice writers, as described above, often end up with "writer-based" prose organized like a memory dump of a computer file, according to the way the writer stored or retrieved his or her information. The narrative or simple descriptive structure of writer-based prose reflects the structure of the writer's knowledge and offers a highly efficient strategy for retrieving information and gen-

erating ideas. Unfortunately, such a structure is often ineffective for the reader who, in business and professional writing, often expects a hierarchically structured discussion focused on an issue or a problem. Moreover, readers don't expect the text to be focused on just any problem, but on one in which they share an interest.

We could, for example, imagine a writer-based plan *To Say* for the Twentieth Century report which might look like this:

A Plan To Say

• In reporting the losses for the current period, we were concerned that shareholders might misinterpret the results.
• We do not see the current loss picture as a cause for concern.
• Long-term investments ride out the fluctuations of the market.
• The market operates in this way:
    Point 1
    Point 2 (and so on)

I have no evidence that the investment staff considered this plan; however, it is typical of many plans I have seen my students in business and professional writing make. In some ways it is quite straightforward, but its egocentric focus on the writers' worries and its combination of a narrative structure followed by textbook recitation makes it visibly insensitive to the rhetorical situation and to the legitimate concerns of the readers.

By contrast, my interviews and the text of the Twentieth Century report let us piece together a quite different plan for the real text. The interesting feature of this plan is how the writers translated their rhetorical goals into a clear, issue-centered text structure. Notice how the major headings for the report also reflect questions the critical reader is likely to have. (The information below in roman type comes from my interviews, that in italics comes from the text.)

A Plan To Do

• We need to deal directly with shareholders' expectations for continued growth or short-term returns.
• Use this loss as an occasion for explaining our philosophy of long-term investment planning.
• Use the egg and tennis ball metaphor to show how our policy deals with market fluctuation.
• *Recognize that the reader is concerned with results, and present the report in terms of how those results are achieved.*
    Point 1. How we choose stocks
    Point 2. Characteristics of Twentieth Century funds (and so on)

How do experts go about instantiating these more global, *To Do* plans in the form of actual words and sentences? Creating reader-based prose requires thought and planning at the text level, too. For example, when we studied differences between well- and poorly written government regulations, we found that effective texts relied on a Scenario Principle that organized ideas around the perspective of the reader.[21] Poorly written texts were focused on formal definitions of key terms and concepts that would be familiar to agency writers but not to readers. By contrast, the more readable, revised regulations created scenarios organized around human agents acting in some context. Instead of defining the features of "eligibility" — a concept the agency writers would be familiar with — these scenarios depicted eligibility in terms of people who did certain things in specified situations. (If you want to sell an illegal or untaxed item such as moonshine, for example, you aren't eligible for a federal Small Business Loan.)

Making and instantiating rhetorical plans also goes on at the sentence level. When a writer tries to move from a rhetorical plan to text production, Witte has shown, a crucial link in this process is the writer's ability to manage the topical structure of sentences and paragraphs. For example, in a recent study Witte follows the planning processes of two students struggling to write an argument for or against a student grade appeal.[22] The unsuccessful writer in this study concentrates on "figuring out" her position on the case (she concludes Jack is innocent). She then tries to write *about* her observations, never seeing that such observations should work as "evidence" within the frame of an argument. Her text is neither coherent nor persuasive, and the writer appears to find the process of ordering her thoughts and sentences a frustrating one.

The successful writer handles the transition from content information to text differently. She starts by forming a rhetorical plan and a sense of purpose (vis-à-vis the faculty board she is addressing). She then places her observations (she, too, thinks Jack is innocent) within the conceptual "frame" of an argument, organized around a top-level proposition which requires evidence. She then uses this discourse frame and its top-level proposition (the discourse topic of the essay) to dictate the topical focus of units of the essay and of individual sentences. As a result, her text not only seems locally coherent, it is also coherent within a larger rhetorical plan.

Witte's study shows us how the path from plan to text can be a series of rhetorical decisions in which the writer's plan and purpose are instantiated in the choice of a top-level discourse topic which is, in turn, elaborated by a series of related sentence topics. The writer's purpose is realized in choices at every point in the hierarchy.

These selected studies can only suggest some of the features of expert planning, but taken together, they illustrate three key points:

1. Important parts of the planning process are conducted at the level of sentence production and text organization. Planning at the text level may call upon writers to reorganize information or to create a topical focus that reflects a more abstract purpose.

2. Creating reader-based prose also calls for planning at other levels. Expert planning can be a demanding cognitive process (even for "experts"). Having given themselves a richly complex problem, and having represented the readers' needs as part of that problem, writers must often reorganize their own knowledge, forge new idea structures, generate new concepts, and infer new relations in order to develop an effective plan for their texts.

3. Rhetorical problem solving and planning, like any demanding cognitive process, takes time, energy, and experience, in part because experts are planning at so many levels. Getting a good top-level plan is a crucial beginning, but expert writers continue to plan and test as they consider various ways to instantiate those grand schemes. This image of planning as a sustained self-conscious activity, focused on building a reader-based plan *To Do* something through writing, may be news to our students, who see business and professional writing as working a formula or generating content.

Reviewing and Testing

Academic writing often "succeeds" if it passes evaluation by a professor or peer group and meets certain discourse conventions for reasoning, evidence, truth, relevance, and so on. The criteria used are established, standard ones (though even these are not always obvious to learners). Business and professional writing introduces an additional criterion that is sometimes harder to meet: The text must *work* for its intended readers. Did the Twentieth Century report work? The authors were satisfied with the message, the writing was polished, and the final product was well designed; but would it do what it was supposed to? Would it educate and maintain the investors' confidence? Would it convince them to invest more? In other words, did it meet its rhetorical goals? Tests for such effectiveness are not always easy to conduct, but in the long run they are the tests that matter.

Many business and professional texts also work as references or informational documents. How effective are the new graphs? They look attractive and they appear informative. But a more practical test might be to find out what happens when new investors try to read them: How long does it take to find data one wants? Do readers comprehend the tables to the right of the graph correctly? Do they read them in such a way that they see the long-term trend? Could they answer comprehension questions on the graph? In some areas, such as instruction-manual writing, writers actually conduct field tests. But these are often expensive and too time-consuming to do once the work is fully completed. Often the writer's problem is to review and evaluate his or her own work from a reader's point of view.

Reviewing and Testing: The Expert Path

To begin with, we must face the fact that even good editors have difficulty testing from the reader's point of view. In a recent study, which compared four different ways to test functional documents, Dieli used a computer manual with known user problems to see how many problems her different methods of testing would detect.[23] The following four methods were used: (1) a computer program style checker called Murky, (2) a group of experienced writer/editors, and two new methods of testing, based on (3) think-aloud reading protocols of potential users reading the manual, and (4) think-aloud user protocols of users trying to actually follow the instructions to do a task on the computer. In these protocols, readers and users think aloud while they carry out the task (they are not asked to interpret or talk about their response but to attend to the task and merely think aloud). The protocols provide a detailed record of readers' efforts to comprehend a text and users' attempts to carry out the instructions and use them to recover from the inevitable errors.[24]

In an earlier study, which tested insurance forms and warranties, Swaney found that experienced editors were able to detect and revise many problems (especially those connected to language and style).[25] However, when the revised texts were submitted to protocol-aided evaluation, they still presented some major comprehension problems for readers. Moreover, some of the editors' revisions actually lowered readers' comprehension and performance on a short test. The Dieli study also found that think-aloud protocols of users detected many problems the editors missed. It went on to make a detailed comparison of the problems each group uncovered and found that editors using such standard methods as checklists often missed crucial problems, such as users' difficulty getting access to information. For example, in using the table of contents, index, or headings of one manual, a reader who wanted to set up or alter a list of figures had to already know the subtle differences between the commands of Paste, Paste Value, and Paste Adjust to even gain access to the manual's instructions. Many users simply never found the information they needed.

However, Dieli found that the editors' ability to detect real user problems improved when she altered their *evaluation process* by training them to focus on user needs and the readers' process rather than on standard text features. For example, users often have difficulty interpreting the meaning of symbolic information (boxes, arrows, color, and special characters). Editors were prompted to note symbolic information as a source of potential problems and to decide whether its intended information would actually be understood by a new user. Editors urged to focus on the users' needs attempted to simulate a reader's response and generated far more information about user problems than did other editors.

Functional writing achieves its goals when it works for the reader. This means that in order to review and test their writing, business and professional writers must often go beyond the standards for well-formed text and ask: Will this text work for my readers (or even for multiple readers)? Testing the text means not only anticipating the reader's expectations (e.g., for a reader-based hierarchical structure) but predicting where the reader might have difficulty. Defined this way, testing the text means simulating the reader's comprehension process. It is not entirely clear how experienced writers carry out this sort of testing, but we can point to some features of the expert review process that stand out as clear and teachable processes:

1. Experts go beyond the surface features. It is well known that student writers stick to evaluating the rule-governed and surface features of a text. Ironically, many guidelines for business writers simply extend those criteria to include report format and "plain" style, but go no deeper than the surface language. Yet, in the highly rhetorical context of business, correct and stylistically "well-written" text is often not enough.

2. Experts review their text at the level of its gist or the gist of sections and at the level of its goals. Witte has suggested that the topic shifts and confused topical structure of student revisions reflect the students' piecemeal understanding of the text.[26] The students never came to grips with the gist of the text before revising. When business students are explicitly prompted to revise their own disorganized drafts, we have found that they often have trouble extracting the gist.[27] The expert path seems to involve first constructing a gist or articulating one's goals and then using these constructions to test the

text. This is not to say that the process is simple or straightforward. The expert writers we studied often went into extended (e.g., three- to four-minute) problem-solving episodes, considering alternate goals for a text and setting up a series of gist statements in order to diagnose and solve a problem.[28]

3. Finally, experts take one more step beyond the text itself and try to simulate a reader's response. In a study of the revision process involving students, professional writers, and writing instructors, we found that the professionals treated the revision task we gave them as a straightforward genre problem whenever they could.[29] (They were asked to revise a text to be used as a handout for freshmen.) However, when genre knowledge didn't specify what to do with a problematic piece of the text, the experienced writers all turned to diagnosis; they tried to define the problem in terms of its rhetorical effects. Furthermore, this diagnosis sometimes took considerable time and effort as the reviser tried to simulate a reader's possible response and then use that simulation to pinpoint the problem.

This observation, in a way, captures the gist of my argument for this paper. When possible, business and professional writers rely on the most streamlined knowledge they possess. If genre or topic knowledge can produce a good plan or a good diagnosis, that is what writers use first. However, the special prerogative of experienced (and effective) writers is their ability to rise to rhetorical problem solving when the occasion demands. My sense as a writer and teacher of writers is that such occasions are not the exception but rather they reflect the rule in business as usual.

The Transfer Dilemma: Realistic Tasks versus Underlying Process

If the picture of business writing and rhetorical problem solving I have painted is accurate, it has a number of implications for teaching. One is that if we want to prepare students for writing beyond the classroom, we must help them to do more than master conventions, correctness, and a "plain style." To develop their skills of rhetorical problem solving they need to work on realistic tasks, not toy problems. I remember vividly giving one of my first professional writing classes a memo assignment I had cooked up on a toy marketing problem and being impressed at the flashy, sophisticated writing they produced. Then a week later I saw a similar memo they were writing for an economics class in which they had a great deal of real information to discuss and integrate. Their apparent writing skills fell apart. They could not *control* the knowledge of rhetorical conventions they did have; they could not bring it to bear on hard tasks that required more than spinning out a verbal formula. We see this same phenomenon in the development of children's abilities: The child can do marvelous things with the support of the teacher or on familiar, engaging topics, but cannot transfer "what worked once" to a new task or to independent work. Writers need to learn on realistically complex problems.

Yet the aspiration to teach to a realistic task (rather than to review more general conventions) creates a dilemma. We simply can't teach the range of situations that turn up in business and the professions. Therefore, our students must somehow generalize our teaching and transfer it to new tasks when we aren't around. Nor is it enough to say that *we* (as teachers and specialists in the field) know there is an underlying principle and could see its application. The student must be able and ready to transfer his or her knowledge in new situations.

The history of education offers us some notable failures in hoped-for transfer. Learning math, for instance, doesn't finally appear to increase a student's ability to think logically about the modern novel. And mastering the short essay on literature in one's freshman composition class fails to transfer not only to business but to much other academic writing. There are many reasons this happens. One is that transfer *across domains,* such as math and reading, is a difficult and rare event. Moreover, when writing is taught in terms of its specific discourse conventions, rather than in terms of goals and strategies, the knowledge a student acquires doesn't appear (to the student) to apply in new genres. The new genre doesn't provide the cues that call up what the writer does, in fact, know. Although strategies for planning an introduction may transfer in theory, they won't transfer in practice unless the student sees the connection between tasks.

I think it is possible to approach this dilemma in two ways:

1. *Teach rhetorical strategies — both general ones and those which underlie the conventions of different kinds of discourse.*

Understanding one's own writing process is one kind of rhetorical knowledge that has great potential to transfer to rhetorical tasks. Knowing how to go about exploring a problem, creating and instantiating a plan, and testing and reviewing a text is a form of rhetorical process knowledge. It may not transfer to math, but it works across many writing tasks. Rhetorical problem solving is itself a specialized kind of knowledge students may learn nowhere else. Although students do strategic thinking in many areas of their lives, they have often not learned to think strategically about their writing and may come to a business writing course expecting to master writing with fast and easy formulas.

It is also helpful to see that many discourse conventions are, in fact, formalizations of rhetorical moves. For example, academic articles typically open with a review of the literature and a statement of a problem for rhetorical reasons: The author needs to show the necessity for the article and to establish his or her own credibility. Seeing conventions not as rules, but as means to an end, opens the door to discovering other, often more appropriate ways to achieve the same end.

_ 2. *Help students develop a meta-awareness of their own strategic process.*

Developing the repertory of strategies mentioned above will be a giant step for some writers. But the expert writer is also knowledgeable about his or her own knowledge. The real hope for transfer — for helping a student to become more self-sufficient as a rhetorical problem solver — lies in the student's own awareness of what he or she can do. All of us have tacit strategic knowledge for writing, although we are scarcely aware of this knowledge and cannot describe it. But in those areas where we possess meta-knowledge — when, for instance, we become aware of some of the alternative planning strategies we control — we have a new power. Unlike the plight of writers who must have a familiar or highly motivating topic in order to write well, writers with increased meta-knowledge have the power to call upon and control the rhetorical knowledge they do have when they need it.

Business and professional writing calls for professional-level rhetorical problem solving. As with any important act of cognition, when writers know the real dimensions of the task and the knowledge it calls for, they are more likely to manage their own writing and thinking with the same awareness they bring to other aspects of their professional life.

Notes

1. For a good discussion of this issue see Charles Bazerman, "Scientific Writing as a Social Act: A Review of the Literature of the Sociology of Science," in *New Essays in Technical and Scientific Communication: Research, Theory, Practice*, ed. Paul V. Anderson, John R. Brockmann, and Carolyn Miller (Farmingdale, N.Y.: Baywood, 1983); Patricia Bizzell, "College Composition: Initiation into the Academic Discourse Community," *Curriculum Inquiry* 12 (1982): 191–207; Elaine Maimon, "Talking to Strangers," *College Composition and Communication* 30 (1979): 366–69; and B. F. Walvoord, *Helping Students Write Well: A Guide for Teachers in All Disciplines* (New York: MLA, 1982).

2. Richard E. Young, "Arts, Crafts, Gifts and Knacks: Some Disharmonies in the New Rhetoric," in *Reinventing the Rhetorical Tradition,* ed. Aviva Freedman and Ian Pringle (Conway, Ark.: L and S Books, 1980).

3. David E. Rumelhart, "Notes on a Schema for Stories," in *Representation and Understanding: Studies in Cognitive Science,* ed. Daniel G. Bobrow and Allan Collins (New York: Academic Press, 1975).

4. R. C. Schank and R. P. Abelson, *Scripts, Plans, Goals, and Understanding* (Hillsdale, N.J.: Erlbaum, 1977).

5. Gary Schumacher, George Klare, and Byron Scott, "Writing Genre: Its Influence on Writing Process" (Paper presented at AERA, Chicago, 1985).

6. G. Spilich et al., "Text-Processing of Domain-Related Information for Individuals with High and Low Domain Knowledge," *Journal of Verbal Learning and Verbal Behavior* 18 (1979): 275–90.

7. Judith A. Langer, "Effects of Topic Knowledge on the Quality and Coherence of Informational Writing," in *Contexts for Learning to Write,* ed. Arthur Applebee (Norwood, N.J.: Ablex, 1984).

8. Sandra J. Bond, John R. Hayes, and Linda S. Flower, *Translating the Law into Common Language: A Protocol Study,* Carnegie–Mellon University, Document Design Project Technical Report no. 1 (Pittsburgh, Pa., April 1980).

9. See also J. A. Langer, "Effects of Topic Knowledge."

10. Richard P. Kern et al., *Guidebook for the Development of Army Training Literature* (Washington, D.C.: U.S. Army Research Institute for the Behavioral and Social Sciences, Human Resources Research Organization, 1976).

11. Linda S. Flower, "A Cognitive Basis for Problems in Writing," *College English* 41 (September 1979): 19–37.

12. See also Janice Lauer et al., *Four Worlds of Writing* (New York: Harper & Row, 1984); Linda Flower, *Problem-Solving Strategies in Writing* (San Diego, Calif.: Harcourt Brace Jovanovich, 1985); Richard Young, Alton Becker, and Kenneth Pike, *Rhetoric: Discovery and Change* (New York: Harcourt Brace Jovanovich, 1970).

13. Herbert A. Simon, "The Structure of Ill-Structured Problems," *Artificial Intelligence* 4 (1973): 181–201.

14. Lee Odell and Dixie Goswami, *Writing in Nonacademic Settings* (New York: Guilford Press, 1985).

15. Carolyn Miller and Jack Selzer, "Special Topics of Argument in Engineering Reports," in *Writing in Nonacademic Settings,* ed. Lee Odell and Dixie Goswami (New York: Guilford Press, 1985).

16. J. F. Voss et al., "Problem Solving Skills in the Social Sciences," in *The Psychology of Learning and Motivation: Advances in Research and Theory,* ed. G. Bower (New York: Academic Press, 1983).

17. See Linda Flower, "The Construction of Purpose in Writing and Reading." *College English* 50 (September 1988), 528–50, and Linda Flower, Karen Schriver, Linda Carey, Christina Haas, and John R. Hayes, "Planning

in Writing: A Theory of the Cognitive Process." (Technical Report) Berkeley, CA: Center for the Study of Writing at University of California, Berkeley, and Carnegie-Mellon University, 1989.

18. Patricia Sullivan, "Rhetoric and the Search for Externally Stored Knowledge: Toward a Computer-age Art of Research" (Ph.D. diss., Carnegie–Mellon University, 1986).

19. A more extended discussion of instantiation appears in Linda Flower and John R. Hayes, "Images, Plans, and Pros: The Representation of Meaning in Writing," *Written Communication* 1 (January 1984): 120–60.

20. Linda Flower and John R. Hayes, "The Dynamics of Composing: Making Plans and Juggling Constraints," in *Cognitive Processes in Writing: An Interdisciplinary Approach*, ed. Lee Gregg and Erwin Steinberg (Hillsdale, N.J.: Erlbaum, 1980).

21. Linda Flower, John R. Hayes, and Heidi Swarts, "Revising Functional Documents: The Scenario Principle," in *New Essays in Technical and Scientific Communication: Research, Theory, Practice*.

22. Stephen Witte and Roger Charry, "Writing Processes and Written Products in Composition Research," in *Linguistic Approaches to the Study of Written Discourse*, ed. C. R. Cooper and S. Greenbaum (Beverly Hills: Sage, 1985).

23. Mary Dieli, "Designing Successful Documents: An Investigation of Document Evaluation Methods" (Ph.D. diss., Carnegie-Mellon University, 1986).

24. See also Marshall A. Atlas, "The User Edit: Making Manuals Easier to Use," *IEEE Transactions on Professional Communication*, PC-24(1) (March 1981): 28–29. Patricia Sullivan and Linda Flower, "How Do Users Read Computer Manuals? Some Protocol Contributions to Writers' Knowledge," in *Convergences: Essays on Reading, Writing and Literacy*, ed. Bruce Peterson (Urbana, Ill.: NCTE, 1986).

25. J. Swaney et al., *Editing for Comprehension: Improving the Process through Reading Protocols*, Carnegie-Mellon University, Document Project 14 (Pittsburgh, Pa., June 1981).

26. Stephen Witte, "Topical Structure and Revision: An Exploratory Study," *College Composition and Communication* 34 (October 1983): 313–41.

27. Mary Sue Garay, "Writers Making Points: A Case Study of Executives and College Students Revising Their Own Business Reports" (Ph.D. Dissertation, Carnegie-Mellon University, 1988).

28. Linda Flower, Linda Carey, and John R. Hayes, "Diagnosis in Revision: The Experts' Option," Carnegie–Mellon University, CDC Technical Report no. 27 (Pittsburgh, Pa.: Carnegie–Mellon University, 1986).

29. Linda Flower, John R. Hayes, Linda Carey, Karen Schriver, and James Stratman, "Detection, Diagnosis, and the Strategies of Revision." *College Composition and Communication*, 37 (February 1986), 16–55.

2 Arranging Business Prose

Jack Selzer
Pennsylvania State University

"Despite the countless number of composition and rhetoric texts dealing with arrangement, we know very little about order in composition. In many texts, arrangement is either neglected or its treatment is woefully inadequate."[1] Frank D'Angelo's comment about composition textbooks just as accurately describes books on business writing. The best books list a few sound principles of arrangement: Marya Holcombe and Judith Stein explain how writers can use first and last positions to good advantage, or maintain a rhythm between general and specific; Ken Davis recommends Rogerian principles, after the example of Young, Becker, and Pike; and several authors remind student writers that certain expository modes, such as narration or comparison, imply certain arrangements.[2] The worst books simply ignore general principles in favor of prescribing stereotypical arrangements for particular types of documents; they either confuse arrangement with format or, worse, merely formulate cookbook recipes and inflexible rules for everything. Claim letters are said to follow one set pattern, sales letters must follow another formula (get the reader's attention, then arouse interest in the product, then instill belief in the product's virtues, and finally, stimulate action — the sale), and other types of reports and correspondence are similarly reduced to formats and recipes — good news should always come first, for example, and negative information should be given only after a positive "buffer" and before positive alternatives.

Such formulas are often sensible enough, of course. The problem is that they work only for very routine messages, often so routine and short that students need little help in learning to compose them or so routine and unimportant that no business professional has the time or inclination to sweat over them. What about longer, more problematical, pieces of discourse: how should one arrange the often interchangeable lengthy subsections of a report, for instance? What about persuasive discourse: in what order should one present a series of arguments that support a specific recommendation? And what about "mixed messages": how should one arrange material in a document with multiple audiences or aims, or the contents of a letter that contains both good and bad news (and that also requests something in return)?

In a sense, it is not surprising that arrangement is treated rather superficially in business writing, for, as Richard Larson has noted, "Form in complete essays has not been the subject of much theoretical investigation."[3] Hence, teachers simply do not have as much advice to give about arrangement as they do about style or substance. This essay is intended, in part, to remedy this neglect. While I will not be offering the results of any theoretical investigation, I do hope to equip business writing teachers (and textbook authors) to give better advice about arrangement. By collecting in one place a list (no doubt still incomplete) of arrangement principles available to writers, by classifying those arrangement options so that they might be presented systematically in a course that approaches writing rhetorically, and by illustrating how those arrangement choices might operate in a couple of short pieces of business prose, I hope to advance the available pedagogy in business writing.

My emphasis will be on patterns and principles that govern the order of paragraphs, paragraph blocks, and even larger segments of business prose; but I believe that many of the principles might also be used by writers as they order sentences within paragraphs, items within sentences, and even of nonfiction prose that does not fall within the domain of business writing. Because my emphasis is on empowering writers more than analysts of prose, I have decided to elaborate on only those arrangement options that seem most productive for writers; while I recognize that rhetoricians have devised many other productive approaches to understanding form in prose, I mean to describe only those arrangement principles that seem most practical to writers as they work. In fact, when I am discussing arrangement, I will be anatomizing something I consider to be somewhat narrower than form, which I take to denote all the aspects of a text that create its coherence. While form includes all those matters that hold a text together for a reader, arrangement, as I understand the term, focuses only on matters of order, especially on the rhetorical principles that govern the order of things beyond the sentence and paragraph.

To put all of this yet another way, form seems to me a characteristic of texts, while arrangement strikes me as more (though not entirely) an activity of writers. Hence, I will treat arrangement as an activity or process performed by writers in the act of writing, even as I recognize that others have seen it as synonymous with form, as characteristic of a finished product, as a set of schemes discovered by analysts, as "the internal set of consistent relationships perceived in any stretch of discourse."[4] Indeed, since my suggestions are, to such a great extent, primarily intended for writers, I will be surprised if any of my observations are very useful to analysts at all. Throughout the essay, then, I mean by arrangement the orderly disposition that a writer gives to parts in prose, the set of ordering principles that a writer uses to shape the sections of a document. And I suggest that those principles might be classified according to five matters involved in any rhetorical transaction: the genre or form of the document, its subject matter or content, its audience, its author, and its setting or social framework.[5] Naturally, there is considerable overlap and interchange among these elements; for example, the conventions of genres and subgenres are affected by social considerations and serve to satisfy audience expectations. But it still seems useful to make sense of arrangement principles by classifying them this way.

Generic Considerations

James Kinneavy has observed that "the structure of any piece of discourse is severely constrained by the medium in which it occurs."[6] Indeed, the expectations aroused by the conventions of various genres and subgenres compel writers of every kind to arrange their work in particular ways. Classical rhetoricians have detailed how early orators arranged public speeches according to the form of a conventional, classical oration. Similarly, professional artists and literary critics have noticed for centuries that particular genres of poetry, drama, and fiction are defined in part at least by their arrangement; anyone composing an epic poem, ode, sonnet, comedy, romance, or satire may ignore conventional arrangements only at the risk of disorienting (or delighting) readers who understand the piece as a species of a general type.[7] Journalists learn to compose news stories according to the conventions of the inverted pyramid: Writers put the most important information first and move to least important so that editors can cut stories to fit space limitations without undermining coherence, and so that readers will know to quit reading when their interest is satisfied. Technical writers structure reports, proposals, and many other documents according to conventions established over time.[8] Academics also understand how scholarly articles are shaped by convention — how the American Psychological Association (APA) publication manual, for instance, codifies the parts (and order) of manuscripts in the social sciences: title page, abstract, introduction, methods, results, discussion, references, appendixes.

And so it is in business writing. A business student joins a firm most likely after constructing a résumé whose parts are ordered in large measure by convention. Once on the job, that person might read contracts and annual company reports to stockholders whose parts are ordered largely by custom; write proposals that might well follow a recognizable format; keep minutes of meetings and arrange them chronologically (although a number of other arrangements might make more sense); and write reports that will look much like other reports. Routine or common documents endemic to a given enterprise (e.g., booklets on benefits packages, environmental impact statements, expense reimbursement forms, etc.) all tend to follow conventional formats.

The stereotypical arrangements for correspondence recommended in business writing textbooks also fit in here; recipe books for various kinds of routine messages have persisted since the *ars dictaminis* of the Middle Ages, and the formats prescribed by textbooks for conveying good news or making sales appeals are largely gleaned from conventional practice. In short, perhaps the first thing business writers should consider when they arrange their documents is how they are constrained by the genre involved. The author of the first Save the Children letter[9] (Appendix A), therefore, follows a formula for sales appeals that is recommended by countless textbooks. It captures attention (with three pictures and a bold caption — "WOMEN — a driving force behind community self-help!"); then it arouses interest, instills belief, and finally stimulates a specific action.[10]

But at the same time that they consider genre, writers should not overemphasize the constraints that conventional forms and formats place upon them. The fact that the Save the Children letter can be rearranged without any terrible damage (Appendixes B and C) suggests perhaps that all sales appeals should capture attention, arouse interest, instill belief, and stimulate action — but not necessarily in that order. The two versions of the other letter included in Appendixes D and E, as well as junk mail everyone receives every day, show just as dramatically how fluid the parts of a sales pitch can be. In addition, résumé writers who make their documents look completely conventional risk rejection. And Charles Bazerman has shown that the "fixed guidelines" of the APA publication manual have not succeeded in fixing the form of scholarly articles; the modern "accepted form" of the scholarly essay in the social sciences has emerged only over time, and that form continues to evolve.[11] Just as a master poet must decide which conventions to observe and which to exploit or ignore, then, so too must business writers, as they arrange, decide whether to observe the constraints of particular genres or to consider other possibilities.

Subject Considerations

Some of those possibilities may be suggested by the writer's topic and method of development. Eighteenth- and nineteenth-century rhetoricians often considered invention and arrangement to be the same process, as Kinneavy and Corbett have pointed out,[12] and W. Ross Winterowd has agreed that "invention and arrangement are so nearly the same that they are indistinguishable; they are basically the same process."[13] While I think that Winterowd overstates, and that arrangement is indeed an operation separate from invention — especially because it properly demands other considerations besides the development of an argument — it is nevertheless undeniable that invention has a vital influence on arrangement. A writer's choices about what information or arguments or supporting details to include imply many things about how that material might be ordered. A writer might articulate those implications through a series of questions:

1. Can I group similar matters (or juxtapose dissimilar ones)?

Leonard Podis has claimed that failing to group similar items accounts for "perhaps half of all organizational problems" in student writing. Whether or not such a figure can be trusted (my own estimate would be far more conservative, and probably reflects a more lenient sense of what constitutes an "organizational problem"), surely this simple precept is indeed "one of the most important organizational principles" in all prose.[14] By grouping like with like, a writer performs a most useful service, for otherwise, readers would have to establish such relationships themselves.[15] All five letters in the appendixes exploit this basic principle of arrangement, in obvious and central ways, both within paragraphs and among them: Each of the three Save the Children letters, for instance, groups information about business enterprises started by women and about family planning efforts; the other two letters group information about faculty and about graduate students.

On occasion a writer might purposely group dissimilar items, either to deliberately disorient a reader for an appropriate effect or to deemphasize certain information or to prepare to demonstrate a fundamental congruity underlying the apparent dissimilarity. (None of the appendixes illustrates this rather rare arrangement choice, however.)

2. Are there hierarchies and subdivisions that I wish to establish?

Once like items have been grouped, a business writer might next consider whether some matters subsume others; he or she might consider whether particular arguments or pieces of information are logically coordinate or whether they are subordinate to larger matters. Such considerations need not imply a formal outline, of course, with Roman numerals, Arabic numbers, letters, indentations, and the other notorious accoutrements of outlines; it does suggest, simply, that writers typically consider through some means the relative significance of the points they include in discourse.[16] Thus, the letters to Dr. Maxwellhouse in the appendixes all make a series of five coordinate appeals about the strength of the graduate program being promoted — placement of graduates, generosity of stipends, future prospects, faculty quality, and recent improvements; each version subordinates other information to these concerns, although that decision is not inevitable. (In fact, the first version attempts in paragraph three to subordinate future prospects to the generosity of present stipends.) The Save the Children letters also create hierarchies and subdivisions: They support their major appeal ("by joining us, you could do much to help poor communities") with a major subappeal ("a gift from you . . . would help other women liberate their villages and themselves"); that subpoint is itself supported by other subpoints (notably, that women are creating economic development and encouraging family planning); and everything else is subordinated still more.

3. Can I move from general to specific, or from specific to general?

Related to the matter of establishing hierarchies is this particular hierarchy: the relationship between general and specific. Notice the rhythm between general and specific that is created in paragraphs four through eight of the first Save the Children letter, for example. First comes the generalization, "I have seen this happen time and time again on my visits to our program areas around the world." Next comes the more specific assertion of the indented paragraph five, before the very specific illustrations of paragraph six: mango jelly enterprises in Honduras, and a weaving business in Santa Isabel, Mexico. Paragraph seven is more general again, and in paragraph eight the writer returns once more to a broad generalization ("ventures like these do wonders. . . ."). Every experienced writer in any writing situation knows how to order discourse by creating similar rhythms between general and more or less general, specific and more or less specific.[17]

4. Does the document contain specific methods of development that presuppose certain approaches to arrangement?

By methods of development I mean traditional modes such as description, narration, and comparison, all of which imply particular arrangements (spatial order, chronological order, and the two arrangement patterns associated with comparison), and the arrangements that follow from certain conventional methods of development: question-answer, problem-solution, cause-effect (see paragraphs nine and ten of the first Save the Children letter). Another method of development, classification, sometimes (although not always) also implies an arrangement. After all, if a writer classifies corporations according to a principle such as size, he or she might well discuss those corporations in ascending or descending order; similarly, if a subject is classified alphabetically or numerically, a certain arrangement follows; if items are classified according to quality, then their discussion might proceed from best to worst; and so on.

5. Are there logical reasons for a particular arrangement?

Formal syllogistic logic appears very rarely in business writing or any other kind of writing; after all, rhetoric deals more often with probable arguments than with certain ones, and with enthymemes far more often than with formal syllogisms. If a writer strives for a syllogistic argument, however, the arrangement of the syllogism obviously influences the order in which premises are presented. The major premise would normally precede the minor premise and the conclusion; or the conclusion would be stated first and then be followed by the major and minor premises.[18]

As for enthymemes — or "inductive arguments" or "nonsyllogistic arguments" or "rhetorical arguments" or "probabilistic reasoning" — they are "logical" too, but their premises need not follow any particular order.[19] That much is illustrated by the letters in my appendixes, all of which are inductive arguments, and all of which order differently their minor premises (and sometimes even their major ones). Thus, the arrangement of the premises of an enthymeme really depends not on conventions of logic but on the other factors considered in this essay: genre and writer and setting and audience. Audience considerations are particularly important, since, as James Raymond has shown so convincingly,[20] the premises of an enthymeme are frequently drawn from an audience's assumptions and presuppositions. So it is appropriate now to consider in general how an audience can affect the arrangement of business prose, and vice versa.

Audience Considerations

So far, I have outlined arrangement patterns that have mostly seemed quite obvious to business writing teachers. After all, business writing has attended to the conventions of genres and has recognized the implications of expository modes for many years. But what might a writer do when the genre does not prescribe a certain arrangement, when a specific logical order is not called for, or when a particular mode does not compel a particular arrangement? To put the matter more concretely, if a report writer wishes to discuss several consequences of a particular act, how should those consequences be ordered? If there are several criteria to be considered in evaluating the feasibility of a product or course of action, how should the criteria be ordered? If a business writer wishes to cite several examples in support of a point, how should those examples be ordered? If a writer is developing an inductive argument, how should the premises of that argument be ordered? In short, what *should* come first when any number of items *could* come first? In these common circumstances, writers must consider their audiences, their own needs, and their social predicament.

Audience probably matters more than anything when a good writer orders business prose. In fact, writers through the centuries have devised (usually on psychological grounds) a number of arrangement strategies (several of them related) calculated to win the assent of neutral or skeptical readers:

1. Can first or final positions be used for emphasis?

Writers and rhetoricians have long agreed that readers remember most what comes first or last, and tend to forget what falls in the middle. To exploit this principle, they recommend that the most telling arguments or most important information should come first or last in a document, in each subsection of the document, in paragraphs, even in sentences; by contrast, relatively unimportant information, less crucial arguments — or discussions of opponents' best counterarguments — might profitably be placed in the middle of things. Note, for example, how the third Save the Children letter packs information about the uses of funds into the beginning and end of the letter, and how the middle is reserved for the explicit appeal for funds. That seems to make good psychological sense.

2. Can a climactic order be used for emphasis?

If journalists are taught to move from most important to least important in order to accommodate editors, then business writers can move from least important to most important in order to build power and drama. By moving to progressively more powerful information or arguments, a writer ensures that a reader will leave with a powerful impression; the risk, of course, is that a weak opener will turn the reader against an argument early or even prevent the reader from finishing the piece. For an example of how this principle works in practice, look at the second-to-last letter in the appendixes: The writer moves from the relatively negative or neutral news about hard times and retirements to his most positive appeals (quality of students, size of stipends, prospects for job placement) in order to leave the reader with a good impression about Hard Knocks. Because the letter is written to an alumnus presumably interested in Hard Knocks, the writer can probably count on his message being read to the end, even despite its weak beginning.

3. Can material be ordered from simplest to most complex, or easiest to most difficult, or most familiar to least familiar (or vice versa) in order to clarify matters (or to obscure them)?

Perhaps a partial application of what linguists call the "given-new contract," a directive that seems to govern the most effective order of items in a sentence,[21] this principle recognizes that writers can also serve readers' needs very efficiently beyond the sentence by moving from what the reader knows already to what he or she does not yet know. Its reverse suggests, of course, that a writer who deliberately wishes to hide or obscure information can do so by moving from most difficult to least, or from least familiar to most.

4. Can the writer move from least controversial or surprising to most controversial or surprising, or vice versa?

Once, while composing a scholarly essay explaining topical allusions in three passages from a medieval poem, I decided to begin my discussion with the third passage: I knew that I was on firm ground in that section of my argument, and I wanted to dispose my audience favorably to me before moving to the more controversial first two passages. Business writers may commonly exploit the same principle in a variety of documents. Proposals might begin with their most conclusive arguments and then move to shakier assertions. Sales letters might begin with conventional uses of a product before discussing exotic ones. Reports might move from the least controversial recommendations to the most controversial. By contrast, the second Save the Children letter might be said to violate this principle because it discusses the relatively controversial issue of family planning before the less controversial matter of economic development. However, I would not claim that in every situation it is unwise to move from controversial to less controversial.

5. Should a presentation be arranged "deductively" or "inductively"?

In other words, should a business writer state a generalization first and then give evidence and arguments for it, or give reasons and evidence before the generalization?[22] In part, of course, this decision is sometimes affected by the conventions of the document involved. When convention does not compel a particular choice, most practical rhetoricians advise writers to begin with the thesis or subthesis when the reader has solicited the communication or seems receptive to the idea in question; on the other hand, the thesis should be withheld until after evidence is presented when the communication is unsolicited or when the reader might seem unreceptive to the idea. The first Save the Children letter in the appendixes is arranged deductively, with its appeal for funds primary. The second one illustrates the risks and the rewards of organizing inductively: on the one hand, the more dramatic opening and closing, the more concrete follow-ups, and the less direct final appeal seem likely to affect a reader positively; on the other hand, readers may never reach the appeal for funds if they quit their reading while wondering why such a communication was sent to them in the first place.

6. Are Rogerian principles called for in a given situation?

A formalized pattern for argument suggested by the work of Carl Rogers makes use of several principles already detailed in this section on audience. Articulated most clearly by Young, Becker, and Pike, this structure is probably most appropriate "whenever commitments to values are powerful and emotions run high" — that is, whenever the stakes are high and the case is in doubt.[23] Report writers whose conclusions or recommendations fly in the face of convention, or threaten the deeply held beliefs of a reader, might well adopt Rogerian tactics. So might tactful letter writers, or a host of other business writers. Indeed, Rogerian argument is in fact a more sophisticated version of a traditional business writing injunction for handling bad news (i.e., provide a buffer, then give reasons for bad news, and only then the message; and close with a counterproposal or some other positive conclusion). Rogerian argument is calculated to eliminate or reduce a reader's sense of being threatened: First, introduce the problem, while conveying to the reader that his or her position is understood; second, delineate the area within which the reader's position is valid; third, state the writer's own position; fourth, state how the reader's position would benefit if he or she would adopt elements of the writer's position. While Young, Becker, and Pike claim that Rogerian argument has no conventional, fixed structure, the four tasks involved in such arguments definitely have as many implications for structure as for invention. And those implications hold as much for argumentative discourse in business settings as in other forums.

Writer Considerations

If genre, subject, and audience are so important in business communication, are there any times when a writer-centered arrangement is appropriate? If novelists on occasion arrange things in the order in which they occur to them or interrupt narratives with flashbacks or intuitive leaps, all in order to recreate a sense of a mind in action, might there also be occasions when a business writer might order things for his or her convenience, or for the sheer fun of doing something playful? At first, such occasions might seem rare. Expressive discourse calls for writer-centered[24] arrangement schemes, but occasions for expressive writing seem exceptional in a business firm. A business professional might arrange the entries in a personal journal or "list of things to do today" in the order in which they strike the fancy, or in a playful way, and the seemingly random order of items in a contract might be another exception, contracts being a form of expressive discourse. But usually the writer-based arrangement "patterns" that, all too often, appear in business or professional prose are regarded as ill-advised by rhetoricians. After all, to play is not often to pursue corporate goals. And for writers to recapitulate their own activities in a report or to reenact the processes they went through to make a discovery or to offer a series of roughly coordinate reminiscences in a document seems to emphasize just the wrong thing: the writer, not the message and its audience. For that reason, consultants rightly take pains to show writers in corporations how their arrangements in reports are indeed writer-centered and then encourage them to employ other patterns.

At the same time, I am wary of discouraging categorically all writer-based arrangements, even in prose that is ostensibly transactional. Rhetoric, after all, aims at the development of knowledge as well as its dissemination; it involves inquiry as well as persuasion. Learning may well be, on many occasions, an individual matter that is then communicated through audience-centered reports, letters, and memos. But learning is also frequently a communal enterprise conducted through language in which those same reports and letters and memos comprise a dialectic that fosters inquiry, incubation, and inspiration. The "writing across the curriculum" movement has demonstrated that writers in various disciplines can use prose not only to make knowledge available but also to generate knowledge in the first place. And that stands in business as well as in any other enterprise. In working with a transportation engineering firm near Chicago I personally observed how an exchange of informal memos — often composed right at the typewriter and often therefore arranged in ways most convenient to the writer — contributed to the resolution of technical problems. It seems to me that we might well encourage such cooperative rhetorical exchanges in business — regardless of whether they take a writer-based form — rather than discourage them completely.

Social Considerations

In addition to genre, subject, audience, and their own convenience, business writers with a rhetorical perspective have one other thing to consider during the arrangement process: setting. For what might be called "social forces" also influence arrangement.

Macrocultural forces: It is probably impossible to catalog all of the patterns for organizing thought that our culture has inherited. Some of those are linguistic: "Rules" for ordering relations between and among sentences are only now being investigated. Others probably have social origins. In fact, it would probably take a detailed comparison of American nonfiction prose and other nations' prose (especially non-Western nations) for linguists to turn up the ways that we have learned to sort out language and meaning.[25] For example, some comparisons of Western prose with Japanese suggest that our conventional agreement to build a beginning, middle, and end into all documents (and most subsections) is indeed only a convention. Prose can move in many other ways. Further study of nonliterary prose by comparative linguists is likely to turn up other such conventions. Still, so ingrained are such conventions in both writers and readers that writers cannot choose to ignore them very often anyway, especially in writing as typically functional as business prose.[26]

Microcultural forces: But there is plenty of choice about "microcultural" forces, those social influences exerted not on an entire society but on its subcultures. The details of those influences on business writing are still sketchy, since only now is a scholarly literature developing on corporate culture; nevertheless, sociologists and anthropologists are already beginning to explain how particular institutions influence customer relations, management practices, and every sort of employee behavior — including writing. In *Complex Organizations*, for instance, Charles Perrow explains how an organization's values affect the language of documents and their structure. Harold Garfinkle has also illustrated how the prevailing interests and activities of an organization affect the content and form of organization prose.[27]

The full implications of organizational theory on rhetoric remain to be detailed. However, it is already clear that business writers in the act of arrangement must ask themselves questions such as these: "How does my boss want this to be presented?" "How do we arrange the parts of a report (or request or proposal, etc.) in this company?" "How did we deal with this problem last time?" And so forth. Not only do particular institutions affect arrangement patterns, but specific disciplines do so as well: As Carolyn Miller and I have tried to show, chemical engineers might learn to construct documents in conventional patterns that are very different from the ways accountants or lawyers might structure prose.[28]

During years of apprenticeship in undergraduate and graduate programs, and in the first months of employment in a given corporation or other institution, business writers themselves learn how to observe appropriate cultural conventions, including conventions that affect arrangement. While it is sometimes difficult for analysts and other "outsiders" to pick up on the social influences that direct a particular workplace, it would be useful if teachers of business writing — and the writers they direct — could grow familiar with how those conventions might affect the arrangement of documents produced at work.

Conclusion

Let me close with some qualifications and generalizations. First, this essay assumes that a piece of discourse is a succession of discrete units, each more or less self-contained, open to being arranged in many different ways; the several versions of letters in the appendixes illustrate the same assumption. I realize, of course, that such a perspective artificially separates form from content, that it fails to acknowledge fully the contribution structure makes to meaning. Perhaps more important, I also realize that such a point of view falsifies in some ways the composing process. Often a legitimate and effective arrangement pattern is less schematic, less "principled," more intuitive than I suggest; frequently, an arrangement represents a movement of the mind that is far more difficult to schematize than I am suggesting; and sometimes highly formal linguistic rules may be influencing arrangement in ways we do not yet know about. I also realize that in some highly conventional prose few arrangement choices may in fact be available to a writer. At the same time, however, I contend that it is valuable for writers to consider formalized principles such as the ones I have laid out. Even if in practice many writers sometimes behave more intuitively than systematically, there is still value in learning systems, especially for writers whose intuitions are largely untutored.

Second, my presentation seems to obviate the possibility of organic plans, of plans that evolve as writers work. Again, I do not mean to do so. I recognize that arrangement occurs as much during formal composition as before it, and I realize that an arrangement choice made early in a composition might in part determine the choices that follow. Nevertheless, I still contend, along with Richard Larson, that "the planning of any piece of writing . . . involves much more than the replication of a previously discerned general pattern of discourse. It requires the choice of an order specially tailored to the subject, to the writer's view of that subject, to the goal sought by the writer, to the reader(s), and to the situation in which it will be perceived."[29]

In short, many arrangements — the products of rhetorical principles — are available for nearly every document that a business writer might compose. In only the most routine and conventional communication is a specific arrangement pattern inevitable. Writers therefore must learn to choose from among the number of arrangement possibilities that have been cataloged here (and the others that have not occurred to me). Sometimes the choice will be simple. More often, however, a writer will arrive at a particular choice only tentatively; for nearly every arrangement has disadvantages as well as advantages, and sometimes the conflicting goals of a writer ("How can I make all my points and still keep this short and emphatic?") will suggest conflicting arrangement principles. Faced with several possibilities, a writer must nevertheless choose. And the choice should be made on rhetorical grounds: Does the arrangement choice gratify the rhetorical need that motivated it? More concretely: Does the arrangement choice *work* better than the other possibilities?

The job of business writing teachers, then, I hope seems clear. Instead of prescribing stereotypical patterns, teachers should present options and suggest alternatives. When reviewing student work, teachers should resist the temptation to judge too quickly; since many arrangements are possible, even plausible, and since the grounds for judging among the possibilities are more often suggestive than conclusive (as the appendixes illustrate), teachers might well concentrate as much on exploring possibilities and expanding students' arrangement repertoires as on directing them to one "best" arrangement.

Finally, business writing teachers might well stay alert for other arrangement patterns besides the ones I have noticed; for only when the catalog is more complete can we be more confident about teaching the arrangement of business writing. Several centuries ago, Ramus separated invention and arrangement from rhetoric and relegated them to logic. Now that rhetoricians have restored invention to a place of eminence, perhaps it is time to welcome back arrangement just as warmly.

Notes

1. Frank D'Angelo, *A Conceptual Theory of Rhetoric* (Cambridge, Mass.: Winthrop, 1975), 55.

2. Marya Holcombe and Judith Stein, *Writing for Decision Makers* (Belmont, Calif.: Lifetime Learning, 1981); Ken Davis, *Better Business Writing: A Process Approach* (Columbus, Ohio: Merrill, 1983), 70–76.

3. Richard Larson, "Structure and Form in Non-Fiction Prose," in *Teaching Composition: Ten Bibliographic Essays*, ed. Gary Tate (Ft. Worth: Texas Christian University Press, 1976), 45. Larson's essay and D'Angelo's book both contain excellent introductory bibliographies on arrangement.

4. W. Ross Winterowd, "*Dispositio*: The Concept of Form in Discourse," *College Composition and Communication* 22 (1971): 34–45. For an innovative recent treatment of form, see Gregory Columb and Joseph Williams, "Perceiving Structure in Professional Prose: A Multiply Determined Experience," in *Writing in Nonacademic Settings*, ed. Lee Odell and Dixie Goswami (New York: Guilford, 1985), 87–128. While not without rich implications for writers, their approach to form (as the title of their essay implies) is rooted primarily in texts and readers. On the difficulty of distinguishing among terms such as *form, structure, organization, design*, etc., see the introductory paragraphs of the same essay.

5. My principle of classification is suggested in part by James Kinneavy, *A Theory of Discourse* (Englewood Cliffs, N.J.: Prentice-Hall, 1971); and by Edward P. J. Corbett, who notes that "the person bent on persuasion will be guided in his decisions about the appropriate disposition of his resources by a number of considerations: (1) The kind of discourse. . . . (2) The nature of his subject. . . . (3) His own *ethos*. . . . (4) The nature of his audience . . ." (*Classical Rhetoric for the Modern Student* [New York: Oxford University Press, 1971]), 300. Neither Kinneavy nor Corbett

considers the social influences that also affect rhetorical choice. Nor do they detail the list of arrangement options as I try to do, or discuss the particular arrangement of business prose.

6. Kinneavy, A *Theory of Discourse*, 151.

7. Kenneth Burke has discussed in some detail the form of literary discourse in *Counter-Statement* (New York: Harcourt, Brace and World, 1931), 124–44.

8. For a study of the effects of established forms on technical writing, see Victoria Winkler [Mikelonis], "The Role of Models in Technical and Scientific Writing," in *New Essays in Technical and Scientific Communication: Research, Theory, Practice,* ed. Paul V. Anderson, R. John Brockmann, and Carolyn Miller (Farmingdale, N.Y.: Baywood, 1983), 111–22.

9. The Save the Children letter was an unsolicited direct mail promotion letter that I received a year or two ago; Appendix B and Appendix C are versions of the letter that I created. The letter in Appendix D was an unsolicited promotion received by one of my colleagues; I have obviously changed names to protect anonymity, but in every other detail the letter is untouched. Appendix E is a version of that original that I constructed. All five appendixes are included here for their illustrative power only; though they seem to me well written, I do not suggest that they are "models" of their genre. Space limitations prevented me from including versions of more and longer documents.

10. The formula is articulated by, among others, Herta Murphy and Charles Peck, *Effective Business Communications* (New York: McGraw–Hill, 1976), 310.

11. Charles Bazerman, "Codifying the Social Scientific Style: The APA Publication Manual as a Behaviorist Rhetoric" (Paper delivered at the Iowa Colloquium on the Rhetoric of the Human Sciences, Iowa City, 1984); and "Reporting the Experiment: The Changing Account of Scientific Doings in the *Philosophical Transactions of the Royal Society,* 1665-1800" (Paper delivered at the Annual Meeting of the Modern Language Association, Washington, D.C., 1984).

12. Kinneavy, A *Theory of Discourse*, 264–65; Corbett, *Classical Rhetoric*, 37.

13. W. Ross Winterowd, *Rhetoric: A Synthesis* (New York: Holt, Rinehart, and Winston, 1968), 121.

14. Leonard Podis, "Teaching Arrangement: Defining a More Practical Approach," *College Composition and Communication* 31 (1980): 199.

15. Of course readers actually *do* construct such relationships for themselves as they read, especially when such relationships are not made explicit in the document.

16. The work of Francis Christensen most fully elaborates this principle of arrangement: See especially "A Generative Rhetoric of the Paragraph," *College Composition and Communication* 16 (1965): 144–56. Christensen's ideas on paragraphs have been extended to whole discourse by D'Angelo and by Michael Grady, "A Conceptual Rhetoric of the Composition," *College Composition and Communication* 22 (1971): 348–54.

17. "Move from general to specific" is of course commonplace advice that students will be comfortable with. Teachers, however, might well find

it more profitable to appropriate the roughly analogous but more generic terms advanced by Columb and Williams ("issue and discussion" or "point and development") because those terms might generate more powerful advice about writing.

18. Richard Young, Alton Becker, and Kenneth Pike plot some of the arrangement patterns contingent on syllogistic logic in *Rhetoric: Discovery and Change* (New York: Harcourt Brace Jovanovich, 1970), 230–35.

19. For a different view, see Lawrence Green, "Enthymemic Invention and Structural Prediction," *College Composition and Communication* 41 (1980): 623–34. Green argues that particular kinds of enthymemes produce distinctive arrangement patterns. My own contention is that Green's fascinating essay describes only very simple (though common) enthymemes that depend on only one minor premise (or "because-clause"), while what most interests me is the arrangement of complex arguments that depend on a series of because-clauses, themselves supported by many examples.

20. James Raymond, "Enthymemes, Examples, and Rhetorical Method," in *Essays on Classical Rhetoric and Modern Discourse,* ed. Robert Connors, Lisa Ede, and Andrea Lunsford (Carbondale, Ill.: Southern Illinois University Press, 1984), 140–51.

21. For a good discussion of the given-new contract with implications drawn explicitly to arrangement, see Columb and Williams, "Perceiving Structure."

22. Actually, the terms *inductive* and *deductive* are misnomers, since both of them in this context describe only inductive arguments — arguments that support a generalization not with formal logic but with specific premises and evidence. James Kinneavy, *A Theory of Discourse,* 151–66, suggests the term "induction" for an argument that concludes with the main thesis and "inverted induction" for one beginning with the thesis.

23. Young, Becker, and Pike, *Rhetoric,* 274. Their description of Rogerian argument is presented on pp. 273–83. For other delineations of Rogerian argument, see Maxine Hairston, *Contemporary Rhetoric* (Boston: Houghton-Mifflin, 1974), 210–11; Andrea Lunsford, "Aristotelian vs. Rogerian Argument: A Reassessment," *College Composition and Communication* 30 (1979): 146–51; Lisa Ede, "Is Rogerian Rhetoric Really Rogerian?" *Rhetoric Review* 3 (1984): 40–48; and Paul Baker, "Aristotelian vs. Rogerian Rhetoric," *College Composition and Communication* 31 (1980): 427–32. For an application to business writing, see Davis.

24. Linda Flower is most commonly associated with the term "writer centered." See *Problem-Solving Strategies for Writing* (New York: Harcourt Brace Jovanovich, 1985), 162–75.

25. The movement in literary criticism known as structuralism has in a sense been dedicated to turning up evidence of cultural patterns in prose that we all observe, mostly subconsciously. See Robert Scholes's primer, *Structuralism in Literature* (New Haven: Yale University Press, 1974), which is based heavily on the work of Lévi-Strauss; and Roland Barthes's *Pleasure of the Text,* trans. Richard Miller (New York: Hill, Wang, 1975).

26. Winston Weathers' *An Alternate Style: Options in Composition* (Rochelle Park, N.J.: Hayden, 1980) explores the features of an "alternate" or unconventional style that he calls Grammar B. Grammar B violates purposely and for specific effects the conventions of "the well-made box" known as Grammar A. Grammar B also affects arrangement: "compositions achieved through the alternate style will obviously be fairly open-ended in structure . . . that is, they will have less well-defined beginnings and endings [and] . . . more frequently open *in medias res* (p. 39). Paragraph conventions are also pushed to their limits in Grammar B. Interestingly, Weathers illustrates Grammar B with several effective (if indeed unconventional) business letters; see pages 47–50 and 89–91.

27. Charles Perrow, *Complex Organizations* (Glenview, Ill.: Scott, Foresman and Company, 1979); Harold Garfinkle, "'Good' Organizational Reasons for 'Bad' Clinic Records," in his *Studies in Ethnomethodology* (Englewood Cliffs, N.J.: Prentice-Hall, 1967), 186–207.

28. See Carolyn Miller and Jack Selzer, "Special Topics of Argument in Engineering Reports," in *Writing in Nonacademic Settings*, 309–41.

29. Larson, "Structure and Form," 60.

Appendix A

Dear Friend:

Knowing of your interest in Save the Children's work, I have been hoping to welcome you into our family of active supporters.

By joining us, you could do much to help poor communities harness their resources of manpower and carry out badly needed self-help projects of all kinds.

But it isn't always "manpower"... often it's *womanpower!*

I have seen this happen time and again on my visits to our program areas around the world.

Here are women whose lives have centered upon raising children and doing farm work. Yet suddenly they find themselves helping to plan large-scale ventures in agriculture, home building, health programs, even small industries... and doing a first-rate job of it!

In Honduras, for example, there's a bakery and a mango jelly enterprise, both initiated and managed entirely by women. Women in the Mexican town of Santa Isabel, having taken a course in weaving, now run a thriving business making and selling multi-colored wall hangings.

In other countries — Colombia, Greece, Korea, Lebanon — women have formed credit unions and launched new enterprises in dressmaking, canning, and poultry raising. Some have founded day-care centers for pre-school youngsters. Others have formed cooperatives to market locally produced food, clothing, and handicrafts.

As you may imagine, ventures like these do wonders to revive the economies of impoverished villages... and do wonders for the self-esteem of women themselves. Their pride and delight in their community involvement is really something to see.

You will also appreciate the initiatives some women are taking in promoting family planning. Having learned methods of fertility control at workshops conducted by Save the Children, they are now working hard to persuade married couples in their villages to practice it.

As a result, family planning is winning slow but steady acceptance in nearly all of our program areas. And much credit for this belongs to women who volunteer to serve as "motivators" among their friends and neighbors.

Yes, women today stand proudly in the forefront of our community development programs in 17 different countries. And I think you'll join me in saying... more power to them!

Come with us today, won't you? A gift from you would help still other women not only liberate their villages from the bonds of poverty... but also liberate themselves from bonds of inferiority imposed by culture and tradition. On their behalf, I thank you most warmly for your contribution.

Sincerely yours,

Marion Fennelly Levy
Women's Program Consultant

Appendix B

Dear Friend:

Do you know that family planning is winning slow but steady acceptance in impoverished areas around the world? Much credit for this belongs to women who volunteer to serve as "motivators" among their friends and neighbors. Having learned methods of fertility control at workshops conducted by Save the Children, they are now working hard to persuade married couples in their villages to practice it.

As you may imagine, ventures like these do wonders to revive the economies of impoverished villages . . . and do wonders for the self-esteem of women themselves. Their pride and delight in their community involvement is really something to see.

In Colombia, Greece, Korea, Lebanon — women have formed credit unions, launched new enterprises in dressmaking, canning, and poultry raising. Some have founded day-care centers for pre-school youngsters. Others have formed cooperatives to market locally produced food, clothing, and handicrafts.

In Honduras there's a bakery and a mango jelly enterprise, both initiated and managed entirely by women. Women in the Mexican town of Santa Isabel, having taken a course in weaving, now run a thriving business making and selling multi-colored wall hangings.

Here are women whose lives have centered upon raising children and doing farm work. Yet suddenly they find themselves helping to plan large-scale ventures in agriculture, home building, health programs, even small industries . . . and doing a first-rate job of it!

I have seen this happen time and again on my visits to our program areas around the world.

Yes, women today stand proudly in the forefront of our community development programs in 17 different countries. And I think you'll join me in saying . . . more power to them!

Won't you consider joining Save the Children's family of active supporters? You could do much to help poor communities harness their resources of womanpower and manpower, to carry out badly needed self-help projects of all kinds.

Come with us today, won't you? A gift from you would help still other women not only liberate their villages from the bonds of poverty . . . but also liberate themselves from bonds of inferiority imposed by culture and tradition.

On their behalf, I thank you most warmly for your contribution.

Sincerely yours,

Marion Fennelly Levy
Women's Program Consultant

Appendix C

Dear Friend:

In my visits to Save the Children program areas around the world, I have seen women whose lives have centered upon raising children and doing farm work. Yet suddenly they find themselves helping to plan large-scale ventures in agriculture, home building, health programs, even small industries . . . and doing a first-rate job of it!

In Honduras, for example, there's a bakery and a mango jelly enterprise, both initiated and managed entirely by women. Women in the Mexican town of Santa Isabel, having taken a course in weaving, now run a thriving business making and selling multi-colored wall hangings.

In other countries — Colombia, Greece, Korea, Lebanon — women have formed credit unions, launched new enterprises in dressmaking, canning, and poultry raising. Some have founded day-care centers for pre-school youngsters. Others have formed cooperatives to market locally produced food, clothing, and handicrafts.

As you may imagine, ventures like these do wonders to revive the economies of impoverished villages . . . and do wonders for the self-esteem of women themselves. Their pride and delight in their community involvement is really something to see.

That is why I have been hoping to welcome you into our family of active supporters.

By joining us, you could do much to help poor communities harness their resources of manpower and carry out badly needed self-help projects of all kinds.

But it isn't always "manpower" . . . often it's *womanpower*!

You might especially appreciate the initiatives some women are taking in promoting family planning. Having learned methods of fertility control at workshops conducted by Save the Children, they are now working hard to persuade married couples in their villages to practice it.

As a result, family planning is winning slow but steady acceptance in nearly all of our program areas. And much credit for this belongs to women who volunteer to serve as "motivators" among their friends and neighbors.

Yes, women today stand proudly in the forefront of our community development programs in 17 different countries. And I think you'll join me in saying . . . more power to them!

Come with us today, won't you? A gift from you would help still other women not only liberate their villages from the bonds of poverty . . . but also liberate themselves from bonds of inferiority imposed by culture and tradition.

On their behalf, I thank you most warmly for your contribution.

Sincerely yours,

Marion Fennelly Levy
Women's Program Consultant

Appendix D

UNIVERSITY OF HARD KNOCKS
Someplace, Somewhere 12345

Department of English
Graduate Division
7000 English Building

December 15, 1982

Dear Dr. Maxwellhouse:

This is to send you greetings and some information to supplement what I hope are fond memories of your experience at the University of Hard Knocks. As we all know, these are difficult times for the Humanities in academia, but at Hard Knocks we do not despair, for we have been able to maintain a vigorous and distinguished faculty and we continue to attract committed and bright students. There are fewer of them, but we would be less than honest if we promised immediate careers to more, considering the brutal realities of the marketplace.

Still, we have been fairly successful at placing our graduates. According to the *Chronicle of Higher Education,* graduate English departments have averaged a placement of no more than forty percent of their graduates in teaching positions. In the past two years at Hard Knocks 26 candidates have received their doctorates. Of these, 19 have entered full-time teaching positions. Five others have gone into editing, publishing, or civil service.

This fall we have 108 Ph.D. candidates and 51 M.A. candidates. The students you advise about graduate programs should know that we have several fellowships available for M.A. candidates and that 73 of our Ph.D. candidates have teaching assistantships. Our assistantships remain among the best paying in the nation — currently about $8,000 a year for 50 percent of full-time. The horizon will probably brighten in the future. In 15 years the great number who came into the profession in the early 1960s will be reaching retirement. So within the next decade, students with a nose for the future might begin graduate work in the Humanities with a reasonable anticipation of academic careers.

The recent retirements of Joseph Morgan, Jonathan Bench, Christine Mathewson, and Mary Williams, and the departure of George Foster, have left our Renaissance and nineteenth-century American areas weakened, but we anticipate recent junior appointments and increased support from the College of Letters and Science to repair these losses. In all other areas we have been able to maintain or increase the Department's traditional eminence.

There have been several changes in the graduate program in recent years which we believe make it better able to prepare the students to confront the tasks ahead. We now require a course in Critical Theory of the students so that all their instructors can anticipate a knowledge of research skills and experience in practical criticism. We have also instituted a Field Examination so that a student must display a competence in one of three broad historical periods, as well as the narrower focus in one traditional historical area of concentration. Finally, we have increased the seminar requirement from one to four courses so that the students now gain more experience in the give-and-take of intellectual inquiry and in literary research.

I hope that this information will be a help to you when advising your own better students who may be considering a career in teaching and scholarship. Please post our enclosed brochure. I would be happy to answer any further questions you may have.

Sincerely,

George A. Anderson
Director of Graduate Studies

GAA/sg

Enclosures: Graduate Programs Brochure
            Program for the M.A. in English
            Program for the Ph.D. in English

Appendix E

UNIVERSITY OF HARD KNOCKS

Someplace, Somewhere 12345

Department of English
Graduate Division
7000 English Building

December 15, 1982

Dear Dr. Maxwellhouse:

This is to send you greetings and some information to supplement what I hope are fond memories of your experience at the University of Hard Knocks. As we all know, these are difficult times for the Humanities in academia, but at Hard Knocks we do not despair, for we have been able to maintain a vigorous and distinguished faculty and we continue to attract committed and bright students.

The recent retirements of Joseph Morgan, Jonathan Bench, Christine Mathewson, and Mary Williams, and the departure of George Foster, have left our Renaissance and nineteenth-century American areas weakened, but we anticipate recent junior appointments and increased support from the College of Letters and Science to repair these losses. In all other areas we have been able to maintain or increase the Department's traditional eminence.

There have been several changes in the graduate program in recent years which we believe make it better able to prepare the students to confront the tasks ahead. We now require a course in Critical Theory of the students so that all their instructors can anticipate a knowledge of research skills and experience in practical criticism. We have also instituted a Field Examination so that a student must display a competence in one of three broad historical periods, as well as the narrower focus in one traditional historical area of concentration. Finally, we have increased the seminar requirement from one to four courses so that the students now gain more experience in the give-and-take of intellectual inquiry and in literary research.

There are fewer students now, but we would be less than honest if we promised immediate careers to more, considering the brutal realities of the marketplace. This fall we have 108 Ph.D. candidates and 51 M.A. candidates. The students you advise about graduate programs should know that we have several fellowships available for M.A. candidates and that 73 of our Ph.D. candidates have teaching assistantships. Our assistantships remain among the best paying in the nation — currently about $8,000 a year for 50 percent of full-time.

The horizon will probably brighten in the future. In 15 years the great number who came into the profession in the early 1960s will be reaching retirement. So within the next decade students with a nose for the future might begin graduate work in the Humanities with a reasonable anticipation of academic careers.

In fact, we have already been fairly successful at placing our graduates. According to the *Chronicle of Higher Education*, graduate English departments have averaged a placement of no more than 40 percent of their graduates in teaching positions. In the past two years at Hard Knocks 26 candidates have received their doctorates. Of these, 19 have entered full-time teaching positions. Five others have gone into editing, publishing, or civil service.

I hope that this information will be a help to you when advising your own better students who may be considering a career in teaching and scholarship. Please post our enclosed brochure. I would be happy to answer any further questions you may have.

Sincerely,

George A. Anderson
Director of Graduate Studies

GAA/sg

Enclosures: Graduate Programs Brochure
            Program for the M.A. in English
            Program for the Ph.D. in English

3 What Classical Rhetoric Has to Offer the Teacher and the Student of Business and Professional Writing

Edward P. J. Corbett
The Ohio State University

The problems associated with any kind of specialized course in writing ultimately turn out to be the fundamental problems that attend the composing of any written text designed to communicate with an audience. Whether the writing is scientific, technical, professional, business, or any other kind of specialized writing, the main and persistent problems resolve themselves into a concern for finding something to say and then selecting, organizing, and expressing what has been found. Those concerns are traditionally the concerns of the academic discipline known as rhetoric, a discipline that can most broadly be defined as "the art of effective communication in the oral or the written medium."

In recent years, experienced teachers of writing have been publishing articles in which they point out the relevance of particular rhetorical systems to technical writing. Some of those teachers have demonstrated the usefulness of even the classical system of rhetoric perfected by the ancient Greeks and Romans. Andrea Lunsford, for instance, has shown how useful the standard six-part structure of the classical oration was in helping her students organize their technical reports.[1] Michael Halloran and Merrill Whitburn have argued that a better model for the kind of plain style that is regularly recommended for scientific and technical writing can be found in Cicero's rhetoric texts than in the later rhetoric texts that were influenced by the pronouncements of John Locke, Francis Bacon, and the Royal Society.[2] Halloran and Annette Bradford have argued for the appropriateness and the effectiveness of the classical figures of speech in scientific and technical writing.[3] I myself once gave a talk at a national convention of English teachers in which I discussed how helpful my knowledge of classical rhetoric was when I first started to teach technical writing.[4]

Lately, teachers of business and professional writing have begun to recognize the usefulness of even the ancient classical system of rhetoric

65

for those engaged in this kind of utilitarian writing. Craig Kallendorf and Carol Kallendorf, for instance, in an article entitled "The Figures of Speech, *Ethos,* and Aristotle: Notes Toward a Rhetoric of Business Communication" have convincingly demonstrated the pertinence of Aristotelian rhetoric to business writing and have displayed evidence of the presence, in contemporary business documents, of the kinds of rhetorical strategies and devices taught in the classical rhetorics.[5] I want to show here that business and professional communication has its own rhetorical system but that this system has been shaped not only by the natural demands of any kind of verbal interchange among human beings, but also by the enduring principles of classical rhetoric.

The basic notion underlying classical rhetoric is that any act of verbal communication between human beings comprises four components: (1) a speaker or writer, (2) listeners or readers, (3) a message or text, and (4) a reality or universe that the message or text is talking about. All four of those components play a part in business and professional communications; but of those four, the one that gets primary consideration is audience — that is, the listeners or readers. One consequence of the audience being a prime concern in such communication is that the writer or speaker must carefully adapt the message to fit the receivers of it. A message must always be shaped in some measure, of course, to fit the audience; but in business and professional communications, the audience is more often than in many other kinds of specialized discourses the chief determinant of the means adopted to effect the end. Assessing that audience, whether it be primarily an in-house audience or an out-of-house audience, requires a great deal of skill and sensitivity on the part of the author. C. H. Knoblauch has reminded us of the complexity of the process by which we gauge the temper of the heterogeneous audience that reads and responds to business and professional communications.[6] Because of the complexity of that process, we can all profit from the lessons that classical rhetoric can teach us about the dynamics of audience relationships.

Prominent among those lessons are the elaborate instructions that classical rhetoric provided for developing an appropriate and effective style. Because the audience for out-of-house communications is likely to be very heterogeneous, the style of those communications must be consonant with the temper and the capacity of a wide range of listeners and readers. The use of jargon may sometimes be inescapable, and even preferable, in scientific and technical writing, but in business and professional writing, even a smattering of jargon could ruinously obscure the message being transmitted to an individual or a group from the so-called "general public." Of the three levels of style that the Roman rhetoricians talked about — the plain, the moderate, and the grand — the plain style is most often the suitable style in business and professional communications.

But to say that the plain style is most often the suitable style for such communications is not to say that this style must never be adorned. The aforementioned articles by Halloran and Whitburn, and by Craig and Carol Kallendorf, disabuse us of the entrenched notion that the style of utilitarian discourses must never be infected with emotional diction, rhythmical sonorities, or bewitching figures of speech. The figures of speech, for instance, often serve to enhance rather than diminish the clarity of one's prose. The figures of speech and other graces of style can also exert subtle emotional effects on the audience — effects that help to promote our purpose. Of all the rhetorical systems that have appeared down through the ages, classical rhetoric had the most to say about style, so that if we want to consciously cultivate style, we will get the most help from the classical rhetoric texts, which took style seriously. A confirmation of the appropriateness and effectiveness of an adorned plain style for business and professional communication can be found in the typical ad copy that regularly issues from Madison Avenue. Such copy is laden with — among other graces of style — the schemes and tropes of classical rhetoric. For example, in these two sentences quoted by the Kallendorfs from a report by TIMEBASE, a computer software company, there are, besides the two metaphorical tropes (*stranglehold* and *covey*), instance of the schemes known as *antimetabole* (repetition of words, in successive clauses, in reverse grammatical order), *anastrophe* (inversion of the natural or usual order), and *parallelism* (similarity in a pair or a series of words, phrases, or clauses):

> The days are gone when a handful of young designers could get a stranglehold on the production of new programs. Gone, too, are the days when a covey of software companies published virtually everything on the market.[7]

In the previous paragraph, I mentioned the subtle emotional effects of style, but classical rhetoric taught its students how to appeal directly to the emotions of the audience. Aristotle devoted the major portion of Book II of his *Rhetoric* to an analysis of contrasting pairs of the common human emotions (for example, fear/confidence, pity/indignation) and of the strategies for arousing or subduing those emotions. Teachers of business and professional writing may not want to subject the students to such an elaborate, formal study of the human emotions, but they would do well to at least eradicate their students' typical deep-seated suspicion of appeals to emotion and make them aware of how potent the appeals to emotion are in moving people to action. Aristotle maintained that the general function of appeals to emotion was to put the audience into proper disposition to receive a message (*Rhetoric*, Book I, Ch. 2).[8]

How important such conditioning of the audience is can readily be seen in one of the common forms of business writing: responding to a letter of complaint from a customer. The customer who wrote the letter of complaint is probably in a hostile emotional state already and consequently may be quite unreasonable about the issue in the letter. The respondent's cool recital of the case could very well fail to placate the angry customer. For such an occasion, it would be well if the respondent had even a rudimentary knowledge of "(1) what the state of mind of angry people is, (2) who the people are with whom they usually get angry, and (3) on what grounds they get angry with them" (*Rhetoric*, Book II, Ch. 1).

The ordinary person can gain some measure of that kind of rudimentary knowledge about the mechanism of human emotions by examining his or her own psyche, but he or she can gain a great deal of insight into the human psyche reading Chapters 2–11 of Book II of Aristotle's *Rhetoric*. Aristotle was certainly an amateur psychologist, as most of us are; but because he was a keen observer of human behavior, he learned some valuable lessons about what makes the human animal tick.

In that same Book II of *Rhetoric*, Chapters 12–17, Aristotle examined the characteristic temperament of people at various stages of their life (youth, middle age, old age) and in various circumstances (the fortunes of birth, wealth, social position, political power). Again, the kind of knowledge of human behavior that Aristotle gained from keen observation of the men and women he came in contact with can be invaluable to people in business, industry, and the professions who have to correspond with members of the general public.

Maybe the most valuable lesson that speakers and writers can learn from classical rhetoric is the lesson about the vital importance of the image of themselves that they project to their audience. Aristotle treated this matter under the term *ethos,* one of the three modes of appeal that he posited in his *Rhetoric,* and most later classical rhetoricians picked up on this idea and elaborated on it or modified it. When we are made to consider the dynamics of the so-called "ethical appeal," we may come to agree with Aristotle's pronouncement that the personal character of the speaker or writer may indeed be the most potent means of persuasion (*Rhetoric,* Book I, Ch. 2).

Since the purpose of much business and professional writing is to be persuasive, projecting a favorable *ethos* is vital to the success of such writing. In technical and scientific writing, the image of the author can be, and in many cases should be, low-keyed and unobtrusive. The widely accepted notion about technical and scientific writing is that it should be rigorously impersonal and objective. For that reason, the use of the first-person pronouns *I* and *we* is discouraged, and the use of the passive voice of the verb is tolerated, if not encouraged. The emphasis or the focus of such writing should be kept, we are told, on the subject or the product being dealt with.

In business and professional writing, on the other hand, readers should be able to catch at least a whiff of the *ethos* of the person addressing them. The "voice" of the writer should not come through as strongly as it does in such expressive forms of writing as personal narratives, confessions, familiar essays, letters to relatives and friends; but some impression of a trustworthy persona must come through. In seller/buyer relationships especially — and much of this writing is based on such relationships — it is vitally important that the buyer trust the seller. And that trust is largely established by the *ethos* that the seller establishes and projects in the verbal text.

Aristotle revealed himself to be amazingly perceptive about human nature when he made this observation:

> There are three things which inspire confidence in the orator's own character [ethos] — the three, namely, that induce us to believe a thing apart from any proof of it: good sense [phronesis], good moral character [arete], and goodwill [eunoial]. Men either form a false opinion through want of good sense; or they form a true opinion, but because of their moral badness do not say what they really think; or finally, they are both sensible and upright but not well disposed to their hearers and may fail in consequence to recommend what they know to be the best course. These are the only possible cases. It follows that anyone who is thought to have all three of these good qualities will inspire trust in his audience (*Rhetoric,* Book II, Ch. 1).

Aristotle is talking here about the qualities essential for a speaker bent on persuading an audience, but he could just as well be enunciating the Code of Conduct for Success in Business and the Professions. Both Cicero and Quintilian took up this notion of the importance of a favorable *ethos* and even went as far as to pronounce that the teacher of rhetoric (the *rhetor*) had to be responsible not only for the intellectual training of his pupils but also for their moral formation.

There are no mysteries about how the speaker or writer establishes the kind of *ethos* that Aristotle is calling for. Once you become aware of the need for, and the efficacy of, a favorable *ethos*, the method for establishing that kind of image of yourself flows from common sense: *What* you say and *how* you say it must consistently inspire your audience with confidence that you are an honest, intelligent, and benevolent person. So you may not make patently outrageous claims; you may not make generalizations that obviously violate logic or belie the known facts; you may not flout the basic values endorsed by the major portion of your audience; you may not arouse incongruous emotions in your audience; in short, you may not create the impression that you are stupid, unfair, unscrupulous, or malicious.

And in order to establish and preserve your *ethos*, you must take care with the *manner* in which you say what you say. *Tone* is the key word here, a word that originates in contemporary rhetorics but a notion that was implicit in classical rhetorics. *Tone*, of course, is a word associated primarily with the spoken medium, and the classical rhetoricians treated this notion most prominently when they dealt with delivery, the oral presentation of the oration. Delivery in classical rhetorics dealt partly with *pronuntiatio*, the vocal enunciation of the speech, and partly with *actio*, the postures and the gestures that accompanied the oral delivery. The *sound* of the speech, its *tone*, had to be audible, mellifluous, and varied. A skillful, impressive delivery sometimes made up for weaknesses in the content and the organization of the speech and thereby helped to rescue the speaker's threatened *ethos*.

In the written medium, the proper tone is created and preserved largely by the style of the discourse, about which I said something earlier. Style was never just ornament for the classical rhetoricians, even though they might admit that an elegant style could adorn an otherwise lackluster text. For them, form and content were intimately related. Style was basically part of the form, but a *good* style was delicately blended with the content. And tone is a perfect example of this blending of matter and form. A style that was appropriate to the subject matter, the occasion, the author, and the audience helped to establish and preserve the ethical appeal of the discourse. If the writers of business and professional prose were made aware of how the classical rhetoricians viewed style, they might be induced to be more concerned about their style.

Writers of business and professional prose must also be made aware that physical appearance plays a part in creating the image of the speaker or writer. In the oral medium, the mere physiognomy of the speaker affects the attitude of the audience toward the speaker; and how the speaker dresses could dispose the audience either favorably or unfavorably to him or her. The equivalent in the written medium is the physical appearance of the manuscript or the printed text in which the discourse is delivered to the readers.[9] Neatness — to pick just one aspect of the physical appearance of the text — may not be next to godliness, but its presence or absence in a written text unquestionably influences the reaction of the readers and determines the kind of *ethos* that the writer projects to the readers. Correct spelling and correct grammar and usage are also part of the "appearance" of a manuscript. As part of the *delivery* system — to use the term from classical rhetoric for the manner in which a text is transmitted to an audience — neatness and correctness reflect the *ethos* of the writer and affect the kind of reception the text gets from the readers. It is safe to say that the neatness and correctness of the text are more crucial in business and professional writing than in any other kind of writing.

For a long time, texts on business and professional writing paid little or no attention to the crucial importance of *ethos* in those forms of discourse involving a relationship between a seller and a buyer or between a professional and a client; but in recent years, some of those texts have been discussing the function of *ethos* in those relationships — even though they may not actually use the term *ethos*. This attention to *ethos* is just one of many pieces of evidence that the classical rhetorics are beginning to exert a delayed and indirect influence on the consciousness and practice of modern writers.

But many of the other lessons that I have talked about in this essay are beginning to have an impact in the modern classroom. Serious students of writing are developing sophisticated rhetorical skills. Many of them are totally unaware that the principles and techniques that have helped to shape their rhetorical craft stem from the ancient rhetoricians, and so they have had to develop their rhetorical skills either through their own instincts or through the mediation of knowledgeable teachers or sound textbooks. It would help to solidify their skills if they were introduced to the Greek and Roman rhetoricians who first formulated the basic principles.

It is not that the ancient rhetoricians laid down the principles and techniques of effective communication once and for all. No, indeed. Much of what they prescribed in their rhetoric texts is outmoded and superseded, and much of what is still valuable in their texts could be learned more readily in modern textbooks.[10] The chief value of classical rhetorics for modern teachers and students of business and professional writing is that they often touch on aspects of the communication process that modern textbooks ignore or that they give us a new perspective on fundamental principles and strategies. It is a rare modern rhetoric, for instance, that sanctions and encourages the use of emotional appeals, as Aristotle did. The classical treatment of *ethos* gives us a fresh perspective on the process that modern textbooks treat under such terms as *persona, image, charisma, tone.* All of us need help in honing our communication skills. We should be disposed to accept that help from whatever source is available to us. Classical rhetoric is a source that has been available to us for thousands of years, and it is an immensely rich and rewarding source.

Notes

1. Andrea Lunsford, "Classical Rhetoric and Technical Writing," *College Composition and Communication* 27 (October 1976): 289–91.

2. S. Michael Halloran and Merrill D. Whitburn, "Ciceronian Rhetoric and the Rise of Science: The Plain Style Reconsidered," in *The Rhetorical Tradition and Modern Writing,* ed. James J. Murphy (New York: MLA, 1982), 58–72.

3. S. Michael Halloran and Annette Morris Bradford, "Figures of Speech in the Rhetoric of Science and Technology," in *Essays on Classical Rhetoric and Modern Discourse,* ed. Robert J. Connors, Lisa S. Ede, and Andrea A. Lunsford (Carbondale: Southern Illinois University Press, 1984), 179–92.

4. Edward P. J. Corbett, "A Rhetorician Looks at Technical Communication," in *Technical Communication: Perspectives for the Eighties,* ed. J. C. Mathes and Thomas E. Pinelli (NASA Conference Publication 2203, Part 1), 213–18.

5. Craig Kallendorf and Carol Kallendorf, "The Figures of Speech, *Ethos,* and Aristotle: Notes toward a Rhetoric of Business Communication," *Journal of Business Communication* 22 (Winter 1985): 35–50; see also Craig Kallendorf and Carol Kallendorf, "A New Topical System for Corporate Speechwriting," *Journal of Business Communication* 21 (Spring 1984): 3–14.

6. C. H. Knoblauch, "Intentionality in the Writing Process: A Case Study," *College Composition and Communication* 31 (May 1980): 157.

7. Kallendorf, "The Figures of Speech, *Ethos,* and Aristotle," 38.

8. Aristotle, *The Rhetoric and the Poetics of Aristotle,* bk. 1, c. 2, introduction by Edward P. J. Corbett (New York: Random House, 1984).

9. See Robert J. Connors, "Actio: A Rhetoric of Manuscripts," *Rhetoric Review* 2 (September 1983): 64–73.

10. See C. H. Knoblauch and Lil Brannon, *Rhetoric Traditions and the Teaching of Writing* (Upper Montclair, N.J.: Boynton/Cook, 1984).

4 Interactive Writing on the Job: Definitions and Implications of "Collaboration"[1]

Barbara Couture and Jone Rymer[2]
Wayne State University

The way writers work together is a new topic among researchers of writing in the workplace. On the one hand, it is not surprising that most academics who study written communication have taken little interest in investigating how writers work with others. For most of us, writing is, after all, a solitary activity — a struggle between self and the empty page, or, perhaps, the blank screen. On the other hand, it should not be surprising that "collaborative writing in the workplace" is of special interest to scholars now.

There are several reasons for this change. First, collaborative learning, demonstrated to be a most useful pedagogical technique across the disciplines, has been applied very successfully to the teaching of writing.[3] Second, the success of group critique and peer review in teaching writing has encouraged teacher-scholars to perceive anew the phenomenon of writers working together on the job and to conduct research on workplace group writing. Empirical surveys of writing practices at work have suggested that on-the-job writers collaborate with others frequently, and that collaboration may be even more prevalent than individual writing for some professionals.[4] Finally, scholarly interest in collaborative composing complements current teaching methods in professional communications, methods emphasizing both the process and the context of composing.

Research on the ways writers compose together is still so new that scholars have not yet defined exactly what they are investigating. "Collaboration" is the broad term currently used to designate writing in which more than one person contributes to the effort, but the nature of each participant's interaction with the others and "contribution" to the end product are far from clarified. In fact, current methods for investigating collaborative writing in the workplace may be inhibiting us from achieving that goal.

73

Many researchers begin their studies with an assumption about collaboration that is based on an academic model: the process of two or three equals who plan, draft, and revise cooperatively.[5] Although this approach provides some insights into collaborative writing by students and teachers,[6] it may be too limited a model for the workplace because it excludes some typical configurations of people producing documents together on the job — for example, the junior engineer who regularly drafts sections for feasibility reports authored by the project manager.

In this chapter, we assume a broader perspective than is typically implied by the term "collaborative writing" so that we may examine more comprehensively how writers in the workplace interact with each other. In doing so, first, we review the research on collaborative writing in the workplace, noting the critical need to define the specific kinds of interaction covered by the term "collaboration." Second, we report on our own research, distinguishing varieties of interaction in composing for routine and special writing tasks as practiced by two exclusive groups which we have defined as "professionals who write" and "career writers." Third, we outline the implications of our findings for future research and for the teaching of professional writing.

What Does Current Research Tell Us about Collaborative Writing in the Workplace?

Empirical research and pedagogical practice suggest that collaborative writing is widely practiced in the workplace and highly valued in academia. Although surveys of collaborative writing at work have been few and results somewhat ambiguous, this research seems to suggest that collaborative writing is pervasive on the job. For example, Faigley and Miller, reporting that 74% of the writers they surveyed collaborate at least some of the time, conclude that "multiple authorship" typifies the writing process for technical and other professionals.[7] Ede and Lunsford, reporting that 87% of workplace writers they surveyed "sometimes wrote collaboratively," conclude that "professionals regularly write as members of a team or group."[8] Paradis, Dobrin, and Bower note that writers in a research and development firm say about one-fifth (19%) of the writing they do is collaborative.[9] Such results appear to confirm the importance of a practice that pedagogy has enthusiastically endorsed for several years.

Textbooks and articles on professional writing include many experiential accounts asserting that team and project writing is frequent and typical on the job, and should be addressed in the classroom.[10] Often such accounts buttress rather elaborate pedagogical plans for students to write together.[11] Such publications have tended to strengthen the assumption that "collaboration" is the norm for writing at work. Of course, collaborative activity in composing has been proclaimed as a productive learning tool by composition teachers, as well as by professional writing instructors. The former cite the advantages of collaboration in the composing process, especially in such activities as critiquing one's peers, playing "reader" (that is, viewing writing in its social context), creating a supportive community for practicing communication, and modeling others' processes and products.[12] Originally, collaborative activities in the classroom focused on students' reviewing each other's independent work; currently, the trend is toward students working together as writers, sharing responsibility for the final document as well as assisting each other in its production. Altogether, teachers' judgment of collaboration as an effective technique for improving writing has provided one kind of legitimacy for teaching group writing in professional writing classes, once more reinforcing the notion that writing on the job is typically collaborative.

Case studies also support the view that collaboration is common. In detailed descriptions of writers composing in specific contexts, scholars have shown that collaborative writing at work is quite diverse. Broadhead and Freed, for example, demonstrate that collaboration in writing in some organizations is the natural outcome of specific contextual constraints — for instance, the necessity for writers to account for and incorporate the views and reviews of others into their own documents.[13] Other researchers, however, have found collaborative writing at work to be true "multiple authorship."[14] Far more than a response to contextual constraint, here collaboration is a powerful catalyst, enriching both the inventive and communicative aspects of composing.

Research on collaboration in writing at work seems to encourage the emphasis on collaborative composing in professional writing classes. But the research is far from conclusive in determining either the extent or nature of collaborative writing at work. The ethnographic studies, of necessity confined to individual cases, limit opportunity for broad generalizations. The survey respondents at work may have quite different notions of "collaboration" than the collaborative models practiced by students/scholars; consequently, results indicating that collaboration is typical on the job may be misleading.

One problem researchers have is how to define "collaboration." To business persons, "collaboration" means many things beyond our definition of it in academia. For example, "collaboration" may describe the cooperation of full equals on some special project or it may have a much broader sense, reflecting the participative management philosophy of "Theory Y."[15] In academic circles, "collaboration" has no common definition. It can cover learning through peer review and feedback on manuscripts, so typical in writing classes; or it can mean multiple authorship — the division of labor on a project too large for an individual or one that demands varying expertise (typical on large grant proposals); or it can designate fully shared planning, drafting, and revising by equals (typical of academics writing a manuscript together). In short, the very term "collaboration" is problematic in distinguishing a specific kind of writing behavior, a problem that survey researchers themselves readily admit.[16]

Further, some problems in interpreting survey results arise when studies have combined data about the practices of career writers (persons hired to write) with data about professionals who write as *part* of their jobs (engineers, accountants, financial analysts).[17] Our own research on career writers and on members of other professions demonstrates that the writing practices of these two groups differ sharply in many ways.[18] Results that combine responses of these two groups may identify practices that are not, in fact, typical of either one.

Collaborative writing is undoubtedly a significant factor in the composing processes of both career writers and professionals who write as part of their jobs. Group writing activities should be part of our classrooms, not only because they represent sound pedagogy, but also because writing with others reflects the reality of workplace writing. However, our teaching should be informed by actual workplace practices, not by assumptions about what happens on the job that are modeled on behavior familiar to us. We need to know the nature of interaction in composing on the job in order to truly describe "collaborative writing," how typical it is for persons in the business professions, and what characteristics it assumes for their different writing tasks.

What Does the Writers' Survey Show about Interaction in Composing on the Job?

Our research is an attempt to define collaborative writing at work. It is based upon results of the "Writers' Survey," a study of more than four hundred professionals, judged as competent writers by their organizations, who responded to a detailed questionnaire about their writing on the job. The survey was part of the Professional Writing Project (PWP), a research and curriculum development effort at Wayne State University.[19] The sample population included professionals from seven major job categories: administrators, writers and technologists, engineers and architects, scientists, health professionals, police and corrections officers, and social scientists. In surveying this group of employees, we tried to avoid the academic perspective and language about writing with others. Rather than asking respondents to interpret "collaborative" or "group writing," we examined these professionals' specific interactions with others in the process of producing documents. For example, we asked them how often they got feedback from others on their writing before sending it out. Further, we asked them to apply such questions to two kinds of writing tasks: first, to their *routine writing* — writing for which speed is more important than quality; and second, to their *special writing* — writing for which quality is more important (or as important) than speed.

We collected data from enough respondents to enable us to compare the collaborative activities of writers across professions. In particular, we compared the activities of career writers (technical writers, public relations specialists, editors) with those of "professionals who write" (engineers, general managers, scientists, accountants, health technologists), the term we use to distinguish respondents in professions that demand writing as part of the job.

From the results of the Writers' Survey, our analysis, and the interpretations of members of a PWP Advisory Board from industry,[20] we have begun to construct a picture of workplace writing practices of the individual who acts not alone, but with others. The Writers' Survey suggests that writers on the job do frequently collaborate, but that this "collaboration" usually does not involve producing a document with a group. Rather, it typically represents simple interaction — either before or after drafting — about a special document, an assignment in which quality is more important than efficiency. (When writers at work prepare their more important reports, for example, other people frequently review the drafts and give them advice to guide revision.) If "collaboration" can mean only group writing, then our respondents do not collaborate very much, but if collaboration means that someone other than "the writer" is involved in the production of a text, then they do collaborate often and in a variety of ways.

Much Writing at Work Is Interactive

Results of the Writers' Survey show that people other than the "writer" often influence writing at work. Despite differences among writing tasks and writers' professions, most writers at work interact during the composing process. Explicitly, the survey demonstrates the following:

> Professionals who write (hereafter referred to as "professionals") and career writers both interact more frequently with others while preparing their special documents than they do during their routine assignments.

> Professionals and career writers interact frequently with others before and after drafting, but career writers interact more often.

Others are frequently involved in professionals' significant writing, both at the planning stage and during revising (Table 1). Three-quarters of professionals (76%) occasionally, or more often, "talk over with others what they will write before they begin" their special writing tasks. In fact, only a quarter of our respondents (23%) typically do *not* interact before they begin drafting special projects. Routine writing presents a different picture, with half of the professionals never or rarely discussing their routine tasks with others. In short, before they draft, professionals interact more frequently about their special documents than about routine assignments. For the 52% of the respondents who indicated a difference, 86% said they discussed their work ahead of time more often for special tasks (p = < .001 by a test of the equality of two proportions).

Table 1

A Comparison of Professionals' Routine and Special Writing: Discussing before and Getting Feedback after Drafting (N = 348)

	Never/Rarely[a]	Sometimes	Often/Very Often
	Percent[b]		
Discuss before			
Routine (NA[c] 4%)	50	28	18
Special (NA 0.3%)	23	30	46
Get feedback after			
Routine (NA 6%)	47	25	22
Special (NA 3%)	20	25	53

[a] All responses were on a 5-point Likert scale of never, rarely, sometimes, often, and very often. Presentations here are grouped into three categories: never/rarely, sometimes, and often/very often.
[b] Rows may not add to 100 percent because of rounding.
[c] Not applicable responses.

In addition to getting advice before drafting, many professionals receive "feedback on their writing before it goes out" (Table 1). The majority of professionals (78%) get feedback on special writing occasionally or more than occasionally. However, fewer than half (47%) do so for routine writing. For the 48% who claimed a difference in their practices, depending on whether quality or efficiency was their major objective, 88% said feedback was more frequent for their special tasks ($p < .001$ by a test of the equality of two proportions).

Although interaction figures prominently in the composing processes of professionals in all disciplines, it is pervasive in the procedures of career writers. Most career writers (94%) discuss their plans *before* writing special assignments (84% often/very often; 10% some; 6% never/rarely; $N = 62$).[21] Their interaction before drafting is much more frequent than that of professionals (46% often/very often; 30% some; 23% never/rarely; NA .3%; $N = 350$ [$p < .001$ as determined by a Chi-Square test]). Career writers also interact more frequently *after* composing a draft for a special document than do professionals. Almost all career writers (95%) get feedback after drafting their special writing (84% often/very often; 11% some; 5% never/rarely; $N = 62$); about three-quarters of the professionals do (53% often/very often; 25% some; 20% never/rarely; 3% NA; $N = 350$ [$p < .001$ by a Chi-Square test]).

People hired as writers are engaged in composing tasks that typically demand discussion and consultation, both before and after drafting. The very nature of their writing is to fulfill the objectives, needs, and criteria of others, and the Survey results bear this out. Even the routine writing of career writers gets others' attention, though to a lesser extent than special documents: 70% talk over their everyday tasks before beginning to write (34% often/very often; 36% some; 3% NA); three-quarters of the respondents (77%) get feedback after drafting routine items (50% often/very often; 27% some; 3% NA).

These results indicate that, while routine writing on the job is frequently interactive, special writing is more often situated in an interactive context, one that for both professionals and career writers is approximately as dynamic prior to drafting as during revising. In fact, in view of the Survey's highly explicit statements defining others' involvement, it may be fair to conclude that significant writing is enveloped in talk.

Interaction in Writing May Be Voluntary or Involuntary

The Writers' Survey focused on defining writers' actions rather than on uncovering their motives, so results on others' involvement in their composing procedures do not clarify who initiates the interaction. Results showing high rates of involvement with others may represent writers tapping a resource, as when asking for a supervisor's opinion of an outline before beginning to draft. This is surely typical, as one PWP advisor commented on the reason he seeks out others' views: ". . . to get the agreement, to make sure that you're on the right track, so you don't write something and have it not meet everyone's expectation."[22] However, high rates of interaction may reflect routine supervisory control, such as securing a "signoff" on a report. Another PWP advisor tried to explain the differences between her own involuntary and voluntary interaction:

> It's supervisory if I, as the supervisor, know what I want and I say, 'Give me X, Y, and Z in this.' Very little is like that because, frankly, if I know X, Y, and Z, I can write it or dictate it. . . . [It's collaborative when my boss and I voluntarily exchange various drafts and] we sit down, we talk for fifteen minutes, we get two grammatical pieces, neither of which meets the objective. So we go to another draft and hopefully that one will be close enough so that he can add a sentence, or change an order, or be able to see perfectly what he wants.

But whether writing involves collaboration or supervision may not be a case of "either/or." As other researchers have pointed out, it seems likely that some interaction in writing at work represents a simultaneous response to both the supervisor's and the writer's needs;[23] or it may merely reflect the conventions of the organizational culture — "the way we do things around here." Initial studies on collaborative writing should aim to uncover all the various interactive procedures in which writers engage, whether they appear supervisory, collaborative, or conventional, even formulaic. Future research might explore the motivation of specific interactions in workplace writing.

Some Interaction in Writing Is a Result of Required Supervision

Many of the "others" who influence the writers' composing practices by discussing plans or giving feedback are acting in supervisory capacities. Much writing at work, rather than being the writer's choice, is prepared because somebody else assigns it. The Writers' Survey shows that professionals believe that they write very frequently on assignment, but that they also write a great deal on their own initiative, for both their routine and special writing tasks. In sharp contrast, our results show that career writers believe most of their writing is on assignment — particularly their special tasks. In short, whereas professionals have a strong impression of writing frequently both "at somebody else's request" and "on their own initiative," career writers perceive almost all their special documents, and a majority of their routine tasks, as being assigned.

Professionals' special documents are produced at the request of others at about the same frequency as those produced on their own initiative. These results concur with Anderson's findings.[24] Three-quarters of our respondents (77%) claimed that their special writing responds to someone's request (44% often/very often; 33% some; 20% never/rarely; 3% NA), and about the same number (74%) claimed to do their special tasks on their own initiative (48% often/very often; 26% some; 20% never/rarely; 6% NA). On the other hand, routine tasks are more often than not produced on the writer's initiative. Although a majority of professionals (65%) said their everyday writing is assigned at least some of the time (30% often/very often; 35% some; 31% never/rarely; 4% NA), 80% claimed they do it on their own initiative (60% often/very often; 20% some; 15% never/rarely; 6% NA).

In contrast to professionals, career writers produce documents on assignment. Even many career writers do routine writing at someone else's request (61% often/very often; 24% some; 15% never/rarely), and nearly all career writers claimed that their special writing tasks are assigned (90% often/very often; 3% some; 6% never/rarely [N = 62]). In contrast to professionals (who answered 44% often/very often; 33% some; 20% never/rarely; 3% NA [N = 351]), career writers prepare their special writing at others' requests significantly more often ($p < .001$ by a Chi-Square test).

Our results show that professionals regard their routine writing at work as done frequently both at others' requests and on their own initiative. This may be so because it is difficult for many writers at work to distinguish when a task is voluntary or involuntary. The fact that professionals perceive that they do routine writing on their own initiative slightly more than special writing is not surprising. Routine documents are typically part of larger, assigned projects; when viewed in isolation, however, they may seem to be done on the writer's own initiative. Commenting on these results, members of the PWP Advisory Board confirmed our speculation that much writing at work cannot be clearly classified as either assigned or unassigned. For example, an advisor representing a public accounting firm explained:

> I do [writing] on my own initiative because I'm the supervisor on the job . . . but the manager is going to see it before it's actually handed in, so [you could say] it was done at someone else's request.

Another Advisory Board Member commented:

> I don't think, in my experience . . . that I do anything at my own
> initiative. . . . My boss and I will discuss overall objectives
> and . . . what I do within those goals are within my own initiative.

In sum, memos, letters, progress reports — the typical documents of
the professional who writes — are part of the writer's overall responsibility for some larger objective. A management-set goal often governs
the shape or direction of such documents, even when it appears to
the writer that he or she is preparing them on his or her own initiative.

Although professionals view their writing as originating both from
others and from themselves, career writers claim that their writing
most often responds to others' requests. The fact that nearly all career
writers claim special writing is often assigned reflects their very job
definition. Career writers, unlike professionals who write, are hired
specifically to prepare documents at someone else's behest. This fact
alone may differentiate their procedures in completing a similar writing
task. Compare the project engineer, who may decide to write some
software documentation to assist a subordinate in using a computer
program, with the technical writer, who prepares a manual for a client
of a software firm.

But despite differences in professionals' and career writers' perceived
autonomy in initiating writing, their relative responsibility for that
writing appears quite similar. For both professionals and career writers,
someone other than the writer frequently assumes responsibility for
essential functions that academics typically associate with a writer's
prerogatives — for example, deciding *whether* to write and *when* to
write. According to our Advisory Board, this "other person" often
designates the audience, sets the objective, and describes the contents.
Then, this person (or somebody else) often reviews the writer's plans
and drafts, providing feedback which influences the writer's strategies,
as well as the shape and substance of the final document. Finally, this
other person may play a significant role in revising the document,
even to the point of actually assuming the writer's role as reviser or
editor (discussed in the section below). As one PWP advisor explained,
the writer's interaction with someone else, whether a supervisor or a
peer, is part of the necessary process of "gaining acceptance of the
document before it is produced."

Interaction Figures Prominently When Writers Revise

Much interaction about writing at work occurs during the revision
stage, some of it undoubtedly arising from supervisors' critiques. In

another report on the Writers' Survey, we show that both professionals and career writers typically do revise their writing after it is drafted.[25] In this chapter, we report results showing that other people frequently influence those revision practices.

Most frequently, the individual professional or career writer revises the draft; but occasionally, others do the revising.

Both professionals and career writers frequently revise their writing in response to critiques, using others' advice more for their special writing tasks than for routine work.

Career writers tend to revise on others' advice more frequently than professionals do.

Both professionals and career writers draft documents that are subsequently revised by others, but career writers engage in this practice more often.

Here again, professionals claimed to follow quite different procedures, depending on the significance of the task: If the writing is important, they tend to use others' opinions in making their revisions. Although professionals believe that they do considerable revising in response to feedback for all their writing tasks, they clearly revise routine documents less often than they do special assignments. A great majority (81%) of the professionals said they revise their special documents to reflect the views of others at least some of the time (49% often/very often; 32% some; 16% never/rarely; 4% NA [N = 348]). In contrast, when preparing run-of-the-mill memos, letters, and reports, only half (56%) of the professionals revise to meet others' comments (25% often/very often; 31% some; 34% never/rarely; 10% NA [N = 349]). Of the 39% who said their procedures differ, 81% claimed to revise in response to others more frequently when the task is special ($p < .01$ by a test of the equality of two proportions). Integrating others' perspectives and adhering to others' standards seems to be conventional behavior for professionals when they are writing valued documents.

Despite a tendency among professionals to revise according to the wishes of others, they do not admit to much revision of their work by anyone else. Only a third (31%) claimed that others revise their special writing (16% often/very often; 15% some; 64% never/rarely; 5% NA), and a small minority said that others revise their routine documents (8% often/very often; 9% some; 75% never/rarely; 8% NA). Although the documents of professionals are occasionally revised by others, more frequently the authors use others' advice to revise their writing themselves.

Career writers, who typically revise more often than professionals,[26] tend to interact with others while they revise. Ninety-five percent of career writers reported revising their own special writing in response to others' critiques at least some of the time (74% often/very often; 21% some; 5% never/rarely [N = 62]), while 77% reported doing so for routine writing (47% often/very often; 31% some; 19% never/rarely; 3% NA [N = 62]). Clearly, they interact more often when preparing their special documents ($p < .001$ by a Chi-Square test).

Not only do career writers typically revise their own work, but others frequently do the task for them. Career writers' drafts are often revised by others, with a majority (52%) claiming that others revise their special documents at least occasionally (34% often/very often; 18% some; 48% never/rarely [N = 62]); 42% claim such attention even for their routine manuscripts (23% often/very often; 19% some; 53% never/rarely; 5% NA [N = 62]). Career writers' documents typically must meet the perspectives of such heterogeneous "others" as technical professionals, editors, marketing managers, and clients, so multiple revisions by various hands are commonplace. Although many respondents among both professionals (64%) and career writers (48%) claimed that even their special documents are rarely or never revised by others, the data above show that career writers do claim more frequent revision by others than do professionals ($p < .01$ by a Chi-Square test).

In surveying respondents about their interaction with others in the revising process, we did not investigate the motivations behind that interaction. Thus, if respondents indicated that they revise according to a critique, they did not distinguish whether the advice was freely sought or imposed. Some respondents' writing may be reviewed because it fails to meet the quality criteria of a supervisor (though our screening procedures limited the sample to competent writers); others' writing may be critiqued because it does not adequately represent some stakeholder's perspective; still others' may be "red-penciled" because it differs from what some superior believes to be good writing; and many others' writing will undergo review to meet company policy or standard operating procedures. On the other hand, some respondents may ask peers for their views or typically seek the opinions of superiors, perhaps because their experience has proven this to be an effective strategy or simply because "that's the way we do things around here."

Regardless of who initiates the revision process, the Writers' Survey suggests that skilled communicators in the workplace do revise a great deal and that others frequently assist them in the revision tasks. Only occasionally, however, do other people actually take over the revising.

The more common practice for both professionals and career writers is to revise their documents themselves. Thus, the commonly held myth among novices that an editor or technical writer will be on hand to rewrite their reports is effectively dispelled.

Some Interaction about Writing Takes Place in Groups

Some interaction among our respondents is formally configured in groups where various people assume responsibilities typically associated with the role of "writer." The Writers' Survey covered two typical models of such writing groups: a planning group where one member drafts, and a writing team where each member contributes a section of the text. Overall results show that our respondents claim infrequent participation in such collaborative endeavors:

> Professionals occasionally work in groups to plan their documents, but they rarely participate in fully collaborative writing teams where several members draft.

> Career writers participate much more frequently in document planning groups than do professionals, but they too are rarely involved in collaborative writing teams.

> Professionals and career writers do not show substantially greater participation in writing groups for their special documents than they do for their routine tasks.

Half the professionals (51%) rarely or never participate in planning groups, even when preparing their significant documents (Table 2). Career writers, however, do so quite often for special assignments and occasionally even for their routine writing. See Table 2 for a comparison of the frequency of professionals' and career writers' participation in groups in which they "plan a document together but do the writing themselves." Responses of the professionals and career writers differ significantly both for routine and special writing ($p < .001$ as determined by Chi-Square tests). Results showing little collaborative planning in groups by professionals may be somewhat surprising. However, results showing more of such collaborative planning among career writers seem congruent with conventional notions of the career writer's role as the drafter and the editor in group projects.[27] Neither professionals nor career writers typically engage in fully collaborative writing teams "in which each member writes a section or part of a document." Results are similar for both routine and special tasks. Career writers, however, did claim somewhat more frequent

Table 2

A Comparison of Professionals' versus Career Writers'
(N = 348 vs. N = 62)
Collaborative Planning for Routine and Special Writing

	Never/Rarely[a]	Sometimes	Often/ Very Often
		Percent[b]	
Routine			
Professionals (NA[c] 14%)	64	16	6
Career writers (NA 10%)	45	15	31
Special			
Professionals (NA 13%)	51	24	13
Career writers (NA 3%)	19	32	45

[a] All responses were on a 5-point Likert scale of never, rarely, sometimes, often, and very often. Presentations here are grouped into three categories: never/rarely, sometimes, and often/very often.
[b] Rows may not add to 100 percent because of rounding.
[c] Not applicable responses.

participation in such collaborative writing groups when engaged in special assignments.

Most professionals denied working in collaborative writing groups with any frequency. Whereas a quarter (24%) did say that they engage in such teams for their special writing, a majority claimed that they never or rarely participate in them, even for special tasks (10% often/very often; 14% some; 65% never/rarely; 11% NA [N = 348]). Results for routine writing are similar (6% often/very often; 7% some; 74% never/rarely; 13% NA). These results suggest that team writing in which several members contribute drafts toward a single document is not commonplace for professionals.

Career writers' experience with collaborative writing groups is quite similar, with a majority (56%) responding that they never/rarely work with such teams on their special assignments and with three-quarters (73%) saying the same for routine. For special writing tasks, however, career writers did note somewhat more frequent team writing experiences, with 36% claiming to practice such collaborative composing (10% often/very often; 26% some; 56% never/rarely; 8% NA [N = 62]). (Data for routine: 6% often/very often; 10% some; 73% never/rarely; 11% NA [N = 62].) Of the 34% who said the tasks differ, 76%

said they work with such groups more for special documents ($p < .02$ by a test of the equality of two proportions).

Results of the Writers' Survey on formally configured writing groups show very low rates of such activity compared with the expectations created by the pedagogical literature (which refers to such teams as commonplace)[28] and compared with the results from earlier empirical studies of collaborative writing at work.[29] The latter discrepancy may arise from the very general nature of the previous studies' questions, contrasted with the highly explicit and limited number of alternative groupings presented in the Writers' Survey. Our questionnaire described only two distinct types of writing groups (excluding, for example, such a common phenomenon as an editorial group),[30] and it narrowly defined the respondents' participation (excluding, for example, involvement in groups where other members do the drafting). Hence, the results from the Writers' Survey permit us to draw conclusions about only two configurations out of an unknown array of possible alternatives open to writers.[31]

Our PWP Advisory Board members suggested additional reasons why our respondents reported collaborating so little. As one advisor explained, some collaboration evolves only during the writing process: "... a lot of the writing that takes place maybe doesn't start off being collaborative. ... It may have turned out that way, but it didn't start off that way, so [respondents may not have known] how to answer your question." (Or perhaps, they may not have thought of the activity as a group writing arrangement if it were not called that.) Another reported that some writers do collaborate with others in a group, but no matter how much others contribute to the writing, the writer perceives that he or she is the only writer: "Yes, I work with a group, but nobody else in the group writes. ... I do the writing." These interpretations suggest that professionals' involvement in formally configured writing groups may be higher than our results indicate.

Certainly the low rates of participation reported for writing groups contrasts sharply with the frequency of writers' interaction with others during composing. Apparently, collaboration in the writing process reflects a continuum, with simple interaction before drafting and written or oral feedback afterward far more frequent in many respondents' experiences than formal group work where participants engage in full-scale collaboration or "multi-authorship." However, given the limited number of configurations covered by the Writers' Survey, we can draw no conclusions about the full extent of professionals' participation in collaborative writing groups.

What Are the Implications of the Writers' Survey for Future Research and for Teaching Professional Writing?

The findings of the Writers' Survey suggest many questions that researchers might investigate. For instance, we need to know the frequency of collaborative writing groups in the workplace and the typical configurations of such groups: Are simple interactions between workers and supervisors the predominant "collaborative" activities of writers on the job? Is "collaboration," in the sense of people fully participating in writing teams, as commonplace in business and industry as previous research suggested? Researchers might examine the extent to which workplace writing is immersed in "talk" and the nature of these exchanges. For example, they might investigate the ways writers "collaborate" with managers for whose signatures they write; or perhaps they might examine the frequency of interaction throughout the composing process — during inventing, planning, organizing, drafting, revising, and editing. We should determine whether professionals voluntarily seek the ideas and advice of their peers and superiors when composing and whether they voluntarily ask for their feedback on drafts. More case studies could help define the interactions that occur while planning and drafting are in process, demonstrating, for example, how closely some pairs of writers collaborate and whether their sense of authorship becomes merged.

In short, we need to know much more about the significance of collaborative writing teams in the workplace and how they function: Which kinds of groups are typical? What is the nature of their group composing processes? Which effective group composing techniques do experienced writers recommend to novices? Which special writing problems do groups face? Answers to these questions may help us address others that go beyond composing to the writer's sense of rhetorical control. Detailed research will help us learn how preparing team documents may affect a writer's sense of professional ethos, revealing, for instance, whether a writer can represent himself or herself with integrity as a professional while adequately accommodating the stance of the group.

The results of the Writers' Survey also have implications for teaching future members of the business professions. Although the classroom should not merely simulate the world of work (education is not an apprenticeship and many business practices are not worthy of imitation), instructors can incorporate into their teaching the significant factors typically characterizing "collaboration" on the job. We know from the Writers' Survey that the following are true:

Writers interact about their writing during the composing process, both before and after drafting.

Writers interact with those who have a stake in the written product — some vested interest in it.[32]

Writers get feedback on their documents before sending them out, but usually take responsibility for revising their own texts.

Clearly, these behaviors differ sharply from many classroom interactive practices where the instructor spells out the specifications for an assignment, the student plans and drafts alone, and a disinterested peer group reviews the manuscript.

Given how workplace practices differ, students may not need to experience elaborate team writing projects at school, but they do need to learn how to interact effectively about their writing with others who are involved in the document and engaged in the effectiveness of the final product. They need, for example, to learn to incorporate perspectives from two departments into a single memo, or to suggest revisions that will allow a report authored by someone else to meet their own and the organization's standards, while destroying neither the writer's professional ethos nor his or her self-esteem. In sum, students should discuss their writing in process, and they should receive critiques from people who are involved with the document and represented by it.

Instructors can incorporate such "collaborative" writing activities into a variety of assignments. Students can complete tasks assigned by many persons playing different functional roles (either in a real situation or in a case) and then account for their perspectives in preparing the document, securing their approval, both for their plans and for their products. Of course, a group writing project is an excellent method for teaching students collaborative skills. Structured team writing of some type will be required of many professionals at work, and group work is an excellent method to teach more effective strategies to compose individually as well as collaboratively. Instructors may profitably design a group writing assignment where students divide composing tasks and/or document sections among the team members.

If we do elect to emphasize collaboration in classroom writing, however, and especially if we establish elaborate schemes to serve wider pedagogical objectives,[33] we should not suggest that the structured classroom teams necessarily model students' future writing experience in the workplace. Rather, students should be made aware that writing with a collaborative group is but one way to learn about writing with others and is an important component of writing on the job.

Notes

1. The authors wish to thank Richard T. Brengle, English Composition Board, University of Michigan, and Kenneth Guire, Department of Biostatistics, School of Public Health, University of Michigan, for help in preparing the statistical data.

2. Jone Rymer formerly published under the name Jone Rymer Goldstein.

3. Kenneth A. Bruffee, *A Short Course in Writing*, 3rd ed. (Boston: Little, Brown, 1985); idem, "Collaborative Learning and the 'Conversation of Mankind,' " *College English* 46 (1984): 635–52.

4. Lester Faigley and Thomas P. Miller, "What We Learn from Writing on the Job," *College English* 44 (1982): 557–69.

5. Stephen A. Bernhardt and Bruce C. Appleby, "Collaboration in Professional Writing with the Computer: Results of a Survey," *Computers and Composition* 3 (1985): 37. For a discussion of an academic model of collaboration, see Lisa Ede and Andrea Lunsford, "Why Write . . . Together?" *Rhetoric Review* 2, 1 (1983): 150–57. Indeed, the total integration of cooperative composing from initial idea to final edit is the most familiar practice to us. We have collaborated for over seven years on writing articles, reports, textbooks, chapters, industrial seminars, conference presentations, and now — this chapter.

6. Colette Daiute, "Do 1 and 1 Make 2? Patterns of Influence by Collaborative Authors," *Written Communication* 3 (1986): 382–408; Pauline Gordon Adams and Emma Shore Thornton, "An Inquiry into the Process of Collaboration," *Language Arts Journal of Michigan* 2 (1986): 25–28.

7. Faigley and Miller, "What We Learn from Writing," 567.

8. Lisa Ede and Andrea Lunsford, "Collaborative Learning: Lessons from the World of Work," *Journal of the Council of Writing Program Administrators* 9, 3 (1986): 20.

9. James Paradis, David Dobrin, and D. Bower, personal correspondence to Paul V. Anderson reported in "What Survey Research Tells Us about Writing at Work," in *Writing in Nonacademic Settings*, ed. Lee Odell and Dixie Goswami (New York: Guilford, 1985), 3–83.

10. Dixie Goswami et al., *Writing in the Professions: A Course Guide and Instructional Materials for an Advanced Composition Course* (Washington, D.C.: American Institutes for Research, 1981); Edmond H. Weiss, *The Writing System for Engineers and Scientists* (Englewood Cliffs, N.J.: Prentice–Hall, 1982); Janet H. Potvin, "Using Team Reporting Projects to Teach Concepts of Audience and Written, Oral, and Interpersonal Communication Skills," *IEEE Transactions on Professional Communication* PC-27 (1984): 130–37; Terry McNally and Peter Schiff, *Contemporary Business Writing: A Problem-Solving Approach* (Belmont, Calif.: Wadsworth, 1986).

11. Gerard J. Gross, "Group Projects in the Technical Writing Course," in *Courses, Components, and Exercises in Technical Communication,* ed. Dwight W. Stevenson et al. (Urbana, Ill.: National Council of Teachers of English, 1981): 54–64; D. H. Covington, "Making Team Projects Work in Technical Communication Courses," *The Technical Writing Teacher* 11 (1984): 100–104; Jone Rymer Goldstein and Elizabeth L. Malone, "Journals on Interpersonal and Group Communication: Facilitating Technical Project Groups," *Journal of Technical Writing and Communication* 14 (1984): 113–31; idem, "Using Journals to Strengthen Collaborative Writing," *The Bulletin of the Association for Business Communication* 48, no. 3 (1985): 24–28.

12. Bruffee, "The Conversation of Mankind"; John Clifford, "Composing in Stages: The Effects of a Collaborative Pedagogy," *Research in the Teaching of English* 15 (1981): 37–53; Anne Ruggles Gere and Robert D. Abbott, "Talking about Writing: The Language of Writing Groups," *Research in the Teaching of English* 19 (1985): 362–81; Angela M. O'Donnell et al., "Cooperative Writing," *Written Communication* 2 (1985): 307–15; John Trimbur, "Collaborative Learning and Teaching Writing," in *Perspectives on Research and Scholarship in Composition,* ed. Ben W. McClelland and Timothy R. Donovan (New York: MLA, 1985), 87–109; Harvey S. Wiener, "Collaborative Learning in the Classroom: A Guide to Evaluation," *College English* 48 (1986): 52–61.

13. Glenn J. Broadhead and Richard C. Freed, *The Variables of Composition: Process and Product in a Business Setting* (Carbondale: Southern Illinois University Press, 1986).

14. Stephen Doheny-Farina, "Writing in an Emerging Organization: An Ethnographic Study," *Written Communication* 3 (1986): 158–85; Ede and Lunsford, "Lessons from the World of Work."

15. Douglas M. McGregor, *The Human Side of Enterprise* (New York: McGraw Hill, 1960; reprint, 1985).

16. Lisa Ede and Andrea Lunsford, "Research into Collaborative Writing," *Technical Communication* 32, 4 (1985): 70; idem, "Collaboration in Writing on the Job: A Research Report" (Paper read at the 37th Annual Conference on College Composition and Communication, New Orleans, 13–15 March, 1986); Andrea Lunsford and Lisa Ede, "Why Write . . . Together: A Research Update," *Rhetoric Review* 5, 1 (1986): 72–74; Faigley and Miller, 567.

17. Nancy Allen and Craig Snow, "Collaborative Writing on the Job" (Paper read at the 37th Annual Conference on College Composition and Communication, New Orleans, March 13–15, 1986); Ede and Lunsford, "Lessons from the World of Work."

18. Barbara Couture and Jone Rymer, "The Writers' Survey: Toward a Profile of Professional Writing" (forthcoming).

19. The Professional Writing Project (codirectors, Barbara Couture and John Brereton) was funded by the U.S. Department of Education, Fund for the Improvement of Postsecondary Education (FIPSE). For details of the Writers' Survey methodology, see Couture and Rymer.

20. The external Advisory Board was composed of managers, trainers, writers, and editors from business, industry, government, and service

organizations in Southeastern Michigan. They met regularly with the Wayne State University Professional Writing Project Team. Advisory Board members' comments on the survey results are incorporated throughout this report. See Barbara Couture et al., "Building a Professional Writing Program through a University-Industry Collaborative," in *Writing in Nonacademic Settings*, ed. Lee Odell and Dixie Goswami (New York: Guilford, 1985), 394–96.

21. Responses on a five-point Likert scale of Never, Rarely, Some, Often, and Very Often are grouped throughout the text into three categories: Never/Rarely, Some, and Often/Very Often, followed by any Not Applicable (NA) responses. Some results may not add to 100% because of rounding.

22. Harwood confirms that writers offer each other assistance through voluntary collaborative associations at work where they critique each other's writing. John T. Harwood, "Freshman English Ten Years After: Writing in the World," *College Composition and Communication* 33 (1982): 282.

23. James Paradis, David Dobrin, and Richard Miller, "Writing at Exxon ITD: Notes on the Writing Environment of an R&D Organization," in *Writing in Nonacademic Settings*, 298.

24. Paul V. Anderson, "What Survey Research Tells Us about Writing at Work," in *Writing in Nonacademic Settings*, 25.

25. Couture and Rymer, "The Writers' Survey."

26. Couture and Rymer, "The Writers' Survey."

27. James R. Kalmbach, Jack W. Jobst, and George P. E. Meese, "Education and Practice: A Survey of Graduates of a Technical Communication Program," *Technical Communication* 33, 1 (1986): 23.

28. Wayne A. Losano, "Editing for Style and Consistency: The Multiple-Author Manuscript," in *Teaching Technical Editing*, ed. Carolyn D. Rude (Association of Teachers of Technical Writing, Anthology no. 6., 1985): 63–71.

29. Faigley and Miller, "What We Learn from Writing"; Ede and Lunsford, "Research into Collaborative Writing."

30. Ede and Lunsford note that they have discovered seven types of collaborative groups in "Why Write . . . Together: A Research Update," 74.

31. This conclusion is supported by the similarity in the results between Faigley and Miller's respondents who "sometimes collaborate" (74%) and our subjects' responses on interactions before drafting (76%) and during revising (78%), as well as the fact that Faigley and Miller do suggest that their study covers all possible kinds and levels of interaction in the term *collaboration*, "What We Learn from Writing," 567.

32. All those who comment on and help shape a document may not play as strong a stakeholder role as a supervisor, of course. Nevertheless, anyone working on the same project, in the same department, or even merely within the same organization is represented by the community's documents. Most persons who give their views or whose advice is

sought by the writer will figure prominently in the document's context and, therefore, have some stake in it.

33. Linda S. Dillon, "Three Approaches to Writing for Group Acceptance," *The Technical Writing Teacher* 11 (1984): 186–89; Caryl Klein Sills, "Adapting Freewriting Techniques and Writing Support Groups for Business Communication," *The Bulletin of the Association for Business Communication* 48, 2 (1985): 12–14; Teresa G. Moore and Margaret P. Morgan, "Collaborative Writing in the Classroom" (Paper read at the 37th Annual Conference on College Composition and Communication, New Orleans, 13–15 March, 1986); Mary Beth Debs, "The Technical Writer and Corporate Influence," idem; Janis Forman and Patricia Katsky, "The Group Report: A Problem in Small Group or Writing Processes?" *Journal of Business Communication*, 23, 4 (1986): 23–35.

II Writing in Corporations, Government, the Law, and Academia

5 Writing in Organizations

Janice Redish
American Institutes for Research

What Are the Problems?

Much poor writing still comes from large organizations. In 1984 a judge on Long Island told a health insurance company that its notices to customers were incomprehensible.[1] In 1985 VCRs became a nation-wide fad, and the media castigated the electronics industry for selling the machines with manuals that no one could understand.[2] We've all had frustrating experiences with documents like Example 1, which you might find enclosed with your gas or electric bill.

Example 1:

THIRD PARTY DESIGNATION NOTIFICATION FORM
Customers 65 or over may voluntarily designate a third party of their own selection to whom notification of past due bills will be sent. Receipt of billing statements or disconnect notifications by a third party places no obligation on such party for payment of the bill nor does it cause deferment or prevention of disconnection of service if payment is not received as required. Completion and signing of the attached pre-addressed, postage-paid third party notification request form will provide the protection afforded by this procedure.

How many elderly people are going to get past the title of this notice to read about a service that might be useful to them? How many are going to understand what it is about or why they might want to sign up for this service?

Cynics might say that the utility company does not want people to understand the notice because the service will cost the company money. My experience in working with utility companies (and many other businesses) does not support the cynics' viewpoint. Although it costs the company to send the extra copies, the company saves because more bills get paid. It costs more to turn off the customer's gas or electricity and then turn it back on than it does to send out extra copies of the notices. Moreover, the bad publicity the company gets when it shuts off service to elderly customers is an intangible expense, but one the company wants very much to avoid.

The notice does not have to read like a traditional legal document to be legally acceptable. It could look like this:

Example 2:

Are you 65 or over?

Would you like to name someone to get a copy of important notices we send to you?

Do you sometimes mislay your bill or forget to pay us? Would you feel more comfortable if we sent a second copy of past-due bills and other important notices to someone else like your son or daughter or a friend?

If you are 65 or over, you can ask for this special service. When we send you a notice that you are late in paying us or a notice that we are going to turn off your gas or electricity, we will also send a copy of the notice to the person you name.

You still have to pay the bill. The other person does not have to pay the bill. We can still turn off your gas or electricity if we do not get paid by the date on the notice. But you will have the protection of knowing that someone can remind you to pay us.

If you would like this service, fill out the attached card and send it to us. Our address is already on the card. We pay the postage.

Poor writing costs businesses and government agencies enormous amounts of time and money. Military equipment goes unused because maintenance technicians cannot understand the repair manuals. A major computer company has to hire customer service representatives to explain installation instructions to new users over the telephone because customers can't find or understand the instructions in the manual.

Poor writing doesn't just happen. Someone (or some group of people) wrote these documents. And they wrote them as employees (or consultants) of an organization whose history and culture influenced what the writers produced.

If we are interested in improving the writing that comes out of businesses and government agencies, we have to look at

- the writers
- the documents
- the institutions

and how they interact with each other and with the readers.

This article focuses on questions such as these:

• Why do writers in business and government produce poor documents?

• What makes so many documents difficult for readers to understand and use?

• How does the organizational setting hinder the writer?

• How can writers and organizations become more sensitive to readers' needs?

• How can teachers of business writing prepare students to be better writers in organizations?

What follows is based in part on research studies that I cite and in part on the work that my colleagues and I have been doing at the Document Design Center for the past ten years — work as researchers, teachers, writers, and advisors in a wide variety of organizational settings, from government agencies to major computer companies.

Understanding Writers and Writing on the Job

1. Professionals in organizations do not define themselves as writers, but they write a lot on the job.

Students in business and technical writing classes often find it difficult to imagine how important writing skills are to securing jobs and promotions. They, like most people in business or in government agencies, don't define themselves as writers. Students see themselves as chemists or economists or marketing specialists. On the job, they will see themselves as sales representatives or product developers or project managers.

Whatever their job titles may be, however, most people who hold professional, technical, or managerial jobs in business and government spend substantial portions of their work week writing. Faigley and Miller surveyed two hundred workers in a variety of job categories in twenty different organizations. On the average, the people in their study reported that they spend 23.1 percent of their time, or more than one full day a week, writing. As Faigley and Miller point out, respondents may have underestimated the time they spend if they are reporting only time spent actually writing and not time spent planning and reviewing what they write.[3]

Other researchers who have surveyed college graduates on the job have reported findings similar to Faigley and Miller's. In a recently published review article, Paul Anderson reports results from his own study of 841 alumni of seven science and business departments at his school (Miami University of Ohio), and he also reports on his review of fifty other surveys of writers on the job. He concludes: "All the surveys that have inquired about the matter find that the respondents spend, on average, approximately 20 percent of their time at work writing." Clearly, whatever their job titles, college graduates will need to know how to write well to do their jobs well.[4]

2. Communication skills become even more important as people move up in organizations.

Moreover, as employees move up the career ladder within an organization, they find that communication skills (both oral and written) become even more important than their technical skills. Managers must be excellent communicators.

Survey after survey confirms that writing skills are a major factor in promotions within organizations and agencies. When Storms surveyed 837 graduates of Miami University of Ohio's School of Business Administration, 88 percent of his respondents said that the ability to write well has an effect on advancement. When Davis surveyed 245 engineers of distinction, 96 percent said that good writing skills had helped their own advancement. Interviews with managers in large organizations and companies may help students to understand the importance of communication skills.[5]

3. On the job, workers write a variety of documents, not just letters and memos.

Anderson asked the people in his survey how often they wrote any of eleven types of documents. Letters and memos were only two of the eleven types (that is, he did not distinguish among different types of letters or memos). More than half of his respondents reported that they write seven of these eleven types at least sometimes.

Memos and letters ranked first and second, but reports were the last of the seven. In between letters and reports, came

• step-by-step instructions
• general instructions
• preprinted forms (to be filled out)
• proposals

An interesting finding for college professors: Articles for professional journals ranked last on the list of eleven document types that Anderson's respondents write.[6]

Anderson reports similar results from other studies: People on the job often write memos and letters, but they also write other types of documents. Nonsurvey case studies support this conclusion. For example, interviews with a department store manager, a college professor, and bank officers indicate that each writes numerous types of material.[7] According to Barrie Van Dyck, an executive in a bank writes the following:

Documents to self or others in the bank:

- Reports of telephone calls, to provide information for others, for the record, or for self at a later time

- Memos requesting services or information, requesting action or commenting on plans or recommendations of others

- Reports of investigations, analyses, or evaluations (Major decisions about the bank's business may be made on the basis of these reports.)

- Reports about a prospective client, analyzing the client's request, recommending lending policy

Documents to others outside the bank:

- Letters to clients from simple acknowledgements to complex explanations of terms of a transaction (rejecting a request for a loan, raising rates, refusing a renewal)

- Agreements for clients to sign

- Proposals to persuade current and prospective clients to use services

4. Many people in organizations did not have college training in writing that prepared them for the writing they do on the job.

Until recently, many of the professional and managerial staff we met in organizations and agencies had not had any pre-job training in the types of writing that they find themselves doing on the job. If they had any writing courses in college at all, the course was likely to have been a typical freshman composition class, covering exposition, literary criticism, and narrative. Aldrich surveyed 254 mid- and senior-level managers; 139 had no training in writing beyond freshman composition.[8]

We can only speculate on why these managers did not take more courses in writing in college or graduate school. They may have gone to colleges that did not offer business writing at all or offered those courses only to business majors. Their major course of study probably did not require any more writing courses, and they may have chosen not to take an elective in writing because they did not appreciate how useful it would be.

Looking back from the vantage point of several years on the job, professionals in many fields rank writing high on a list of critical courses. Managers who did take business writing in college remember it as an important course. Eighty percent of the respondents in a survey of 133 senior managers named business writing as the college course they use most often on the job.[9]

In a survey of more than 4,000 engineers, respondents named technical writing second only to management practices as the course most needed for a professional career. Stevenson reports that graduates of the University of Michigan Law School ranked writing first among the topics that should receive more emphasis in legal education.[10]

Professionals in many jobs think writing is important, yet many people still enter professional jobs without enough relevant training in writing.

5. The lack of training helps to perpetuate poor writing in organizations.

The fact that so many people come to jobs unprepared to write in organizational settings has several negative consequences.

Because they know they have not been taught to write job-related materials, young workers have no background to counterbalance the influence of the organization's tradition and culture. They look to the organization's earlier products as models. When these models are examples of poor writing (as so many are), the new workers perpetuate poor writing.

When new workers in organizations use the training they have had in college, they often write in the wrong genre with an incorrect view of the audience. They may write reports as narratives with lengthy explanations of what happened during the study, building up to the conclusion at the end. That's just the opposite of the way a report should be written for a busy manager. Managers want to see the conclusion first, followed by support for the conclusion. The most they usually want to see about how the study was done is a very brief summary.

Young workers often write technical descriptions that show everything they know about a topic, when their readers, trying to get a job done, need step-by-step procedures organized by task, not by topic.

Because these young workers are used to writing academic papers which go only once to one reviewer for a grade, they find it difficult to share early drafts and to negotiate changes with many reviewers, each of whom represents a different constituency. In many work settings, skills in dealing with people are as important in preparing a useful document as are skills in writing a coherent sentence. Inefficient writing is costly for government agencies and businesses. Moreover, the result is all too often a document that goes unread and unused. Let us turn now to typical business documents. What is it about the documents that make them so ineffective and frustrating?

Analyzing Typical Documents

This section is based on analyzing numerous documents from government agencies and private corporations. We've worked with

- credit notices
- collection letters
- leaflets about drugs
- instructions for forms
- notices about government programs
- benefits handbooks
- insurance policies
- computer manuals
- regulations
- loan applications
- warranties
- appliance manuals
- utility bills and notices
- policy and procedure manuals
- reports of analytic studies

and many types of forms.[11]

Note that most of the documents on this list are not memos or letters. Although business people write letters and memos more often than they write other types of documents, these other documents may have greater importance for the agency or company. The documents on this list have a much longer useful life than a memo or a letter and are likely to have many more readers. Authorship of one of these documents may mean more for a professional's career advancement than would a stack of memos or letters. In many cases, these are the documents that represent an agency or company to its customers. In other cases (such as benefits handbooks or policy manuals), these documents represent the authors and the authors' groups to other groups within the agency or company.

We can group the problems that readers have with many of these documents in five categories.

1. The document is not organized so that readers can find what they want in the time they are willing to spend looking for it.

2. The content of the document is not what readers need.

3. Readers cannot picture themselves in the text.

4. People have to read a sentence several times to understand what it means.

5. Readers do not know the words the document uses, or the words mean different things to the reader and the writer.

1. The document is not organized so that readers can find what they want in the time they are willing to spend looking for it.

People read for different purposes at different times. When Sticht and his colleagues considered the problems in military manuals, they distinguished between "reading to learn" and "reading to do." In reading to learn, the reader's goal is to absorb the material to remember it for future use. In reading to do, the reader's goal is to read enough to act immediately (to make a decision or to follow steps in a procedure).[12]

Researchers have found that readers in school and readers on the job have approximately opposite reading requirements. About 85 percent of the reading in school is reading to learn; only about 15 percent is reading to do. On the job, about 85 percent of the reading most people do is reading to do; only about 15 percent is reading to learn.[13]

Much business and government writing is written as if it were meant to be learned when it is used by busy people — both inside the organization and outside — as reading to do. We don't read business documents cover to cover; we scan them for answers to questions or instructions for action.

A new computer user goes to her computer manual to learn how to move a sentence from one paragraph to another. The table of contents is an alphabetical list of command names (none of which seems to apply to moving text), so she asks the friend who told her about the program instead of reading further. A student who wants a loan to pay for college has a number of questions about whether he is eligible, how much he can get, what he has to do to get the money, and so forth. He has received a sheet of information about the loan, but he does not read it because it has headings like these:

Example 3:

TERMS AND CONDITIONS OF LOANS
DEFERMENTS
REPAYMENT
ELIGIBILITY NOTICE

. . .

Note that, except for one conjunction and one preposition, all the words in these headings are nouns. Nouns name things, they do not explain. They do not draw the reader into the text. The section on "deferments" includes information that probably interests many students (namely, valid reasons for getting an extension on repaying the loan). But few students look at that section. They don't recognize the word "deferments." They don't connect it to the questions they have about the loans.

Note also that the headings are not in an order that is logical to the student. "Eligibility Notice" is the fourth heading, but the first question you would probably have about these loans is, "Am I eligible?" Certainly, you have to know about eligibility before you worry about repayment.

Typical bureaucratic documents, and many documents from private companies, ignore the pragmatics of the interaction between writer and reader. They are "reader-less" descriptions when they could and should be answering readers' questions or explaining procedures to readers. They are "content-oriented" instead of "reader-oriented." Because the writer is concerned only with getting information down on paper and not with addressing a reader's needs and concerns, the information is often put down in the order in which it occurs to the writer. That order may not be logical to the reader.

You can word a document so that it's technically accurate, legally sound, and also workable for readers. Here, for example, are the headings in a different version of the information sheet for student loans.

Example 4:

What is the guaranteed student loan program?
Who is eligible to apply?
To whom do I apply?
How much can I borrow?

. . .

No matter how well written a document is, the information in it won't be used if the reader does not bother to get to the right section. Business writing is not meant to be savored like a novel. Business people (and consumers who receive information from businesses) are too busy to bother struggling through difficult documents. They skim, they scan, they flip pages, but they read only when they think they have found a relevant section.[14] How do you make it easy for them to find the relevant sections?

Five important features that make information accessible to readers include the following:

- an informative table of contents
- useful headings
- context-setting introductions
- page layout that makes information easy to locate
- an index (if the document is longer than a memo or letter)

Include a table of contents and make it useful. The Federal Communications Commission, with help from the Document Design Center, tested two versions of the regulations for owners of two-way radios. In the old version, the table of contents read like this:

Example 5:

Applications and Licensee
    Station Authorization Required
    General Citizenship Requirements
    Eligibility for Station License

In the new version, it read like this:

Example 6:

How to get a license
    Do I need a license?
    How do I apply for my license?

In a controlled comprehension test, people were able to find the correct information in the new version more quickly and more accurately than in the old version. The new version was much shorter because it included only the information that the readers needed to know. The new version made the information easy to find because the headings in the new version matched the expectations of the readers. Readers come to a document like this looking for answers to questions. The new document is, therefore, a useful manual for readers; it is also, like the old one, a legally binding regulation.[15]

Write headings as questions or verb phrases. Other research supports the point I've been making; namely, that nouns by themselves do not help people understand how a text is organized. The nouns may be too vague, too general, or too abstract.

Swarts, Flower, and Hayes studied readers trying to make sense out of a regulation for small businesses. Their subjects could not correctly predict what information would follow the headings nor could they match headings and text. The headings in the document were single nouns and noun strings, such as "Definitions," "General Policy," "Procedure," and "Use of Advance Payment Funds." When the researchers rewrote the headings to be more informative (for example, "Setting Up the Bank Account"), subjects were significantly better at both tasks: predicting the information that would come after the heading and matching headings and text.[16]

In a study of product warranties, Charrow and Redish found that more than 90 percent of the participants preferred warranties with questions as headings to warranties with no headings or with noun phrases as headings.[17] Questions and verb phrases both work well as informative headings. Questions work well for information sheets and brochures. Verb phrases work well for procedural manuals. Consider these two tables of contents from computer manuals.

Example 7a:	Example 7b:
ALLOUT	How to use magnetic tape
AUTOPSY	Choosing an appropriate tape
AUTOSUM	Putting the tape on the machine
BUILD	Assigning the tape to your run
CBT	Copying information to and from the tape
CFT	Marking the end of a file on the tape
. . .	Removing the tape from the machine

Start by showing the structure of the document to the readers. Bransford and his colleagues have shown that readers understand a text much better if they can place what they are reading into a context that is familiar to them. This context can be as short as an informative title. It can be a picture that makes the text familiar. It can be informative headings (which, in turn, create a useful table of contents). It can be a pictorial or written road map of the document.[18]

Make the page layout help readers find information easily. When busy readers use a document (even a memo, letter, or notice that they go back to in order to locate a specific piece of information), they are generally searching for information. They want to find that information quickly without reading the entire document. The page layout and typography can hinder or help the reader's task.

Consider, for example, the two page layouts shown below. Information is much easier to find in the page layout on the right. Readers can scan the left column to find the heading they want. They can flip the pages and look at the line in the bottom right corner (the "running foot") to see where they are.

Example 8a	Example 8b
Poor page layout	Better page layout

Main Heading	**Main Heading**
Heading	
Texttexttexttexttext	**Heading**
Texttexttexttexttext	
Texttexttexttexttext	Texttexttexttext
Texttexttexttexttext	Texttexttexttext
Heading	
Texttexttexttexttext	**Heading**
Texttexttexttexttext	
Texttexttexttexttext	Texttexttexttext
Texttexttexttexttext	Texttexttexttext
Texttexttexttexttext	
3	Section-3

Even though the page layout on the right allows for much less text than the layout on the left, readers prefer it. In a recent project, we took a densely packed 12-panel card and turned it into an attractive, well-spaced, 32-page slim booklet. Readers overwhelmingly preferred the booklet, even though it was thicker. The company accepted the extra cost of producing the larger booklet because it agreed with us that it would reduce the costs of telephone operators to give out the information people should have been getting from the document.

Graphic design is an area that most writing courses totally neglect, but design conveys information just as language does. Even the writer who uses a typewriter can use margins and spacing to make headings stand out, to set off examples, to line up figures. Now that so many students and businesses are using word processing equipment, many more options are available for designing pages and highlighting text. In the past few years, desktop electronic publishing has become commonplace. (That is, writers are able to design and print pages that look like professionally produced books just by using a microcomputer and a laserjet printer.)[19]

Most documents also include more information than is necessary. The dense prose on the tightly packed page in example 8a might be replaced by the sentences that fit on the same page in example 8b. (For more on this point, see the next section on choosing the right content for the readers.)

Include an index in a manual, report, or handbook. Business writing courses that limit themselves to memos and letters do not touch on many of the issues that are important in creating longer documents. One of these issues is the difficult task of creating an index. A report, manual, or handbook needs an index; a useful index can make the difference between a document that sits on the shelf and one that readers refer to often. Redish, Battison, and Gold give specific hints for indexing technical and business documents. For example, they suggest indexing verbs as well as nouns and including in the index words that readers will bring to the document even if those words aren't in the document. (As one example, in a computer program with a FIND function, you might also have index entries for LOCATE and SEARCH with cross-references to FIND.)[20]

These five guidelines can help writers reorganize typical content-oriented bureaucratic and business documents into reader-oriented documents; but that is not sufficient. The content as well as the organization has to be appropriate for the readers. The second problem with many business documents is that they contain the wrong content for the readers.

2. The content of the document is not what readers need.

Writers who write in the noun-based, content-oriented style that is typical of traditional business, government, technical, and legal writing often include content that readers do not need and leave out content that readers do need. The problem is that they are focusing on putting down what they know rather than on addressing the reader's concerns.

For example, one document we worked with explains the rules for a government program that gives out grants. The original was a dense compilation of paragraphs, in no particular order, written in legalese. When it was first published, it did not include any information on who is eligible for the grants. If the writers or reviewers had looked through the rules as a reader would, they would have immediately looked for information on "Am I eligible?" and they would have realized that a critical piece of information was missing.

Just as reading in college and reading on the job serve different purposes, so do writing for college courses and writing on the job. In college, students learn to put down all the information they can to impress a teacher who already knows the material. On the job, writers are giving information to very busy people who do not know the information but who need to make quick decisions or to act immediately on the information.

We all tend to overwrite. We are excited about what we know and want to impart that information to people. But research on nonacademic writing continually finds that business people and consumers do not read long pieces. Recent research on how people use computer manuals has produced a concept of the "minimalist reader" and the "minimalist manual." For example, Sullivan and Flower studied people as they oriented themselves to a computerized library catalog, using the computer and the manual to accomplish realistic tasks such as finding out if the library had a particular book. In this situation, the researchers found that no one read carefully (that is, read most of the words) more than two sentences at a time. They also found that most readers did not read any section in its entirety.[21]

One key to good business writing is to provide only the information that busy people need to accomplish their tasks. Another is to give them that information in a writing style that makes it easy for them to use the information. In the next sections, I explore the problems in the writing style of many documents from large organizations and businesses.

3. Readers cannot picture themselves in the text.

Bureaucratic and business writers overuse nouns. They make nouns out of verbs; use inanimate nouns instead of pronouns or names; and string nouns together, making nouns serve in place of adjectives or prepositional phrases. The resulting style is so formal and abstract that the people who have to use the document often do not understand it because they cannot figure out from the text who can or should do what to whom. Here is an example of the traditional, topic-oriented, noun-based style:

Example 9a:
Issuance of a TOP command results in a line zero condition.

This sentence talks about a topic (the TOP command). It does not talk to the reader; it does not explain, in the reader's terms, when or how to do a task.

In a very interesting study, Flower, Hayes, and Swarts found that the nominal, passive style of business and bureaucratic prose does not match the way that readers work with documents. They asked people to read and interpret a typical bureaucratic passage. The readers had a difficult time with the passage. Moreover, in trying to understand it, they did not merely rephrase the sentences. They created "scenarios"; that is, they translated the abstract, nominal text into active sentences with people performing actions.[22]

The "scenario principle," as Flower and her colleagues named their finding, is simple and powerful. If writers focus the text on people, actions, and situations, they can improve their prose significantly. Here, for example, is a scenario-based translation of the previous example:

Example 9b:

If you want to see the beginning of your file, type TOP and press ENTER.

The typical bureaucratic or formal business style, with a passive or an empty verb, no agents at all, and with the focus on an object or an idea, is the way that most writers were taught to write. Although this style has been called "writer-based," it is really "content-based." Not only is the writer not addressing the reader, the writer is trying to remove himself or herself from the document so that the document is "neutral" or "voiceless."

The problem with this style is that it does not succeed as communication. Readers do not go to these documents to learn about topics; they go to find out how to do tasks or to make decisions or to get answers to their questions. When they cannot figure out from the text who is supposed to do what, they turn to other sources for the information. Businesses must then provide costly extra services to help people get the information that they cannot get (or will not spend the time to get) from the document.

The scenario principle supports and explains several of the basic guidelines for clear writing, namely the following:

• Write in the active voice.

• Address the reader directly. In procedures, use "you" or imperative verbs. In reports or rules, name the actors.

• Use action verbs, not nouns made out of verbs.[23]

Example 10:

Nouns made out of verbs:
Completion and *return* of the attached form will assure *participation* in the program.

Action verbs (scenario):
If you want to *participate* in the program, *fill out* the attached form and *send* it *in*.

4. Readers have to read a sentence several times to understand what it means.

In addition to overusing nouns, bureaucratic and business writers tend to run ideas together, piling up concepts in a single sentence that becomes very difficult to read. It often seems as if the writer's goal is to sound as erudite as possible rather than to communicate information to readers. What is your image of the writers of these two sentences?

Example 11a:

The purpose of this project is to create an awareness on the behalf of the consumer as to how one must proceed to effectively impact upon regulatory agency policymaking processes.

Example 11b:

XYZ agency wants people to know how they can participate when the agency is considering a new regulation.

Researchers have known since the 1950s that long or convoluted sentences overtax the human brain's capacity to process information.[24] More recent research has shown that it is not just the length of a sentence that affects how easily readers can understand it. Material presented in concrete terms is easier to understand than material presented in abstract terms. (Look again at Example 11.) Material which presents new information in a context of previously given information is easier to understand.[25] Sentences with extra information at the end (or in another sentence) are easier to understand than sentences with extra information at the beginning or imbedded in the middle.[26]

Again, the problem in many bureaucratic and business documents is that the sentences are written not to be read but simply to present information. How many writers read their material out loud before they send it off? If they did, they would probably rewrite much of it.

On the level of the paragraph and the sentence, as well as on the level of the document as a whole, the writer's task should be to help the reader find the relevant information as quickly as possible. Just as the title, headings, and page layout help readers see the structure of the document as a whole, lists, numbered steps, and tables help readers see the structure of paragraphs and sections. Research shows that people extract information more quickly and easily when it is presented in lists and tables than when it is presented in prose.[27]

If you were a busy executive, which format would give you the information you need in the time you want to spend?

Example 12a:

This program is only available to companies that have more than 200 but fewer than 500 employees and if no more than 20 percent of the employees are in nonexempt categories. In addition, they can have employees in up to ten different locations as long as any one location has at least 50 employees.

Example 12b:

This program is available only to companies that meet these criteria:

• You have between 200 and 500 employees.

• No more than 20 percent of your employees are in nonexempt categories.

• You have no more than 10 different locations.

• Each location has at least 50 employees.

5. Readers do not understand the words the writer uses.

The problem that many people focus on when they think of bureaucratic and business writing is jargon — specific words. As we have seen, however, other problems in organization, content, noun-based style, and convoluted sentences are just as important, perhaps more important, problems for readers.

A specialized vocabulary (jargon) can serve both a social and a communicative function.[28] In its social function, jargon distinguishes those who belong to a group from those who do not. It is often difficult to convince newly trained lawyers or policy analysts or computer programmers to write in plain English because they are still proving that they belong. Since they have just made the effort to learn a specialized vocabulary, they do not want to give it up. Those involved in senior management, who feel more comfortable in their profession, are more comfortable being bilingual — using the jargon with colleagues, but using ordinary English with other people.

Jargon can serve a useful communicative function within the group.[29] It takes many more words to explain to a computer novice what the experienced programmer immediately understands with the instructions: "Boot the computer. Load the program. Enter OPEN filename."

Jargon causes problems in at least three situations:

First, the specialist is writing for a general audience. To communicate, the specialist must forego the jargon and write in common, everyday words. But specialists forget that many of the words they use all the time are not common words. They cannot imagine that other people don't also know them. Therefore, writers need to get feedback from readers who are outside their group, readers who represent the audience for the materials and who can remind them of the words that the audience does not know. The writer may also need the help of a writer or editor who can serve as a translator or transformer.[30]

Second, the specialist is writing for more than one audience at the same time. Most bureaucratic and business documents have multiple audiences. A document must be read by engineers and chemists, by technicians and sales reps, by accountants and managers, by insurance agents and ordinary customers. The mistake that most business writers make is to write for the part of the audience that is like themselves. Three possible solutions include the following:

- If the material is highly technical, and if different audiences need different information, consider writing two documents or putting the more technical information into an appendix.

- If the technical vocabulary is not needed, write for the more general audience.

- If the technical vocabulary is needed (for legal reasons or because the technical people will be looking for that term), define the technical term in the text.

Example 13:
You must pay the premium within 31 days of the day it is due. (We call this 31 days the "grace period.")
The booklet will be saddle-stitched (stapled through the spine).

Third, the specialist is writing for other specialists, but they don't share the writer's jargon. Most writers think that many more people share their specialized vocabulary than is usually the case. Lawyers in different specialties do not understand each other's jargon. Business analysts in one major corporation use different words from their counterparts in other major corporations. I show examples on "view-graphs"; IBMers use "foils"; many professors use "transparencies" — three terms for the same object.

How Do We Foster Change?

If these are the problems, what are the solutions? In order to improve writing in organizations, we have to

- understand how to improve writing
- understand how to make change happen

We know a lot about what makes writing work for readers. We know less about how to get institutions to produce that sort of writing.

Making change happen means

- teaching people new ways and how to change
- making people want to change

Again, we know more about the former than the latter.

Helping Writers Empathize with Readers

As we have seen, the major difference between traditional organizational writing and the writing we are trying to foster is that the former focuses on content and the latter on the needs of the reader.

Students in business writing courses have to be taught not only to be writers of business documents, but to be readers of these documents as well. If we and the students acknowledge the difficulties that we all have as readers of many business documents, we can begin to see the difficulties that other people may have when they read what we write.[31]

Suggestions for a business writing course

Have students portray the busy executive who gives one minute to each memo. Allow the students to reject any memo from which they cannot get the information necessary for a management decision in the time allotted. Have the students rethink and rewrite the memos to convey the necessary information within the time limit.

Have students write descriptions of the range of readers who will have to deal with a given document. Discuss the realism of the students' written portraits of their audiences. Discuss the important characteristics of the audience (the time they will give to it; their attitude towards it) versus the characteristics that students often think of but that turn out to be less important (age, education level).

Have students act as readers of each other's drafts. If possible, include at least two types of readers for each document — one who comes from the same subject matter field and one who represents a more naive reader. Encourage students to be honest but constructive in their reactions. (Knowing how to be a constructive reviewer of documents is an important skill in business writing.)

Include assignments in which students analyze documents as readers and as users of the documents, as well as assignments in which students write the documents. You can find many documents for which students might be relevant readers (users), including the following examples:

- an application form for a car loan
- a consent form for hospital patients

- the manual for a word processing program
- the announcement of a government fellowship program
- the college's contract for room and board
- the credit notice on the back of a bill
- inserts that come with gas, electricity, telephone, or credit card bills

If the students find these documents difficult to understand, you have an opening for a discussion of how and why they, as writers, should attend to readers' needs.

Participants in my workshops often lament that they'll never be able to read a document again without analyzing it. I think that's great. More discerning readers make better writers. Readers who acknowledge the frustration they feel with poorly organized, poorly designed, incomprehensible documents are more likely to be concerned with making their own documents work for their readers.

Teaching Formats within a Process Model

Writing is a process. Expert writers plan before they write, revise their plans as they write, monitor what they are writing against their plans, and revise as they write and after they have developed a draft.[32]

Students need help in understanding that process and in developing strategies for all the aspects of the process, not just for writing clear, coherent sentences. One way to help students is to give them a flow chart of the writing process and to use it as a job aid in analyzing each assignment as a document design problem. The Document Design Center's model (Figure 1) is one example of such a flow chart.

Since I first developed the model in 1978, my colleagues and I at the Document Design Center (and many friends who have asked to use it) have found that it works extremely well. It works as a teaching tool with college students and with people writing on the job. It works as the framework for document design projects with a wide range of clients and documents.

Note that the picture on the previous page is not an attempt to model the cognitive processes that a writer goes through.[33] Our process model is a way to show students how much there is to a writing task and a way to help them work through all the steps in the task.

The model is not the only possible picture of the writing process. Duffy presents an alternative model with four phases; Anderson presents a model that includes testing and evaluation at almost every stage.[34]

The model is not a complete course; it only brings out many of the issues that writers must think about. Of course, the model must be

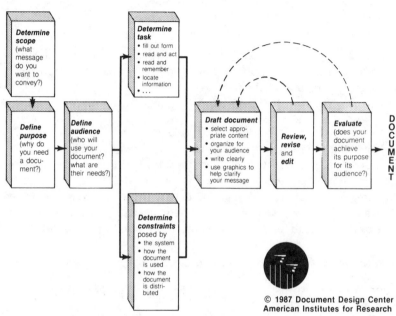

Fig. 1. The process model of document design.

supplemented with more specific questions on each issue, techniques for answering the questions, and heuristics for creating and evaluating documents based on the answers. (For one example of how to do this, see the Document Design Center's course Writing in the Professions.)[35]

Despite these limitations, the process model is helpful in teaching writing for many reasons:

- The model shows that writing is a process that does not begin with putting words on paper.
- It shows that producing a document takes time.
- It stresses planning and raises specific planning issues.
- It asks writers to think about the document both from the writer's point of view (purposes) and from the reader's point of view (reader's task).

- It stresses conscious consideration of the constraints that institutions place on writers.
- It introduces design at the first draft stage.
- It shows that multiple drafts are the norm. (More arrows would clutter up the picture, but I always stress that all the boxes should be connected with arrows. The process of writing is iterative, not linear.)
- It includes a review phase, opening the door to teaching students how to review other people's drafts and how to handle themselves during a review of their drafts.
- It says that you must test a document with its audience before you know whether you have an effective document.

Note that the model also helps to explain why readability formulas do not work. Readability formulas do not take into account different combinations of purpose/audience/reader's task. They do not consider content, organization, or design. When you see the range of issues that are relevant to successful document design, you can easily understand why readability formulas are too limited to be useful.[36]

Broadening the Scope of Business Writing Courses

The discussion in this chapter suggests that business writing courses should be expanded in at least three ways.

1. Courses should focus on generalizable strategies, not on formats.

A product orientation will not serve students as well as a process orientation. No teacher or student can predict exactly what that student will be writing on the job five or ten years from now. In our highly mobile society, your students are likely to have several jobs, even careers, during their working lives. Even if a person stays in the same organization, he or she is likely to have many different positions over the years. Business writing courses should focus on teaching skills that students can transfer from one writing situation to another. Please don't, however, interpret my advocacy of a process orientation as a suggestion that business writing teachers dispense with formats entirely. You can't. A process model and rhetorical problem solving cannot be taught in the abstract; they must come with examples. Specific examples (a complaint letter, an answer to a complaint, a letter of rejection to a job applicant, a computer manual) should be taught within the framework of a process model.

The final product that you expect from students may be the same whichever teaching methodology you adopt. The difference is the set of skills that you expect the students to have when they leave the course. In a product-oriented course, the objectives are for students to know how to write a résumé, a bad-news letter, and so forth, because they have seen examples of good résumés and have practiced writing ones that look like the good examples. In a process-oriented course, the objectives are for students to be able to

- analyze a writing task as a problem to be solved
- plan the task to meet the writer's and the institution's goals
- organize the writing to meet the reader's needs
- select writing and design guidelines to meet the plans and goals
- implement those writing and design guidelines to produce a clear, coherent, and grammatically correct product
- review and revise the writing with input from others within the institution
- know when the writing is successful

The goal is to make students think about the assignment as well as to have them produce a product. Formats are important in the process orientation, but as examples of the process rather than as ends in themselves.

2. Courses should cover longer documents, not just memos and letters.

Most of what Flower (see chapter 1) calls significant pieces of writing are not letters or memos. Longer documents, of the type I have been talking about in this chapter, bring out problems that may not be covered in a course that restricts itself to short pieces such as letters or memos.

3. Courses should try to create more links to business.

Writing in business organizations has many features that are absent from the typical classroom, including collaborative writing, diverse audiences, hierarchical review of materials, and real consequences to the writer of ineffective documents. For all of these aspects of business writing, an understanding of the sociology of large businesses and skills in working with other people may be as important to success as the ability to write clearly.

Suggestions for a business writing course

Have each student find a "client" company for the course and use that company as a case study throughout the course.

The client company must be real. Others have used

- an office on campus that is putting out a new catalog or set of instructions
- a local agency
- the office of a local political figure
- a business

A useful beginning exercise is to have the students work with someone in the company early in the semester, creating a list of all the writing that person does over a two-week or month-long period. Seeing the wide range of documents, audiences, and purposes that the client must write often motivates the students to broaden their writing skills.

As a later exercise, the students can work with the client to write or revise a document that has real audiences, real reviewers, and real consequences.

You can also bring some aspects of the business setting into the classroom.

- Create collaborative writing assignments.
- Have heterogeneous classes to provide students with a diversity of audiences within the classroom.
- Use elaborate case studies to simulate working situations.[37]

Notes

1. "Federal Judge Overrules Gobbledygook," *Simply Stated* 47 (July 1984): 3. *Simply Stated* is the newsletter of the Document Design Center, American Institutes for Research, 1055 Thomas Jefferson St. NW, Washington D.C. 20007.

2. "Consumer Products Need Better Manuals," *Simply Stated* 52 (December 1984–January 1985): 1, 3.

3. Lester Faigley and Thomas Miller, "What We Learn from Writing on the Job," *College English* 4 (1982): 557–69.

4. Paul Anderson, "What Survey Research Tells Us about Writing at Work," in *Writing in Nonacademic Settings*, ed. Lee Odell and Dixie Goswami (New York: Guilford Press, 1985): 3–83. The quote is on page 30.

5. C. Gilbert Storms, "What Business School Graduates Say about the Writing They Do at Work: Implications for the Business Communication Course," *ABCA Bulletin*, 46, 4 (1983): 13–18. R. M. Davis, "How Important Is Technical Writing? A Survey of the Opinions of Successful Engineers," *The Technical Writing Teacher* 4 (1977): 83–88. Both cited in Anderson, "Survey Research" 43, 42.

6. Anderson, "Survey Research" 23.

7. Barrie Van Dyck, "On the Job Writing of High Level Business Executives" (Paper read at the 31st Annual Conference on College Composition and Communication, Washington, D.C., 1980). Charts from Van Dyck's study

and the other cases mentioned here are in Dixie Goswami et al., *Writing in the Professions: A Course Guide and Instructional Materials for an Advanced Composition Course* (Washington, D.C.: American Institutes for Research, 1981).

8. Pearl Aldrich, "Adult Writers: Some Factors that Interfere with Effective Writing," *The Technical Writing Teacher* 9 (1982): 128–32.

9. R. H. Simonds, "Skills Businessmen Use Most," *Nation's Business* 48, 11 (1960): 88, quoted in Anderson, "Survey Research," 41.

10. Engineering survey reported in Anderson, "Survey Research," 41; law school survey reported by Dwight W. Stevenson, "The Ideal Pre-professional Writing Course: Some Unmet Objectives in Need of Attention," in *Proceedings of the Maryland Composition Conference 16 April 1982*, ed. S. Kleimann and A. Franzak (College Park: University of Maryland, 1982), 111–34.

11. For earlier treatments of the problems in bureaucratic and business documents, see Janice C. Redish, "The Language of the Bureaucracy," in *Literacy for Life: The Demand for Reading and Writing*, ed. Richard W. Bailey and Robin M. Fosheim (New York: MLA, 1983), 151–74. Also see Veda R. Charrow, "Language in the Bureaucracy," in *Linguistics and the Professions*, ed. R. J. DiPietro (Norwood, N.J.: Ablex, 1982), 173–88.

   The classification of readers' problems in this section is built on a classification that I presented in 1981. See Janice C. Redish, "How to Write Regulations (and Other Legal Documents) in Clear English," in *Drafting Documents in Plain Language, 1981*, Richard A. Givens, chairman (New York: Practicing Law Institute, Handbook 254), 207–66. This paper is also available as a separate publication from the Document Design Center (American Institutes for Research, 1055 Thomas Jefferson St. NW, Washington, D.C. 20007).

12. Thomas Sticht et al., *The Role of Reading in the Navy*, Navy Personnel Research and Development Center, Technical Report no. 77–40 (San Diego, Calif.: NPRDC, 1977).

13. Thomas Sticht, "Understanding Readers and Their Uses of Text," *Designing Usable Texts*, ed. Thomas M. Duffy and Robert M. Waller (Orlando: Academic Press, 1985), 315–40.

14. Janice C. Redish, Robbin M. Battison, and Edward S. Gold, "Making Information Accessible to Readers," in *Writing in Nonacademic Settings*, 129–54.

   Patricia Sullivan and Linda Flower, "How Do Users Read Computer Manuals? Some Protocol Contributions to Writers' Knowledge," in *Convergences: Transactions in Reading and Writing*, ed. Bruce T. Peterson (Urbana, Ill.: National Council of Teachers of English, 1986), 163–78.

15. Janice C. Redish, Daniel B. Felker, and Andrew M. Rose, "Evaluating the Effects of Document Design Principles," *Information Design Journal* 4, 2/3 (1981): 236–43.

16. Heidi Swarts, Linda Flower, and John R. Hayes, *How Headings in Documents Can Mislead Readers*, Carnegie–Mellon, Document Design Project Technical Report no. 9 (Pittsburgh: Carnegie–Mellon University, 1980), available from ERIC as ED 192 344. Some of the important

points of this study are also explained in the Flower, Hayes, and Swarts paper on the scenario principle (see n. 22) and in Linda Flower's paper in this book (Chapter 1).

17. Veda R. Charrow and Janice C. Redish, *A Study of Standardized Headings for Warranties*, American Institutes for Research, Document Design Project Technical Report no. 6 (Washington, D.C.: American Institutes for Research, 1980), available from ERIC as ED 192 341.

18. J. Bransford and M. Johnson, "Contextual Prerequisites for Understanding: Some Investigations of Comprehension and Recall," *Journal of Verbal Learning and Verbal Behavior* 11 (1972): 716–17.

19. For a brief primer on design, page layout, and typography in technical and business documents, see Philippa J. Benson, "Writing Visually: Design Considerations in Technical Publications," *Technical Communication* 32, 4 (Fourth Quarter 1985): 35–39. Another good article is James Hartley, "Eight Ways of Improving Instructional Text," *IEEE Transactions on Professional Communication* 24, 1 (March 1981): 17–27.

   For book-length primers, see James Hartley, *Designing Instructional Text*, 2nd ed. (New York: Nichols, 1985); or R. F. Rehe, *Typography: How to Make It Most Legible* (Carmel, Ind.: Design Research International, 1981).

   Relevant articles also appear from time to time in *Simply Stated*, a publication of the Document Design Center. See in particular, "Highlighting Text: Techniques that Work," *Simply Stated* 64 (March 1986); and *Simply Stated* 30 (October 1982), a special issue on graphics.

   Forms design is a special and very important case of document design. Most forms in large corporations are designed by subject matter specialists, not by graphic designers. See Joanne Landesman, "The FISAP Before and After," *Simply Stated* 15 (March 1981), reprinted in *The Journal of Business Communication* 18 (1) (Fall 1981): 17–21.

20. Janice C. Redish, Robbin M. Battison, and Edward S. Gold, "Making Information Accessible to Readers," in *Writing in Nonacademic Settings*, 129–54.

21. Patricia Sullivan and Linda Flower, "How Do Users Read Computer Manuals? Some Protocol Contributions to Writers' Knowledge," in *Convergences: Transactions in Reading and Writing*, 163–78.

22. Linda Flower, John R. Hayes, and Heidi Swarts, "Revising Functional Documents: The Scenario Principle," in *New Essays in Technical and Scientific Communication: Research, Theory, Practice*, ed. Paul V. Anderson, R. John Brockmann, and Carolyn R. Miller (Farmingdale, N.Y.: Baywood, 1983), 41–58.

23. These and other guidelines in this section come from the Document Design Center's handbook, *Guidelines for Document Designers* (American Institutes for Research, 1055 Thomas Jefferson St. NW, Washington, D.C. 20007). *Guidelines* covers twenty-five principles for organizing documents for readers, writing clearly, using typography wisely, and using charts and tables well. Each principle includes an explanation, guidelines for when and how to use it, examples, and research support.

24. George A. Miller, "The Magical Number Seven, Plus or Minus Two: Some Limits on Our Capacity for Processing Information," *Psychological*

Review 63 (1956): 748–62. Walter Kintsch and J. Kennan, "Reading Rate and Retention as a Function of the Number of Propositions in the Base Structure of Sentences," *Cognitive Psychology* 5 (1973): 257–74.

25. S. Haviland and J. Clark, "What's New? Acquiring New Information as a Process in Comprehension," *Journal of Verbal Learning and Verbal Behavior* 13 (1974): 512–21.

26. W. Larkin and D. Burns, "Sentence Comprehension and Memory for Embedded Structures," *Memory and Cognition* 5 (1977): 17–22; J. Fodor and M. Garrett, "Some Syntactic Determinants of Sentential Complexity," *Perception and Psychophysics* 2 (1967): 289–96.

27. Lists are generally superior to prose in helping people figure out complex conditional sentences. Patricia Wright and F. Reid, "Written Information: Some Alternatives to Prose for Expressing the Outcomes of Complex Contingencies," *Journal of Applied Psychology* 57 (1973): 160-66. Algorithms can help people if they know how to use algorithms. V. Melissa Holland and Andrew M. Rose, *A Comparison of Prose and Algorithms for Presenting Complex Instructions*, American Institutes for Research, Document Design Project Technical Report no. 17 (Washington, D.C.: American Institutes for Research, 1981), available from ERIC as ED 213 027.

28. Janice C. Redish, "The Language of the Bureaucracy," in *Literacy for Life*, 151–74.

29. Thomas N. Huckin, "A Cognitive Approach to Readability," in *New Essays in Technical and Scientific Writing*, 90–108.

30. Michael Macdonald-Ross and Robert Waller, "The Transformer," *Penrose Annual* 69 (1976): 141–52.

31. Janice C. Redish, "The Plain English Movement," in *The English Language Today*, ed. Sidney Greenbaum (Elmsford, N.Y.: Pergamon Press, 1985), 125–38.

32. "Plain language Pays," *Simply Stated* 63 (February 1986): 1, 4.

33. Lee Odell, "Beyond the Text: Relations between Writing and Social Context," in *Writing in Nonacademic Settings*, 249–80; Lee Odell et al., "Studying Writing in Nonacademic Settings," in *New Essays in Technical and Scientific Writing*, 17–40.

34. John D. Gould and Clayton Lewis, "Designing for Usability: Key Principles and What Designers Think," *Communications of the ACM* 28, 3 (1985): 300–11.

35. Carol B. Mills and Kenneth L. Dye, "Usability Testing: User Reviews," *Technical Communication* 32, 4 (Fourth Quarter 1985): 40–45. David Schell, "Testing On Line User Documentation," *IEEE Transactions on Professional Communication.* 29, 4 (December 1986).

36. A 1986 NCTE collection focuses on bringing reading and writing together in the college curriculum. See Bruce T. Peterson, ed., *Convergences: Transactions in Reading and Writing*.

37. John D. Gould and S. J. Boies, "Writing, Dictating, and Speaking Letters," *The Psychology of Written Communication* (London: Kogan Paul, 1980): 92–97. Linda Flower and John R. Hayes, "The Pregnant Pause: An

Inquiry into the Nature of Planning," *Research in the Teaching of English* 15 (3) (1981): 229–43.

38. If you are interested in a cognitive model of the writing process, see the work of Linda Flower and John R. Hayes of Carnegie-Mellon University. For example, Linda Flower and John R. Hayes, "A Cognitive Process Theory of Writing," *College Composition and Communication* 32 (December 1981): 365–87.

39. Thomas M. Duffy, "Organizing and Utilizing Document Design Options," *Instructional Design Journal* 2, 3/4 (1981): 256–66.

40. Dixie Goswami et al., *Writing in the Professions: A Course Guide and Instructional Materials for an Advanced Composition Course* (Washington, D.C.: American Institutes for Research, 1981).

41. If you are tempted to use a readability formula, first read any of these articles: Janice C. Redish and Jack Selzer, "The Place of Readability Formulas in Technical Communication," *Technical Communication* 32, 4 (Fourth Quarter 1985): 46–52; Janice C. Redish, "Readability," in *Document Design: A Review of the Relevant Research*, ed. Daniel B. Felker (Washington D.C.: American Institutes for Research, 1980), 69–94; Jack Selzer, "Readability Is a Four Letter Word," *The Journal of Business Communication* 18, 4 (Fall 1981): 23–24; Thomas M. Duffy, "Readability Formulas: What's the Use," in *Writing Usable Texts*, ed. Thomas M. Duffy and Robert M. Waller (New York: Academic Press, 1985), 113–43; Bertram Bruce, Andee Rubin, and K. Starr, "Why Readability Formulas Fail," *IEEE Transactions on Professional Communication* 24, 1 (March 1981): 50–52.

6 Understanding the Writing Context in Organizations

Linda Driskill
Rice University

New attention has recently been given to writers' knowledge of situations and procedures in organizations. The success of many business documents seems to depend on factors outside the genre features taught in textbooks or beyond commonly investigated cognitive processes. Studying the writing decisions of analysts in a state agency, Odell found that knowledge of other departments' needs, an understanding of the agency's interests, and experience with readers' reactions to similar documents affected individuals' writing goals as well as many decisions on content, organization, and word choice.[1] The chief value of context is its usefulness in explaining the types of meanings writers attempt to express, and readers expect to interpret, in specific situations.

The Importance of the Writing Context

The way the writing context can influence the creative and interpretive processes of writers and readers can be seen in the example of a new mutual fund's brochure headline. The new fund used a market timing approach to investing, which means that it followed technical indicators to attempt to invest in stocks only when stock prices were rising. The headline for the direct mail piece sounded full of punch to the advertising agency writer:

> When you want both safety and growth for your capital, timing is everything! And the time is right, right now.

The interplay of different meanings for *timing* and *time* were better than so much of that dry investment language, the writer thought, and he went on with another subheading: "The easy and strategic way of taking advantage of stock market trends." The headline looked

125

attractive to the marketing people, who were eager to spread their enthusiasm for their new fund.

However, the lawyer for the industry's regulatory body, the National Association of Securities Dealers (NASD), judged the language unacceptable and did not approve the piece. The language implied that the reader stood only to benefit by investing in this fund. Further, it implied that the investor's money would be safe as the value of the investment grew. The risks of the investment were not mentioned. As a result, despite talent and creative effort, considerable expense and time were lost.

The error was both the fault of the agency writer, who lacked knowledge of the NASD's standards, and of the company, which had not hired writers with legal expertise or structured its review process to assure detection of the unacceptable language.[2] Many investment brokers use only literature that has been approved by the NASD because they fear lawsuits by investors. A plaintiff would surely have a greater chance of success if unapproved literature were involved.

An awareness of the effects of specific situations, company procedures, and factors inside and outside the company has come to be known as the "business savvy" that only the experienced can apply in a writing situation. Many writing instructors, for example, would not know of the NASD and its standards for the literature of investment companies. Such awareness can be the difference between an expert writer and a novice, yet not all experienced workers are expert writers. Employees and managers, as well as teachers, consultants, and researchers, need good analytic tools and guides for writing decisions. This article presents a conceptual tool to help writers systematically tap the contextual sources of corporate savvy that affect communication success. It first discusses current theoretical models' inattention to the context for writing and the meaning of documents. It then presents components of a model of the organizational context for communication and discusses how the model can systematize organizational savvy for the benefit of teachers, consultants, and writers in companies.

Why Current Models Neglect Context

Current models and theories of business communication tell little about the effects of context on writing processes. Most theoretical positions seem to have one of three orientations: One group attends to *particular aspects of communication events*, including genres (such as letters, reports, meetings, and presentations), the individual writer's processes, or communication technologies. The second emphasizes *communication systems and their abstract properties*, such as flexibility and direction of flow. The third, recently proposed by Faigley, urges interdisciplinary research into the social aspects of writing.[3]

Approaches Attending to Particular Aspects of Communication

Genres and traditional rhetorical modes (comparison, analysis, etc.) have been the bases of communication courses focusing on types of communication events or genres: the formal report, the interview, the sales letter, etc. Many textbooks are organized to serve such courses, which emphasize features of format and abstract patterns of organization, rather than (1) what is meant or understood, and (2) how these meanings matter in the context of the organizational situation.[4] These courses focus on the means for expressing meaning, not the meanings themselves.

Another narrowly focused approach has been the study of individuals' writing behavior, usually in a laboratory setting with fictional writing assignments. Courses based on this approach have emphasized individual writing strategies, especially for invention and arrangement. Studies of individuals' cognitive processes can help distinguish between experts' and novices' strategies and identify types of writing plans. Most of this research has involved fictional settings because of a desire to standardize the situation and facilitate comparison.

Recently, attention has been focused on the effects of different technologies, such as electronic mail, dictating systems, and word processing on communication. These studies tend to overlook context and to focus instead on the technology as the source of behavior. These studies sometimes are linked with investigation of individuals' processes or with surveys of workplace practices.[5] Each of these focused approaches may reveal valuable insights, but each is likely to be incomplete, to overlook some aspects of the writing context.

Systems Approaches to Organizational Communication

Although the systems approach seems to involve writing contexts, its theorists are concerned neither with meaning nor with transactions among individuals. For example, the structural-functionalist communication scholars, whose assumptions are consistent with structural-functional management theory, think of the company as a large, abstract machine:

> Structural-functionalism requires that traits or concepts that are vital to the continuance and performance of the organization be

specifically identified. Furthermore, the investigator is charged with the task of specifying the *mechanisms* within the organization that bring about the desired levels of those traits. Consequently, if degree of flexibility, directionality of message flow, message initiation, innovation/maintenance messages are the traits under scrutiny, structural-functionalism requires one to search for those key factors that lead to different levels of each trait. As more is learned about the factors, it becomes more feasible to bring the traits under control, and so effectively "manage" communication in the organization. (emphasis added)[6]

The structural-functionalists, like many other organizational communication theorists, were heavily influenced by the communication model published by Shannon and Weaver in 1949.[7] Based on telecommunication systems, their theory is concerned with the generation of information, its flow rate along its channel, and ways to mathematically encode information to reduce "noise" in the system (Figure 1).

Shannon and Weaver were not concerned with why people needed to communicate with one another or with the content of the messages. Although Osgood subsequently criticized the Shannon-Weaver model because it did not deal with meaning, the model was irresistibly easy to grasp for people familiar with transportation systems, and it was adopted by scholars from many fields, including biochemistry, genetics, chemistry, and business communication.[8] This model influenced the works of major communications scholars, such as Berlo, Lasswell, McCroskey, and Schramm, each of whom modified the model somewhat.[9]

Schramm revised the Shannon-Weaver model in three elaborations designed to indicate that communication takes place in an environment, involves people (not just information sources), and produces feedback. Schramm's modifications certainly offered a more complete represen-

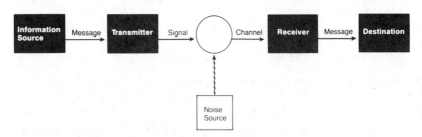

Fig. 1. Shannon-Weaver model of communication. The model does not represent meaning or intentions of persons. Source: Shannon and Weaver 1949, 7. Copyright 1948 by the Board of Trustees of the University of Illinois. Reprinted by permission of the University of Illinois Press.

tation of communication than the Shannon-Weaver model did, but the categories of "environment" and "feedback" are still too general to produce detailed analyses of the communication context, communications processes, or products.

In "Nonacademic Writing: The Social Perspective," Faigley reviews the development of genre and cognitive perspectives, but omits the systems approach, which has actually had great prominence in business communication. He suggests a "social perspective" in which writing is defined as an action "that takes place in a structure of authority, changes constantly as society changes, has consequences in the economic and political realms, and shapes the writer as much as it is shaped by the writer." According to Faigley, those taking the social perspective must move beyond the traditional rhetorical concern for audience to consider issues such as social roles, group purposes, communal organization, ideology, and finally, theories of culture.[10]

Faigley's intent is to create categories of research perspectives, each of which includes many specific approaches to the study of writing. He hopes to foster a new appreciation of the relevance of other disciplines' methods and premises for the study of writing by describing developments in several disciplines. Faigley uses *social* in a broad sense that does not reconcile the many specific meanings of the term used by sociology, psychology, anthropology, and other disciplines. The model of context proposed in this article is intended as an example of the approach Faigley would classify as "social." However, this discussion will avoid *social* as a theoretical term because of the multiple definitions it has in other disciplines. Context can help explain what a document means, what ideas it contains, why the writer would try to express his or her ideas in a particular way, and why readers who occupy particular roles in different parts of an organization would be likely to respond to a document in particular ways. Context has this power because it is a source of meaning for writers and readers. Experience in their particular roles in an organizational context has taught them to view specific topics in particular ways, to interpret particular information according to certain formal or informal rules, and to value certain styles as preferred or appropriate.

Meaning in business communication has its primary source in the writing context because communication involves actions and goals; it is instrumental. Writers in businesses seek to create meanings that produce sales, cooperation, approval, compliance, or agreement. Meaning in business writing is not limited to subject or topic knowledge. The professional may indeed have stored in memory academic knowledge learned outside of a business or professional setting, but access to such knowledge is gained via constraints and objectives that occur in a particular situation.

Any subject or issue is framed by the perceived external environment (society, government, competitors, resources, markets) as well as the perceived internal environment of the company (size, structure, technology, culture, individuals, roles, and forms of argument or reasoning). Perceptions of the external and internal environments converge to define the situations in which workers participate. Almost all these situations have rhetorical or communication requirements, because most business functions require communication. Advertising new positions available; soliciting bids from vendors and suppliers; applying for licenses; consulting with lawyers, lenders, and advertising media; promoting and selling products and services: all involve communication.

This emphasis on the external and internal environments as sources of meaning tends to deemphasize the personality of the individual writer or reader as a source of meaning. The persona of the organizational writer is defined by a somewhat different set of features than is that of the poet, political orator, or personal friend who writes in a nonorganizational or academic setting. In most business situations, the roles of writers and readers, their powers of action and expertise as members of the organization, are more important than other aspects of their personal identity. Nevertheless, the writer or speaker does have the creative power to transform the sources of meaning and to develop original solutions to organizational problems and novel writing strategies. The training of the individual in the reasoning methods of specific professional disciplines and the range of writing plans known by the writer may strongly affect the action of the individual writer. The national or regional culture (for example, "good ole boy" cultures) may also be important.

Thus, a rhetorical situation, with its range of reader/audience roles, purposes, sets of proprieties, genres, individuals, and temporal and technological constraints, must be seen as embedded within a complex context that affects both writers and readers. The "subject" or "topic" is not context-free, but situated, involved in what the members of the organization must know, feel, or believe in order to accomplish their goals. Columb and Williams have proposed a descriptive technique for describing the multiple cues writers in professional situations can embed to elicit specific expectations and invoke particular domains of information.[11]

External Sources of Meaning: Mutual Funds Industry Example

Context as a source of meaning can be understood more easily if we separate those sources of meaning external to the firm from those within the firm. These two different types exert different kinds of influences in varying degrees and are involved at different times and in different circumstances. In most firms, external sources matter less frequently; internal sources affect virtually every document. A regulatory body can be called a source of meaning because writers consult its definitions and criteria when representing their ideas.

External sources of meaning are interpreted, not absolute, influences on writers and readers. Some management scholars assume that language and reality are isomorphic, that reality is what language declares it to be. This belief is illustrated by the way management scholars speak about an organization's environment as an independent entity, not recognizing that organizations construct their own definitions of their environments, primarily through language usage. Recent debate

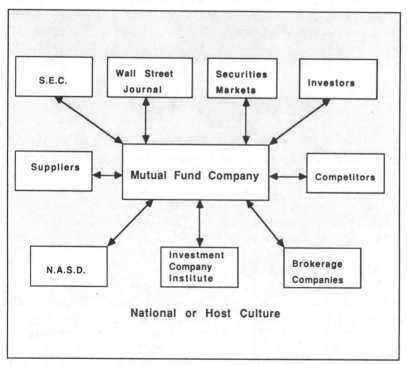

Fig. 2. Model of the communication context showing external sources of meaning in the mutual funds industry.

over the usefulness of economic indicators illustrates how "facts" of the environment, such as the "money supply" and "credit availability," are interpretations, not absolutes, of the firm's environment.

Smircich argues that instead of treating the organization's environment and the organization itself as objects or givens, managers must become aware of the language processes essential to everyday corporate life:

> The possibility of organized action hinges on the emergence and continued existence of common modes of interpretation that allow day-to-day activities to be taken for granted. In the context of group interaction, it is this routinization that we refer to as being organized. When groups encounter novel situations, new interpretations must be constructed to sustain organized activity. The process of negotiating meanings for these events may alter current understandings and thereby change the formerly taken-for-granted way of life.[12]

In the case of the mutual fund industry, mentioned earlier, several organizations, groups, and factors affect how writers in mutual funds companies interpret information and compose documents. A mutual fund is an investment company that sells shares of its investment portfolio to investors and uses the money to purchase securities, such as bonds, stocks, gold certificates, U.S. government securities, or other investment instruments. Writers in such companies may use external sources of meaning (Figure 2) to assess opportunities, obtain information, analyze audiences for company documents, and create writing plans.

The recent history (1984–86) of mutual funds that specialize in U.S. government securities illustrates the dynamic effect of the external environment as a context for writing. Until late in 1984, only a few funds concentrated their assets in U.S. government securities, such as treasury bonds, treasury bills, and mortgage-backed certificates such as "Ginnie Maes." These investment instruments are often traded in units of $100,000 or more, amounts that formerly had kept smaller individual investors from owning them. The attractive features of these funds were (1) the high rates of interest that were being paid and passed along to the owners of the mutual fund shares, and (2) the fact that the securities owned by the funds were backed by the U.S. government, which had never defaulted on any payment of principal or interest when due. The ads emphasized the annualized rate of interest currently paid and they usually included words such as "safety," "security," or "guaranteed," along with such patriotic symbols as the domes of capitols, flags, and eagles[13] (Figure 3).

FRANKLIN

U.S. Government Securities Fund

High Yield and Safety
12.15%

Fig. 3. Partial text from early Franklin U.S. Government Securities Fund advertisement emphasizing yield and safety. Source: *The Wall Street Journal,* November 1983.

In 1985, investment companies created many more of these funds that specialized in U.S. government securities. Advertisements began to appear that attracted billions of dollars into these new funds.[14] The Securities and Exchange Commission (SEC), however, perceived two problems with these attractive new funds. First, since nearly all the funds were new, they had no performance record, over time, on which investors might base their estimates of future performance, and the SEC was worried that investors would rely on the current high annualized rates being advertised. Second, although the government would indeed guarantee that the rate of interest would be paid, the value of the mutual fund shares was *not* guaranteed; instead, it would fluctuate according to interest rates. If interest rates on other investments rose higher than those being paid on the securities owned by the fund, the value of fund shares would decline. This risk, called interest rate risk, was believed to be poorly understood by investors.

The NASD began to send back comments on ads submitted for review and requested qualification of the language in the ads. NASD lawyers, for example, recommended that *safety* be changed to *a high degree of safety* (Figure 4). In the fall of 1985, the SEC asked the mutual fund trade association, the Investment Company Institute (ICI), to deal with the problems arising from misunderstood statements about safety, and to make uniform the widely varying practices in calculating and reporting the yield rates for these funds. Weeks went by as meetings of representatives from more than a thousand mutual fund companies met at the ICI. Concerned about the potential risk of lawsuits, companies began changing their advertising, even before the ICI could reach any agreement, removing the yield figures (and the explanations of how they were calculated), and changing more and

High Income
For Your IRA,
With A High
Degree of Safety

Franklin U.S. Government Securities Fund

12.38%

Fig. 4. Partial text from Franklin U.S. Government Securities Fund advertisement modified to "high degree of safety." Source: *The Wall Street Journal,* March 1985.

more to metaphorical language to suggest indirectly the attractiveness of the product (Figure 5).

Interest rates on government securities declined in early 1986 because the yields dropped on the new certificates and bonds the funds could buy. At the same time, the marketplace was exerting an influence on one marketing point: high yields. By mid-March of 1986, few government securities funds were advertising yields. Only after the ICI memorandum of agreement was completed in June 1986, did yields begin to reappear in the ads, now consistently defined and presented in uniform phrasing and letter heights. The external environment, with its complex structure of audiences, information sources, and influences, had clearly affected what mutual fund companies managing government securities funds decided to say in their publications and how writers of these ads created meaning.

Internal Sources of Meaning: The Challenger Accident Example

Internal as well as external sources of meaning affect writers in companies. The structure, size, and technology of the organization will affect the roles people play and the ways rhetorical situations are defined.[15] In the 1960s the contingency theorists at Harvard showed

**Franklin and GNMA.
It's a perfect fit.**

Franklin U.S. Government Securities Fund

Fig. 5. Partial text and illustration from Franklin U.S. Government Securities Fund advertisement using metaphor. Source: *The Wall Street Journal*, April 28, 1986.

that the volatility and complexity in a firm's environment dictate the amount, type, and frequency of information the organization processes to accomplish its mission. Since a firm's structure is a vehicle for gaining access to and communicating information, organizations try to adapt their structures to secure and disseminate most efficiently the information they need from the environment.[16]

These theorists have been criticized for not paying more attention to other factors within the firm that affect communication, such as corporate culture and the individuals of the firm. Individuals are also sources of meaning and their preferences can affect writing practices. Powerful executives can also affect how writing is produced; their preferences tend to become maxims of the company culture. Space does not permit discussion of all aspects of the model proposed in Figure 6.

Corporate Culture: As management consultants and scholars interested in nonquantitative measures of corporate behavior focused attention on the distinctive practices of individual companies in the late 1970s and '80s, a picture of the power of shared values, norms, roles, rituals, and "the company way" began to emerge. Such features

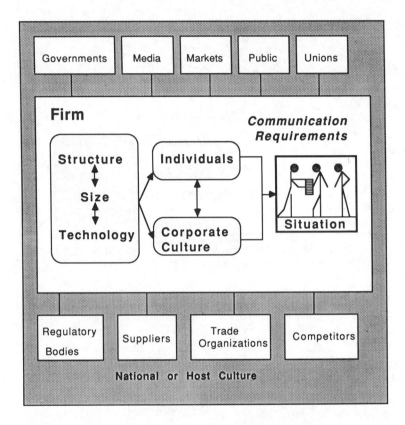

Fig. 6. Model of how external environment and firm's characteristics define business situations and communication requirements.

of a company compose what has been called its *corporate culture*. In a discussion of the variety of anthropological theories of culture whose concepts might be applied to the study of corporate culture, Allaire and Firsirotu define *corporate culture* as *a system of shared and meaningful symbols manifested in myths, ideologies, values, and multiple cultural artifacts*. They show that adopting a particular definition of culture commits one to specific conceptual assumptions and ways of studying culture.[17]

They argue in favor of a definition of corporate culture that separates the sociostructural system of the firm from its cultural system. For the purpose of understanding communication processes, we need to be able to separate culture and structure. If culture cannot be separated from structure, then the effects of these processes on communication cannot be separated. Yet, the structure and the shared values and beliefs of the organization may have quite different effects on writing practices. In a survey of one financial services company, two groups of employees expressed the same attitudes toward problem solving, but they differed significantly in their ability to solve problems. One group had no problem-solving unit or routine process; the other had a weekly meeting at which a special committee could discuss problems and make decisions. Not surprisingly, the second group was much more successful in dealing with problems. Structure, not culture, was the obstacle in that firm.

Like organizational structure, but different in its operation, culture is a powerful determinant of the definition of situation and of rituals and procedures: Who speaks to whom? Who listens to whom, when, and why? Corporate culture contributes many of the interpretive standards that affect writers' choices of content, persuasive approach, and word choice. In one company, I was told to delete *hope* from a draft. "We don't hope for anything around here," I was advised, "We decide what we want and then we make it happen."

Not all organizations have strong cultures — strong values, norms, and beliefs that guide action. Ouchi and others have classified cultures as ranging from those whose members are fully involved to those whose members are only slightly involved.[18] One would expect that in organizations where "anything goes so long as you get the work out," either communication processes would vary or external sources, such as the professional standards for accountants, engineers, and others, would influence communication practices.

It is important to note, however, that not all strong cultures facilitate communication; Bate reported difficulties experienced by companies whose cultures repressed communication about problems, prevented naming of individuals who were the source of trouble, and resisted cooperative problem solving and the expression of emotions. Communication and participation could be improved only by attacking the pervasive beliefs of the companies' cultures; and that is not an easy matter.[19] We need to include corporate culture in our models of communication, not because it plays a uniform role in all corporate communication, but because it accounts for a complex of interdependent factors whose configuration affects what people say, write, and read. Models of organizational communication that assume uniformity in many areas of organization life cannot account for the variety of documents and events in companies. Recognizing corporate culture as a source of meaning will reduce some of the confusion and enable us to identify other influences more easily.

With a variety of techniques, organizational communication scholars could investigate how culture influences the creation of written or spoken language. Rhetorical analysis of transcribed protocols might be able to show how norms and values are transmitted, enacted, negotiated, and affirmed. Scholars also might analyze objects, such as written reports, videotapes, and marketing materials, for cultural properties and for their function in rituals. Rymer has analyzed narratives and anecdotes used by managers to identify important issues, to show relationships among events and actions, and to motivate employees in a midsized manufacturing firm.[20]

Incorporating corporate or organizational culture into models and theories of corporate communication should, therefore, enable us to describe and account for different attitudes toward communication, variations in the meanings expressed by documents, variations in preferences for modes and genres, types of analogies and anecdotes, types of arguments, and roles of writers and readers. Such an array of considerations would substantially expand the degree of organizational savvy that an experienced writer might bring to bear on a single writing task.

Definitions of Situation/Prescriptive Paradigms: Throughout this article I have described the effects of the writing context, both within and without the firm, as though writers consulted their understanding of context directly in making writing decisions. More typically, I believe that these understandings are concentrated in groups of ideas associated with particular definitions of situation. Frequently, writers will respond to questions such as "What kind of situation would you call this?" or "What does a writer do in such a situation?" with lengthy rhetorical prescriptions for audience adaptation, genre choices, production schedules, stylistic preferences, and argument strategies.

Definitions of situation reflect the values of corporate culture, the requirements of organizational structure, the influences of the firm's external environment, and ways of thinking and arguing that derive from the individual's training, education, and professional role. Writers usually define situation in terms of the work of the company or a department's routines and operations. A situation involves nonrhetorical elements: actions such as delivering goods to a particular location, manufacturing, operating machinery, or making calculations. Often associated with this definition, however, are one or more *rhetorical situations*. For each rhetorical situation there is an associated set of roles, terms, concepts, reasoning procedures, and history that serves as a guide to thinking, believing, and acting. The definition of the rhetorical situation controls to a large extent which events or perceptions count as facts, which concepts apply to these facts, and which assumptions are used to evaluate them. The definition of situation determines which words are chosen as appropriate to the subject, which roles are available, which range of actions is appropriate, and with whom one is to communicate and how. The reasoning processes preferred by individuals seem to be heavily influenced by their education and professional training. Engineers frequently create narrative arguments, arguments that are stories explaining what happened when and under what circumstances. Managers more frequently use social science reasoning in which much of the "reasoning" is actually justification of assumptions underlying the model applied to the subject. Understanding the differences between the reasoning of different groups of professionals within a company or organization may be a primary key to anticipating the organization and use of evidence in documents produced by that group or person.

   The Space Shuttle Challenger Accident Case: When a writer implements an inappropriate rhetorical situation, serious, even tragic, problems can occur, as suggested in the report of the Presidential Commission on the Space Shuttle Challenger Accident.[21] The Commission concluded that the mechanical cause of the Challenger accident was the failure of the pressure seal in the aft field joint of the right Solid Rocket Motor (Vol. 1, p. 72). The Commission also found as a contributing cause a flawed decision-making process:

> Testimony reveals failures in communication that resulted in a decision to launch . . . based on incomplete and sometimes misleading information, a conflict between engineering data and management judgments, and a NASA management structure that permitted internal flight safety problems to bypass key Shuttle managers. (Vol. 1, p. 82)

The report suggests that the critical failures occurred during two teleconferences and an intervening caucus or meeting of the Morton Thiokol engineers involved in the production of the Solid Rocket Motor. These electronically conducted meetings were part of the preflight readiness review process held in the 24-hour period before the space shuttle flight began. The NASA managers and the Thiokol engineers appear to have begun the meeting with a shared understanding of the rhetorical situation (purposes, roles, type of reasoning), but in this instance the NASA managers' model-based logic and the Thiokol engineers' analogical reasoning from a few specific instances produced a tragic conflict. Participants from NASA, especially Lawrence B. Mulloy, the Solid Rocket Booster project manager at the Marshall Spacecraft Center who was in charge of the teleconferences, talked about the rhetorical situation as a collaborative probing of the data to determine whether the model of assumptions on which previous launch decisions had been based justified a change in that model. As a consequence of this approach, NASA officials were determined to treat a potential safety problem with the O-ring seals as a deterrent to launch only if data could be presented that invalidated the decision model used in the past. Mulloy looked at the teleconference as an encounter in which NASA and Thiokol would review the "Launch Commit Criteria" and determine whether any of these conditions essential for launching would be violated by the predicted conditions on the morning of January 28, 1986.

The Thiokol engineers recommended that NASA should not launch at a temperature colder than the coldest previous launch (53°F). The implication of this recommendation was that the shuttle should not be launched on the following day, when temperatures were expected to be less than 30°F. Mulloy was very certain in his testimony about the rhetorical moves appropriate to his position in that circumstance:

> *Chairman Rogers:* Didn't you take that to be a negative recommendation?
>
> *Mr. Mulloy:* Yes sir. That was an engineering conclusion, which I found this conclusion without basis and I challenged its logic. Now, that has been interpreted by some people as applying pressure. I certainly don't consider it to be applying pressure. Any time that one of my contractors . . . come to me with a recommendation and a conclusion that is based on engineering data, I probe the basis for their conclusion to assure that it is sound and that it is logical. (Vol. 5, p. 839)
>
> We were simply looking at the engineering data and reviewing those engineering data. The concern, of course, that was being expressed was for the low ambient temperatures that were predicted for the night and the effect those low ambient temperatures would have on the propellant mean bulk temperature and on the joint particularly. (Vol. 5, p. 829)

In Mulloy's judgment, his communications tactics did not constitute pressure on the Thiokol engineers. Mulloy would not allow Thiokol to use any other reasoning process than the provision of data which showed that a launch commit criterion would be violated; but the Thiokol engineers did not have that kind of data at their disposal.

Mulloy had a list of criteria that constituted a model for his decision making; the engineers had limited concrete data from a few flights and laboratory tests. The engineers who had handled the charred O-rings from the coldest previous flights were frustrated by NASA's unwillingness to consider the implications of charts showing the history of O-ring erosion on previous flights and pictures of damaged O-rings, as the testimony of Roger Boisjoly describes:

> And there was an exchange amongst the technical people on that data as to what it meant. . . . But the real exchange never really came until the conclusions and recommendations came in.
> At that point in time, our vice president, Mr. Bob Lund, presented those charts and he presented the charts on the conclusions and recommendations. And the bottom line was that the engineering people would not recommend a launch below 53 degrees Fahrenheit. (Vol. 1, p. 91)
> One of my colleagues that was in the meeting summed it up best. This was a meeting where the determination was to launch, and it was up to us to prove beyond a shadow of a doubt that it was not safe to do so. This is in total reverse to what the position usually is in a preflight conversation or a flight readiness review. It is usually exactly opposite that. . . . (Vol. 1, p. 93)

Although Mulloy maintained that customary argument structure had been followed for review of the evidence (he invited the Commission to call other witnesses who would confirm that he had handled the meeting as usual), the Thiokol people felt that the purpose of the rhetorical situation had been reversed. They were used to arguing inductively from example. Once they had had sufficient examples to provide statistically sound proof for NASA's model of launch criteria, the two reasoning processes, though different, had allowed agreement. When Thiokol had too little data, NASA managers were unwilling to look at the implications of specific examples.

After NASA Manager George Hardy, deputy director of the Marshall Space Flight Center, declared the Thiokol recommendation "appalling," and Mulloy asked whether Thiokol wanted him to wait until April to launch, Thiokol management began to feel the company's interests as sole supplier of the rocket engines were threatened and asked for a meeting among Thiokol people with the teleconference lines switched off. During this exclusive meeting of Thiokol people, a senior manager explicitly revised the rhetorical situation by asking the vice president, Lund, to change roles, "to take off his engineering hat and put on his management hat" (Vol. 1, p. 94). Chairman Rogers followed up on this testimony by asking Lund, "How do you explain the fact that you seemed to change your mind when you changed your hat?" Mr.

Lund was not able to answer this question directly. Apparently, management interests differed sufficiently from engineering interests to produce a different conclusion, and Thiokol subsequently agreed that no launch criteria would be violated and the launch could proceed. Mulloy did not convey these concerns to the top two levels of the review process and the shuttle Challenger exploded shortly after the launch on January 28, 1987.

Organizational Situations and Rhetorical Situations

Because of rapid changes in business environments and within companies, many rhetorical situations must be redefined to achieve greater congruence between organizational situations and rhetorical situations. In the example of the mutual fund's reliance on market timing, the agency writer saw the situation as "writing a brochure for a client . . . essentially, marketing a parity product by claiming extra attention for it, making it stand out on the shelf." The writer perceived investors as breakfast cereal buyers, the sole audience for the message on the box. He needed to understand that, although he was writing a brochure for a client, the rhetorical situation involved audiences other than consumers and marketing professionals. He needed to include in the rhetorical theater other powerful actors, including regulatory associations, competitors, lawyers, investment brokers, as well as investors. By using a broader model of the sources of meaning in the writing context, practitioners and teachers alike can construct more accurate definitions of organizational situations and rhetorical situations to guide their decision making.

Implications for Teaching

Teachers can use the model described and the results of research to improve instruction. Recognizing the force of culture, technology, and situations can enrich our production and use of cases in the classroom. Brockmann identifies six features of a successful case, including "fullness of the rhetorical context," which he associates with purpose, audience, and role.[22] A full rhetorical context should go beyond these three factors to include the relation between the organizational situation and the rhetorical situation, and the culture, values, history, and ways of thinking that determine the criteria for judging communication practice in a real organization.

Further, by studying rhetorical situations, we may identify how these provide roles for individuals trained in particular disciplines, particular ways of thinking and arguing. We can help students anticipate how the skills learned in accounting, finance, real estate, strategic planning, and other business functions will be applied in communication, and we will be able to describe more precisely the relationship between business communication and other management disciplines.

We must teach students to analyze organizational and rhetorical situations and to develop strategies for achieving greater congruence between them, given the culture, size, and technology of the organization. Finally, we should emphasize the excitement and pleasure of dealing with the demands of rhetorical situations. Creativity and personal involvement are essential for meeting the complex challenges of real organizational contexts. Too often, technical and business communication has been taught as a dry, mechanical skill devoid of personal interest. When we recognize the importance of the context for writing in organizations, we see the significance of the issues resolved through communication processes. Writing well is not merely conforming to genre conventions, as some of the genre-based approaches have implied. Communicating in organizational contexts is essential to the vitality, and even to the survival, of organizations and society in a technical era.

Notes

1. Lee Odell, "Relations between Writing and Social Context," in Lee Odell and Dixie Goswami, ed., *Writing in Nonacademic Settings* (New York: Guilford Press, 1985), 249–80.
2. Brief examples throughout the article, such as this one, are drawn from my consulting experience.
3. Lester Faigley, "Nonacademic Writing: The Social Perspective," in Lee Odell and Dixie Goswami, ed., *Writing in Nonacademic Settings*, 231–48.
4. Exceptions to these texts would be Marya Holcombe and Judith Stein's *Writing for Decision Makers* (Belmont, Calif.: Lifetime Learning, 1981); and Mathes and Stevenson's *Designing Technical Reports*, both of which emphasize the effect of the organization's structure and problem-solving activities on meaning.
5. Jeanne W. Halpern and Sarah Liggett, *Computers and Composing: How the New Technologies Are Changing Writing* (Carbondale: Southern Illinois University Press, 1984).
6. Richard V. Farace, Peter R. Monge, and Hamish M. Russell, *Communicating and Organizing* (Reading, Mass.: Addison-Wesley, 1977), 93. *Structural-functional* refers to the relation between a firm's structure and the business functions performed. Most firms attempt to group together

workers with similar goals and expertise to foster cooperation and efficiency.

7. Claude Shannon and Warren Weaver, *The Mathematical Theory of Communication* (Urbana: University of Illinois Press, 1949). The image of reified language in this model has been thoroughly analyzed by Ragnar Rommetveit, "Prospective Social Psychological Contributions to a Truly Interdisciplinary Understanding of Ordinary Language," *Language and Social Psychology* 2; 2, 3, 4 (1983), 89–104.

8. C. E. Osgood, "Psycholinguistics: A Survey of Theory and Research Problems," *Journal of Abnormal and Social Psychology* 49 (October 1954).

9. David K. Berlo, *The Process of Communication: An Introduction to Theory and Practice* (New York: Holt, Rinehart, and Winston, 1960); Harold D. Lasswell, "The Structure and Function of Communication in Society," in John Byrson, ed., *The Communication of Ideas* (New York: Harper and Row, 1948), 37–51; J. C. McCroskey, *An Introduction to Rhetorical Communication* (Englewood Cliffs, N.J.: Prentice–Hall, 1972); Wilbur Schramm, *The Process and Effects of Mass Communication* (Urbana: University of Illinois Press, 1954).

10. Lester Faigley, "Nonacademic Writing."

11. Gregory G. Colomb and Joseph M. Williams, "Perceiving Structure in Professional Prose: A Multiply Determined Experience," in *Writing in Nonacademic Settings*, 87–128.

12. Linda Smircich, "Implications for Management Theory," Linda Putnam and Michael Pacanowsky, ed., *Communication and Organizations: An Interpretive Approach* (Beverly Hills, Calif.: Sage Publications, 1983), 221.

13. Figures 3, 4, and 5 show the ads of funds managed by only one company, Franklin Funds, because of lack of space for additional figures. However, by consulting the *Wall Street Journal* for this period, the reader can see that the statements are generally true about funds of this type.

14. *1986 Mutual Fund Fact Book* (Washington, D.C.: Investment Company Institute, 1986).

15. Effects of size, structure, and technology have been studied for over twenty-five years, especially by the Tavistock group in England and by the contingency theorists at Harvard. The sociotechnical models can be useful for analyzing patterns of communication, but other sources of meaning must be considered as well. T. Burns and G. M. Stalker, *The Management of Innovation* (London: Tavistock Publications, 1961); Joan Woodward, *Industrial Organizations: Theory and Practice* (London: Oxford University Press, 1965).

16. Paul R. Lawrence and Jay W. Lorsch, *Organization and Environment* (Boston: Harvard Business School, 1967). For a historical review, see Henry Mintzberg, *The Structuring of Organizations: A Synthesis of the Research* (Englewood Cliffs, N. J.: Prentice-Hall, 1979).

17. Yvan Allaire and Mihaela E. Firsirotu, "Theories of Organizational Culture," *Organization Studies* 5, 3 (1984): 193–226.

18. Alan L. Wilkins and William G. Ouchi, "Efficient Cultures: Exploring the Relation between Culture and Organizational Performance," *Administrative Science Quarterly* 28, 3 (1983): 468–81.

19. Paul Bate, "The Impact of Organizational Culture on Approaches to Organizational Problem Solving," *Organization Studies* 5, 1 (1984): 43–66.

20. Jone Rymer Goldstein, "Myths and Stories in Corporate Communication" (Paper presented at the Association for Business Communication Convention, Chicago, November 1985).

21. *Report of the Presidential Commission on the Space Shuttle Challenger Accident*, 5 vols. William P. Rogers, chairman (Washington, D.C.: U.S. Government Printing Office, 1986).

22. R. John Brockmann, "What Is a Case?" in R. John Brockman, ed., *The Case Method in Technical Communication: Theory and Models* ([Lubbock, Tex.]: Association of Teachers of Technical Writing, 1984), 1–16.

7 The State of Legal Writing: *Res Ipsa Loquitur*

George D. Gopen
Duke University

When Shakespeare made Hamlet say to the grave-digger:
Why may not this be the skull of a lawyer?
Where now be his quiddities, his quillets,
his cases, his tenures, and his tricks?
he was paying the profession a real compliment; and a compliment none the less because it was intended as a slur. A quiddity is defined by Webster as a "trifling nicety," and the word quillet is another form of "quibble." Both words seem to have been in fairly common use three hundred years ago and Shakespeare used them to express the sharpness of the lawyer and his facility in the use of words even in that day and time. For the ability of the lawyer to confuse others by the use of words has long been the subject of proverbs. The reasons for the distinction — or if you prefer, for this reproach — are not hard to find; they lie in the lawyer's training and in the work he is called upon to do. And yet, no matter what else may be said of him, the lawyer, in his field — even as the physician and the priest in theirs — remains the last resource of other men and women. When the wisdom of common men fails them and disaster is at hand, when the layman's brain is overworked until his mental fuse burns out, when the motor car of "Business" blows out its tires and piles up in the ditches of insolvency, when the human derelict is finally tossed up upon the rocks by the stormy seas of life, then the lawyer is sent for and his "quiddities" and his "quillets" are more than welcome; then the myriad complexities of human frailty, and the baffling chicanery of men, test out all "his cases, his tenures, and his tricks."[1] (Urban A. Lavery, Chief Legislative Draftsman, Illinois Constitutional Convention)

Ask the public: The first thing it associates with professors is tweed; the first with doctors (a tie here) is lots of money or bad handwriting; and the first with lawyers, prose that is impossible to understand. The lengthy quote above is from a 1921 article entitled "The Language of the Law: Defects in the Written Style of Lawyers, Some Illustrations, the Reasons Therefore, and Certain Suggestions as to Improvement," and, ironically, it pronounces on the profession something of a slur, even though it was intended as a real compliment. There is a glory, it seems, in the mystery of a language that can be deciphered only by initiates of the secret society; there is a great sense of power and an even greater actuality of power in controlling a language that in turn controls the most pressing affairs of individuals and communities; and there is a monopolistic safety in being able to manipulate a language which, because it was part of the creation of legal problems, must be part of their solutions as well. It was true in 1921, and it is still true nearly seventy years later. This essay will suggest some possible causes of traditional legal style and then explore some of the recent attempts to do something about it.

Legal Language: Use and Abuse

"Legal writing" is a misnomer. Every rhetorical problem that faces lawyers faces other professionals as well; only the particular *combination* of those rhetorical needs is special to the Law. We continue to use the term "legal writing" because we have not found a simple way of defining that combination, and because (as Mr. Justice Potter Stewart once said of hard-core pornography) we know it when we see it. Is there no "legal writing" of high quality, deep perception, and broad vision? Of course there is. Every firm or legal department I deal with (as a writing consultant) is quick to point out to me the two or three "really fine" writers in their midst; but that seems rather like Boswell's pointing out a tree in Scotland to disprove Johnson's complaint that there were no trees in Scotland. The demonstration of the exception is good circumstantial evidence of the aptness of the rule — or so a lawyer might say.

In one of the best articles on the subject written to date, Professor Robert W. Benson neatly summarizes the major problems of what has come to be called "legalese":

> There is plentiful evidence that lawyer's language is hocus-pocus to non-lawyers, and that non-lawyers cannot comprehend it. There exist scores of empirical studies showing that most of the linguistic features found in legalese cause comprehension difficulties. Legalese is characterized by passive verbs, impersonality, nominalizations, long sentences, idea-stuffed sentences, difficult words, double negatives, illogical order, poor headings, and poor typeface and graphic layout. Each of these features alone is known to work against clear understanding.[2]

When I speak pejoratively of "legal writing," "legal language," or "legal prose," I am referring not only to the recognizable professionalisms or statutory monsters:

> Any person who obtains payment or acceptance and any prior transferor warrants to a person who in good faith pays or accepts that he has no knowledge that the signature of the maker or drawer is unauthorized, except that this warranty is not given by a holder in due course acting in good faith to a drawer with respect to the drawer's own signature, whether or not the drawer is also the drawee. . . .

I am referring as well to the failed attempts to communicate clearly and swiftly:

> Appellant's attempt to characterize the funds by the method of payment (reimbursement), rather than by the actual nature of the payment misses the mark.

Lawyers need to be able to articulate clearly the steps and connections in a logical argument. Lawyers need to be able to maintain clarity of expression, even in the face of complexity of thought. Lawyers need particularly to be able to write with both precision and anti-precision: For some documents they have to nail down particulars in order to avoid vagueness and ambiguity, whereas for others they will have to keep the letter free in order to protect the plasticity of the spirit in the advent of unforeseen circumstances. But none of these rhetorical needs need produce problematic prose; the causes of the problems lie elsewhere. Here are eight of them:

Adjudicated Jargon

Many lawyers will respond to an attack on their obfuscatory legal style by insisting that they *have* to write that way. By this they usually mean that so many words and phrases have been defined by courts or by traditional professional usage as terms of art, that to use simpler synonymous words or structures would raise the presumption that they did not intend to mean what the legal term of art would have meant. Of course, the need for some arcane vocabulary hardly excuses all the other sins of legalese; but within a limited extent, the lawyers have a case.

Historically, there is an extraordinary importance granted to accuracy of detail in legal proceedings. In medieval times, trials often depended on oath-taking and the accurate repetition of precise statements by members of the community. The original "juries" were not fact finders, but rather people who were willing to swear (French "jurer") that a certain thing happened a certain way. In some cases this meant that they each would have to read without error the same previously prepared statement. A single stumble (presumably caused by God, who would not allow injustice to triumph) would indicate the falsehood of the statement and prove conclusive to the proceedings. Not all of medieval English law functioned in this manner; but enough of it did to impute a quasi-religious significance to the existence of particular words in a legal context.

To make matters worse, the English and American common-law systems were developed not by simplification and clarification, but by addition and qualification. Not until 1968 could a case decided by the British supreme court be overturned; a precedent could not be defeated, but only distinguished away. Therefore, the specifically *legal* meanings of words and concepts became the specialized knowledge of the practitioners; before the awesome complexity of the traditions, non-lawyers could only stand in fear and tremble.

There was, in this process of addition and qualification, too, a touch of the religious. In many orthodox religions, it is more common by far for prayers and observances to be added to established rituals than to be deleted. As time goes by, the liturgy becomes longer, more dense, and less understood by the laity; it takes more of its meaning from the fact that it has existed than from the significance it was once intended to convey. Until quite recently, the same has been generally true for the Law. Is granting a piece of property to "X" the same as granting it to "X and his heirs"? Was it always so? If it once was not, can it be so now? And who, besides a lawyer, would know?

So it is true, to an extent: Lawyers have to know their jargon and its probable effects. They are probably safer in using the traditionally effective incantations than in writing their own, more modern, more streamlined tunes. But *must* they be confined to expressing something only as it has been expressed in the past? Example: A small business wants to hire a particular company to handle its investments. To be "legal" about it, the Board of Directors must sign a consent vote to the following text:

> Pursuant to the provisions of applicable law, Chapter 156B of the Massachusetts General Laws, the undersigned, being all of the Directors of Acorn Products, Inc., hereby consent to the following:
> VOTED:
> That the resolutions contained in the attached resolutions for the Thomas Mackay Securities Inc. Corporation Cash Account be and they hereby are adopted as actions of the Corporation, and that the clerk be and he hereby is authorized and directed

to execute and deliver said resolutions and the certificate contained therein in the form attached hereto and made a part hereof.

Lacking the space here to investigate all the history of this off-putting bit of prose, let me point out only the fear and trembling in the "be and hereby are" formula. Quite possibly, someone long ago wrote such a document with the simpler phrase "that the resolutions be adopted" and learned in some court at a later date that the document *meant* "that the resolutions will be adopted at some time in the future but not necessarily now." Not to be burned twice, that someone eliminated the loophole by adding the present tense, thereby resolving the ambiguity between the subjunctive and the future — "that the resolutions be and hereby are adopted." Once that crept into the form books, who would dare put it otherwise? If something works, why take a chance with something else, merely for the increased reading ease of nonprofessionals?

There is no simple way out of this. Leadership in this kind of reform must come from the institutions above, not from the individuals below. Such help is now at hand in many states, where "Plain English" laws are not only allowing but requiring that the ancient band-aid rhetoric be replaced by language that the populace at large can understand — at least for documents such as insurance policies and lay-away plans, which directly affect large numbers of consumers.

Leadership can also come from important law firms and large corporate legal departments which dare to simplify. First, however, they must be convinced that the sanctity of their form books came, not from God, but from convenience, caution, and inertia. I recently succeeded in converting one corporate lawyer in a skirmish that bears repeating here. She had been specializing in her field for eight years but had been with her present firm only one year. I was consulting with the firm about writing skills and had a thirty-minute individual conference scheduled with her. She appeared at the appropriate time but denied that she needed any help, since she mostly spent her time piecing together the appropriate bits of boiler-plate prose she found in the firm's form books. That boiler plate, she argued, had stood up successfully in the courts and therefore was not to be tampered with under any circumstances. I asked her if this firm's boiler plate was identical to that which she had used for seven years in her previous firm; she said no. I asked her how long it had taken her to adjust to the new boiler plate; she said that after a full year she was only just then starting to feel comfortable. So there they were: two completely different sacred pieces of prose, neither of which could be altered in any detail, even though each did precisely the same job. She was willing to take a closer look. Here is the paragraph on which we worked:

> 1.08 *Ownership*
>
> All property and interests in property, real or personal, owned by the Partnership, will be deemed owned by the Partnership as an entity, and no Partner, individually, will have any ownership of such property or interest owned by the Partnership except as a tenant in partnership as provided in the Act. Each of the Partners irrevocably waives, during the term of the Partnership and during any period of the liquidation of the Partnership following any dissolution, any right it may have to maintain any act for partition with respect to any of the assets of the Partnership. The General Partner shall be authorized to provide for the holding of legal title to all or any part of the Partnership property in the name of any entity or person as trustee on behalf of the Partnership; provided, that any such trustee or nominee shall execute a certificate, suitable for recording, acknowledging that the beneficial owner of such property is the Partnership and agreeing to hold and dispose of legal title to such property in accordance with the terms of this Agreement.

We applied certain structural revision techniques (further explored below) sentence by sentence, and in fifteen minutes produced the following, which she now insists differs not at all from the original in substance:

> 1.08 *Ownership*
>
> Partnership property shall be owned by the Partnership entity and not by the Partners individually. Each Partner irrevocably waives any right to partition the property. Although the Partnership owns the property, the General Partner may authorize any person to hold legal title to the property as trustee or nominee for the Partnership. Such trustee/nominee shall execute a recordable certificate in which (i) s/he agrees to dispose of legal title to the property in accordance with this Agreement and (ii) s/he acknowledges that the Partnership is the beneficial owner.

The boiler-plate battle can be won, but it will not even be engaged until the legislatures, the courts, and the leading lawyers become convinced it is worth fighting.

The Problem of Precedent

Lawyers work primarily with legal concepts that have been established by statute or private agreement and have been elaborated upon by court decisions. The lawyers may be called to action by the facts of the present case, moved by those facts, and even convinced by those facts; but those facts will work against the client unless they can be properly and persuasively associated with principles of law that will resolve the issue in favor of the client. Lawyers, therefore, fill relatively little space with interesting, human specifics, and are forced to concentrate instead on the relatively nonhuman (some would say inhuman) legal concepts. Professor Steven Stark has put it nicely:

> But anyone who writes about rules and not facts is going to have a difficult time composing an appealing piece. What intrigues most writers are stories about people; a story is usually the development of a character. For example, what would make the story in *Erie v. Tompkins* [a particularly thorny case, often used to begin courses in Civil Procedure] interesting to the typical reader is what happened to Tompkins, not what happened to the doctrine of *Swift v. Tyson*. But the legal writer must ignore the attractive part of a story and be content instead to discuss the application of rules in a way that tells lawyers what doctrines they should follow. Even Joan Didion would have trouble doing much within those constraints.[3]

Concentrating on what the law has said and how the present facts fit those concepts, lawyers keep foremost in mind the goal of making a totally subjective task (representing their client) agree as much as possible with that legal Chimera, objectivity. Again, Stark:

> Legal language and style make the task easier. To begin with, lawyers can use labels to objectify and simplify: Ms. Jones and Mr. Smith become tort feasors or lessees. Or lawyers can resort to a style of writing replete with logical analysis and dozens of footnotes designed to show the objectivity of the legal process. Finally, because it aspires to objectivity, legal language may refuse to recognize troublesome concepts such as hope, candor, or even love. If the doctrine of standing means anything, it must be that certain perceived hurts are not recognized in conventional legal discourse, perhaps because in an objective world they can have no universal meaning.[4]

The Club

Although many lawyers might feel discomfort in departing from the traditional diction, usage, and constructions of legal language, they also derive a sense of comfort and identity from the language which marks them as a tribe unto themselves. They belong to one of the largest clubs in American society, a group that uses language and technicality to distinguish itself from the public. One has to work hard to be admitted to the training ground and even harder to be accepted into the inner sanctum. The status of the profession comes from its power:

> And yet, no matter what else may be said of him, the lawyer, in
> his field — even as the physician and the priest in theirs — remains
> the last resource of other men and women.[5]

Its livery is its language.

There are practical, historical reasons for the existence of much of the "legal sound." In many cases the reasons have faded away but the language remains. For example, the familiar legal "doubling" (e.g., "cease and desist," or "made and entered into") probably began as a result of the translation of British law from Anglo-Norman ("Law French") into English. It was feared at the time (early sixteenth century) that certain terms of art would be re-expanded in definition and lose their peculiarly legal significance by their translation into English. Where this was feared to be the case, the translation was made, but the Anglo-Norman term was retained as well, thus producing the doubling effect. We no longer need have the fear, but we still have the doubled terms. (Can one "cease" from doing something without "desisting" as well?)

Some lawyers will defend the retention of the doubled terms by recourse to a new fear — that some judge somewhere will insist that neither "cease" nor "desist" by itself will have the same hallowed legal effect of "cease and desist." Personally, I cannot imagine such an event; I suggest rather that lawyers have grown accustomed to their sound and are pleased with the way it sets them off from all others. It will be as difficult in some circles to dispossess the profession of its sound as it was for certain religions to abandon the original languages of their liturgy in favor of the vernacular.

The Hostile Audience

The lawyer's rhetorical task is arguably among the most difficult because, unlike other professionals, lawyers are constantly writing for hostile audiences. When a doctor writes an article for a journal or a report on a patient, the audience tends to spare no pains in trying to interpret the prose as the author intended. But when a lawyer writes, who is the audience? Is it a senior partner, who will play the devil's advocate in order to ensure its combat readiness? A judge, who will subject it to comparisons with the brief on the other side? Or, worst of all, an opposing counsel who, fully cognizant of what the author intended, will spare no pains to demonstrate that it might not, indeed cannot, mean that very thing? This is a great problem, not to be underestimated. It is no wonder that lawyers are so willing to repeat themselves, to plug small holes that might not even exist, to pile on much more information than the argument requires, and in general, to use a shotgun approach (instead of a crossbow approach) to rhetoric.

I would suggest that the main hope for overcoming this substantial problem lies in teaching lawyers structural stylistics. That is, for example, if lawyers can learn where readers tend to look in units of discourse for emphasis, they can fill that slot with their emphatic material, thereby diminishing the possibilities for ambiguity. The same is true for the placement in the sentence of context and action, the placement in the paragraph of the point, and the placement in the document of the thesis. This approach has been used with great success in the past several years by some consultants and at some law schools. (See the section entitled Work in Related Fields.)

Practical Pressures

These are varied. They all explain in part why lawyers turn out prose that is difficult to read, but they do not excuse it. In order to prepare lawyers to face these pressures, we should be teaching them a great deal more than we do about the language and about writing processes.

The most pervasive practical pressure, especially in large firms, is time. Lawyers are almost always up against a deadline or up against the need to finish with the present problem in order to turn to others. Those needs translate into anxiety about speed and a heightened awareness of the passage of time. (Many a new law clerk, having been for so long a student, has had painful difficulties in adjusting to the requirement of accounting literally for each minute of the day's work, a procedure necessary for the accurate billing of the appropriate client.)

These time constraints neither allow for long prewriting processes (at least not without an accompanying sense of great guilt or incompetence) nor encourage patient revision; nor do they foster the kind of fruitful creative fervor experienced by some journalists. Lawyers are regularly producing texts under conditions singularly ill suited to the production of clear, readable prose.

Add to that the pressures that result from camel creation — that is, from writing by committee. In all large firms, most medium-sized firms, and even many small firms, documents are created by several hands. Sometimes the task is divided into subtasks, each handled by an individual; other times, several hands are set to the same problem. In either case the prose may well bounce from one individual to another, then to a committee, then to a senior partner or two, then back to the committee, and so on. In large corporations it might travel up and down several rungs of the corporate ladder several times. Problems arise in such multiauthored prose for two main reasons: (1) It is a hard enough task for any individual to maintain a consistent style; without commonly shared principles of rhetoric, it is excruciatingly difficult for a committee to do it. (2) As prose travels upwards to higher and yet higher authorities, the handgun principle of power sets in; that is, if you have power, sooner or later you will use it just to demonstrate that you have it. A senior partner or a vice president, unaware of the committee's methods of arriving at the proposed text, will send it back down with *some* changes made simply out of this sense of power or, failing that, out of a sense of duty. All too often the final prose product will suffer from incohesions and incoherencies, the explanations for which lie in the needs of each of the participants to be heard.

On the other hand, there is another practical pressure, which most of the anti-legalese literature overlooks: Writing on legal subjects is usually immensely difficult. Combine the nature of the substantive material with the complexity of the concepts, the hostility of the audience, and the time pressures of production, and which of us would 'scape whipping? It is always easier to note the flaws in someone else's work than to produce that revised quality from scratch. While we criticize legalese — justifiably and needfully — let us not condescend unnecessarily. There but for the lack of a law degree go most of us.

The combined effect of these practical pressures is especially overwhelming for lawyers who write (as far too many of us tend to write) by ear. With Time's winged chariot hurrying near, the committee chattering, the boss complaining, and the clients whimpering, one cannot *hear* very much. Again, the solution must lie in the mastering of *methods* of argumentation and *principles* of style.

The Toll Booth Syndrome

A great many lawyers misconceive the nature of the writing task. In this the lawyer is not alone; any writer who neither enjoys the writing process nor is uplifted by the intellectual challenge presented may suffer from it as well. I call it the Toll Booth Syndrome.

Picture the following as vividly as you can: You are a lawyer. You arrived at the office in New York at 6:30 a.m. to work on the big case. You have worked straight through to 9:00 p.m. You have redeemed your car from the parking lot and have fought both the traffic and the incipient inclement weather up into Connecticut. You approach a toll booth. The sign says "40¢ — Exact Change Left Lane." You search in your pocket and come up with a nickel, a dime, and a quarter — all the change you have. You enter the Exact Change lane. In front of you is a shining red light, but no barrier; to the left of you is the hopper. You are tired and irritable as you roll down the window, the wind and rain greeting you inhospitably. You heave the change at the hopper. The quarter drops in; the dime drops in; but the nickel hits the rim and bounces out. What do you do? Do you put the car in "park," get out, and grovel in the gravel for your nickel? Do you put the car in reverse and change to another lane where a human being can make change for your dollar bill? No. You go through the red light.

You go through the red light, I would argue, because of a misconception of the purpose of tolls. At this anxious moment, you are not feeling that before you continue on that road the government must receive from you 40 cents, with which it will keep the roads in good repair and pay the toll booth operators. Instead you believe that before continuing on that road you must be dispossessed of 40 cents. You have been dispossessed of 40 cents. It is therefore moral, if a bit risky, for you to plunge further into the Connecticut darkness.

That is the misconception lawyers (others too, but especially lawyers) have concerning the writing task. So much work has preceded the actual writing: You may have interviewed the client, discussed the case with your associates, delegated tasks to your assistants, done the research, conceived of the strategies, taken the depositions, and organized the entire project. The thinking is done; now you have only to *write* it. You cast all of your knowledge on the subject out of your mind onto the paper, not caring if the audience will actually receive your 40-cents-worth of wisdom, but caring only that you unburden yourself of it. It's all out there — on the paper, in the gravel — and that is what matters.

Of course that is *not* what matters. The writing process is not to be separated from the thinking process; it *is* a thinking process. That concept, commonplace enough in English Departments nowadays, has not reached the majority of our lawyers. They get all the relevant information down on the paper; they refer to all the possible issues and suggest a number of different approaches and counter-approaches; and all the while they have no perception of how a reader not already knee-deep in the case will be able to wade through it all.

The Lure of Money and Power

In *Woe unto You, Lawyers!,* Fred Rodell thunders:

> In tribal times, there were the medicine-men. In the Middle Ages,
> there were the priests. Today, there are the lawyers. For every
> age, a group of bright boys, learned in their trade and jealous of
> their learning, who blend technical competence with plain and
> fancy hocus-pocus to make themselves masters of their fellow
> men. For every age, a pseudo-intellectual aristocracy, guarding the
> tricks of its trade from the uninitiated, and running, after its own
> pattern, the civilization of its day.[6]

There are no greater powers than those of creation and dissolution.
Lawyers have both, on a daily basis, because of the nature of their
relationship to language. They create binding relationships between
people where none existed before — a god-like task, making something
out of nothing. They create whole entities (corporations) by the Adam-
like power of naming. Those powers remain with the lawyers as long
as nonlawyers cannot pierce the veil of legal language.

Once one has power — especially a power mysterious to others —
one is tempted to use it to advantage. Law professor Robert Benson
confesses:

> Every lawyer's personal experience bears witness to the fact that
> legalese can be a weapon. Is there a lawyer among us who has
> not employed the magic of legal language as a psychological
> device to dominate some lay person? I confess I have done so
> many times — particularly when dealing with recalcitrant bureau-
> crats and corporate clerks — and I have frequently seen my
> comrades-in-law do the same. If there breathes a lawyer who is
> free from this taint, I shall immediately nominate him or her to
> receive the next Saint Thomas More Award from my law school.[7]

Along with that power comes the pay. In teaching lawyers how to
clarify their language, I have often heard them express the fear that
if their prose were to lose its arcane, ponderous, and technical qualities,
their clients would be likely to protest the stunningly high costs
incurred. For those who are not up on such things, in 1986 lawyer's
fees of $200 per hour were quite common in many places, and $400
per hour was by no means out of the question. Starting positions in
firms on Wall Street now offer as much as $65,000 a year to the new
graduates of law school. Clients who pay such prices, the argument
runs, want to see their received value in terms of the degree of difficulty
of the product. It is annoying when immoral arguments find their
basis in truth.

Here, perhaps, is the core of the matter: It is in the lawyer's self-interest to keep legal prose unreadable. If money, power, and prestige are all protected by keeping the layperson confused and awestruck, why should any lawyer voluntarily opt for clear, concise, communicative prose? I can see only two possibilities: (1) If governments make it illegal to be obscure, then lawyers will be forced to clean up their prose; and (2) if lawyers discover that they can make a profit from the time saved in reading and writing clear prose, then they will accept the idea as a new professional challenge. Both projects are under way.

Lack of Linguistic Awareness

A lawyer who has risen above all of the problems already mentioned may still be a poor writer. That is, the lawyer who knows which bits of legal language are essential to maintain and which are not; who has learned to disdain the clubbiness of linguistic obfuscation; who has learned to deal with the hostile audience and the practical pressures; and who is able to keep in mind at all times both the right of the audience to straightforward communication and the need of the audience to receive that which it gets thrown — that lawyer will still write poorly if he or she has not somehow (either by intuition or education) become expert at fitting the substance of the thought to the linguistic structures and expectations that are inescapably part of the English language.

Some people pick this up by ear; they "hear" what good writing sounds like and are then able to imitate what they think is style (but is more often structure) in their own prose. Others pick this up (with considerably more stress on the lower lumbar region) through education. Unfortunately, those two groups combined do not represent a large percentage of the populace. Few read enough good prose to have an opportunity to use whatever ear they might have been born with; not many more have been lucky enough to study writing under a pedagogy that is effective for those without the good ear.

Working on the Problem: Attacks on Several Fronts

Despite all the above problems and abuses, there is still a sense of hope in the air.

Public concern for the problem has never been more evident. There is actually a "Plain English movement," which has managed to foster several successful attempts to have "Plain English" legislation passed in many states.

There are signs of progress in education: Some effort is being made to awaken pre-law students to the need to study writing more seriously than their classmates; greater efforts are evident at the law school level, although few schools are claiming successful breakthroughs; and both law firms and state bar associations are investing substantial sums in Continuing Legal Education programs in writing.

The Law has recently come to be perceived by Humanists as an excellent field for cross-disciplinary attention. Particularly interesting work is being done in the new fields of "Law and Literature" and "Law and Language."

Academic and intellectual interest has been sparked. The number of books and articles on the subject has been increasing dramatically since 1960.

Manifestations of Public Concern

In recent years we have heard a great deal from the "Plain English movement," a somewhat organized, already effective, partial response to the problem of unreadable legal writing. It is difficult to date its inception because the critics of legalese have been legion through many centuries now. Shakespeare's "The first thing we do, let's kill all the lawyers" (spoken by a butcher turned revolutionary) was not the first outcry by any means.[8] At least as early as the thirteenth century there were provisions for citizens who lived far from London (and therefore far from most lawyers) to write their legal complaints in plain language instead of using the proper legal forms and formulas. (These complaints were called Bills in Eyre, and they give remarkable insights into medieval English life that the far more formal writs do not.)[9]

We are not the first to try to do anything about the situation. In 1566 the judge in *Milward v. Welden*[10] was incensed at a lawyer's having expanded what should have been a short pleading to 120 pages. He ordered a hole cut in the middle of the document, through which the offender's head was thrust; this interlocking pair was then to be led around Westminster Hall during court sessions as an example to future padders and expanders. Thirty-four years later Sir Francis Bacon was able to bring into effect Chancery Ordinance Rule 55 which simplified the punishment somewhat: "If any bill shall be formed of an immoderate length both the party and the counsel under whose hand it passeth shall be fined." Neither of these bold attempts seems to have had a lasting effect on the profession.

Sir Thomas More, Dean Swift, Jeremy Bentham, Charles Dickens, and a host of others have attacked lawyers for their language in the plainest and sometimes most acrimonious terms. (The lawyer has for four centuries been so much a stock character on the stage as not to require a proper name; "the lawyer" will do.) Bentham, in particular, had at the lawyers for "poisoning language in order to fleece their clients," calling the resulting prose "excrementitious matter" and "literary garbage."[11] In our century Fred Rodell led the way with a whole book on the subject, *Woe unto You, Lawyers!* David Mellinkoff followed with two fine books, *The Language of the Law* (1963) and *Legal Writing: Sense and Nonsense* (1982), filled with debunking good sense and scholarly evidence.

We have gone beyond complaining to actually doing something about the problem. Minnesota led the way in 1977, shortly to be followed by Maryland, by insisting through statute that insurance contracts be written in language the average consumer of insurance contracts could understand. For all their predictions of disaster, many insurance companies have done a fine job of it, without suffering any long-term ill consequences. In 1978 New York passed a broader law, expanding the requirement to cover consumer contracts in general. As of mid-1986, twenty states[12] had passed legislation requiring readability in insurance policies, and twelve states[13] had yet more generalized laws.[14] These are real victories, not to be underestimated.

But there are problems, even with this high-principled, well-intentioned effort. What exactly is meant by the term "plain English" in this context? George H. Hathaway, chairperson of the Plain English Committee of the Michigan State Bar, offers the following:

> Plain English is the writing style that (1) all legal writing textbooks recommend, (2) the ABA Committee on Legal Writing recommends, (3) all law students study in their law school course in legal writing, and (4) many law students and lawyers give lip service to, but often ignore for the rest of their law school and entire legal careers.[15]

The combination of hyperbole and wishful thinking exhibited in (1) through (3) here suggests one of the problems with the movement: There seems to be a belief that such a writing style can actually be identified and that we all could learn it from existing sources and practice it by the sheer will to do it. The facts are that (a) most writing textbooks recommend what the product should look like without offering helpful advice on how to achieve it, and (b) a great majority of the legal writing courses in our law schools are poorly taught, reluctantly taken, undercompensated on all parts, and therefore abject failures. Plain English, I would argue, is not quite as available a commodity as Mr. Hathaway suggests; nor, in the gray area cases, will we be sure to know it when we see it. Foes of plainer English will eventually attempt to use this imprecision to impede the progress of reform.[16] It behooves us to make sure that we prepare a valid defense.

Mr. Hathaway goes on to name "ten typical elements of Plain English":

1. a clear, organized, easy-to-follow outline or table of contents
2. appropriate captions or headings
3. reasonably short sentences
4. active voice
5. positive form
6. subject-verb-object sequence
7. parallel construction
8. concise words
9. simple words
10. precise words

One can only be pleased with the general intent of such attempts at definition; however, some of the details viewed more closely leave something yet to be desired.

1. A clear outline or table of contents: often of great help. However, the worst-offending legalese document imaginable might still boast a stunningly clear table of contents.

2. Appropriate captions or headings: indeed. But once again, many offenders do well in this category.

3. Reasonably short sentences: a real problem. Much of the Plain English movement's activity has been geared toward getting lawyers to write shorter sentences. Readability tests, especially that of Rudolph Flesch, have been used to argue that since sentences which contain more than twenty-nine words are hard to read, then lawyers should not write many sentences longer than twenty-nine words. The logic here is false.[17] If sentences with more than twenty-nine words are often harder to read, it is frequently because they were written by people who did not know how (in Joseph Williams's words) to "control the sprawl."[18] Simple declarative sentences can be kept within twenty-five words with little difficulty. But lawyers spend much of their writing effort trying to articulate the connection between two simple declaratory thoughts. They cannot afford to juxtapose "here's a fact" with "here's

a legal concept" and expect an impartial judge or hostile opposing counsel to supply the appropriate logical process which will lead to the desired conclusion. In order to link the facts to the concept, or the concepts to other concepts, and therefore to a specific conclusion, the lawyer must articulate the connection; that necessarily produces longer sentences. The problem is not how to make lawyers write shorter sentences, but rather how to get them to manage long sentences far better than they now are able. In the process, the redundancies, the loophole plugs, and other assorted "fat" will naturally be trimmed away. The typically long legal sentence is a manifestation of our lawyers' rhetorical inabilities, not its cause.

4. Active voice: trouble here. Just because the passive voice is grossly abused by most professional writers, legal or otherwise, we have no cause to exclude it as a rhetorical strategy. Authoritarian powers (most high school teachers, some governments, a few religions), who condescend to their populations as indiscriminating children, find it easier to forbid all of an activity than to instruct the children how to choose between good and bad. If 85 percent of all passives are bad passives, then ridding prose of all passives will be a net gain of 70 percent (the 85 percent gain minus the 15 percent loss of good passives). We ought to shoot for 100 percent instead.

If agency is unknown, and that particular lack of knowledge is not the point in question, the passive does well. ("The note was left before 4:00 p.m.") If agency is known but would be intrusive if articulated, the passive does well. ("Each horse will be tested for drugs at the end of each race.") If the passivity of a person is the point to be emphasized, then the passive does well. ("The Senator was led by his theory to the following ludicrous conclusion: . . .") These are just a few examples of correct usage of the passive voice.

It is true that lawyers tend more than most to hide agency by recourse to the passive. It is also true that because of this, lawyers have learned to "hear" legal arguments as being predominantly set in the passive, and therefore by imitation diminish yet further the use of the active. However, we should not let the fear of abuse lead us to do away with such a useful rhetorical device; instead we need to teach people when and how to use it effectively.

5. Positive form: not always possible, but where possible, usually better.

6. Subject-verb-object sequence: ?? Nearly every grammatical English sentence that is not a question proceeds syntactically in this order. Native speakers of German have a problem now and then, and some

poets (Milton, for one) delight in moving things around; but nearly all lawyers write nearly all their sentences, good ones and bad ones, in the subject-verb-object sequence. There is no problem here.

7. Parallel construction: a good technique to master. Of course, the construction by itself has no virtue. It works well only where the substance is parallel in nature. On occasion, the substance might be antithetical in nature, which would better be served by chiasmus (xyyx) than by parallel construction (xyxy). Such exceptions aside, a greater awareness and skillful use of parallel construction would help to remedy certain problems with legal prose.

8. Concise words: they would help.

9. Simple words: yes, but only where simplicity is attainable without sacrificing accuracy and depth.

10. Precise words: certainly. But to concentrate on the most evident manifestations of legal prose (here, the jargon) is to miss that far more destructive force of dilapidated structure. If all the units of discourse in an atrocious legalese document were restructured so that the relationships among the various words, actors, acts, and concepts were clearly delineated, then the presence of elongated and complex words would matter relatively little. (The restructuring would necessitate the choosing of precise words.) At the least, we would know quite specifically what questions to ask (e.g., "What is meant by 'bailee'?").

My criticisms here are aimed not at the intent of the Plain English movement, but at the lack of sophistication of some of its linguistic precepts. Our gratitude to those involved in the leadership of the movement should not be allowed to render us uncritical. We must take care not to treat the symptoms in place of the diseases, and we must not neglect a prime source of the problem — the widespread absence of effective programs for teaching the art and craft of clear writing to law students and lawyers.

Efforts to Improve the Teaching of Writing to Lawyers

Writing Courses for Pre-Law Students

I find it curious that relatively little effort has been made to train pre-law students with advanced composition courses. One would think this was the ideal opportunity to deal with some of the questions of language that seem to law students an unnecessary burden added to legal studies. Yet there are few articles on the subject[19] and only one textbook produced specifically for this purpose.[20]

Stranger still than this silence was the structure of the nation's leading (perhaps only) pre-law major program at Rice University. The program was founded about ten years ago, lived a vibrant, intriguing life, and now is being dismantled for lack of faculty availability. (Apparently, the student interest is still high.)[21] The program offered every area of pre-law study imaginable, with one exception: There was no composition course. In the light of statements from law school deans across the country that the most important pre-law abilities to develop are those of critical reading and critical writing, this absence of a writing course from the Rice program remains a mystery.

Schools that have offered special composition courses for pre-law students (Illinois, Utah, Wayne State, Loyola of Chicago, amongst several others) have generally found them well received and over-subscribed. Here, clearly, is a fertile area for expansion.

Writing Courses and Programs at Law Schools

Here, much has been written about, tried, discarded, reinstated, and reconsidered. The main strivings have been toward discovering the perfect structure for law school writing instruction. The results have not been encouraging, with a few notable exceptions. Many courses have been established, but few programs have resulted.

The typical nonprogram in writing at law schools is shaped something like this:

1. First year
   a. Fall semester: Legal Methods, Research, and Writing (1 or 2 credits in contrast to 3 for other courses). Much time spent on tasks other than writing; instructor either a part-time adjunct not trained in writing pedagogy or an upper-class student, equally untrained.
   b. Spring semester: Moot court experience (1 credit or no credit), for which a brief is written; criticism offered by upper-class students.
2. Second year
   Nothing.
3. Third year
   a. Either one twenty-page paper written in conjunction with a seminar; little or no attention paid to the writing process; revisions rarely allowed.
   b. Or nothing.

Even in schools where the first-year program has some efficacy, students tend to lack reconfirmation of their newly gained skills because of the lack of subsequent writing opportunities. In light of the importance to lawyers of controlling the language and the particular rhetorical difficulties that confront the legal profession, this absence of care and of competence in the teaching of writing at law schools is stunning. Absolutely everyone at these schools complains — the students about having to take a course undervalued and poorly taught; the instructors about not knowing how to engage their students and manage the task effectively; and the administration about having to schedule, staff, and pay for the whole affair.

As one might expect, the major variations (and many of the published articles) concern who will do the teaching: Upper-class law students? Part-time faculty (either lawyers who have an interest in teaching or English teachers who cannot find other employment)? Full-time faculty hired specifically for the purpose? Or regular law school faculty? These variations are explained and well documented in two review articles.[22]

A few of these variations in structure have achieved a certain measure of success. Some law schools, such as John Marshall (Chicago) and the University of Puget Sound, have added writing requirements in the second year. Others, such as Harvard and Indiana, offer elective writing seminars with great regularity, the popularity of which are due in great part to the skills of the instructors, Steven Stark and Perry Hodges, respectively, who have taught there for several years and have established substantial reputations as part-time members of the faculty. Significantly, this sense of permanence (or at least of continuous presence) seems to be the one factor that distinguishes attempts like these which work from those that do not.

Through that stability of a sense of continued presence, Notre Dame has found a successful formula for a course, if not yet for a whole program. Six years ago it hired Theresa Phelps, an English Ph.D. with no legal training, to run a legal writing course that was, for the first time, to be separate from the legal research and methods instruction. After two successful years under one-year contracts, Phelps was offered a tenure-track position to teach legal writing in the required first-year course (160 students), to offer a law-and-literature elective on the upper levels, and to be available for individual tutoring six hours weekly. Notre Dame thus legitimized instruction in writing by establishing a potentially permanent spot on its faculty for an appropriate specialist.

To my knowledge, only one law school in the country has been bold enough to do what logic and sound pedagogy demand — to implement a three-year writing requirement for all law students. That school is Chicago-Kent, affiliated with the Illinois Institute of Technology; the director of the program is Ralph Brill, former associate dean and former acting dean — in other words, a person of stature in the school, no underpaid "specialist" invited from the outside and given a part-time salary and half an office.

In their first year at Chicago-Kent, students take a two-semester writing course, three hours each term, in which they learn to do research, to write memos, to revise effectively, to construct appellate briefs, and to argue orally. In the second year, all students again take two writing-intensive courses. In the fall they study legal drafting with local practitioners in real estate law, commercial law, or in general practice. In the spring they take a course called "Advanced Research," which deals with substantive law in one of several fields (tax, securities, labor, environmental or international law); it requires two fifteen-page papers and several smaller research exercises. Students fulfill the third year's writing requirement either by taking an independent study course with a faculty member or by taking one of a number of seminars; both choices require a twenty-five-page paper.

Reports on this program are uniformly positive. It owes its success, it seems, to the following: (1) The directorship is in the hands of a respected senior faculty member; (2) full credit is given for student effort at every stage of the requirements (to a maximum of eleven credits total); (3) much of the instruction is done by full-time faculty, some of whom specialize in teaching writing; and (4) more than a quarter of a million dollars is spent on this instruction yearly.

From the few successes we have seen to date, it appears that certain elements are required for a writing program to work at a law school:

1. Sufficient money must be expended on competent faculty specialists (that is, on people trained or experienced in the teaching of writing).

2. Sufficient credit must be given to students for their labors to allow them to expend as serious an effort on improving writing as they do on learning Torts or Trusts or Tax Law.

3. A certain amount of writing instruction must be made available, preferably required, in all six terms of law school, not just in the first half of the first year.

4. Perhaps most importantly, a consistent methodology must be adopted by the program as a whole, so that students of any one section or year may talk intelligibly with any faculty and all other students about the standards of cohesive and coherent prose.

"A consistent methodology": perhaps it is the consistency that is essential here, the methodology being an orderly way of achieving it.

Cunning writers assess their audience before adopting a tone and a strategy. Students are forced by their roles in life to be amongst the most cunning of writers (whether or not they are the most capable). Bright undergraduates spend the first half of any course figuring out what that particular teacher wants and the second half of the course producing it. The subtle but pervasive cynicism in our students (which often develops into a straightforward anti-intellectualism) stems in great part from their perceiving their education as a series of audience-detection problems. For the cause of that perception we have but to consider our own peevish idiosyncracies concerning their writing.

It may or may not be too much to expect an entire faculty of an undergraduate college to agree on how to approach the criticism of written work. (Programs christened "Writing Across the Curriculum" are now in the process of trying to effect this at many institutions.) It should not be too much to expect a law faculty to give it a whirl. Legal audiences are limited in number and character: thorough senior partners, impartial judges, partial administrators and politicians, cautious allies, hostile adversaries, and questioning clients. The genres of legal writing are even more limited in number and character: memos to files and to collaborators, letters to clients and to adversaries, contracts both precise and anti-precise, briefs of persuasion. Surely there must be ways of regarding and manipulating language — which after all is a system of functioning structures — that would most adequately fulfill these particular and somewhat well-defined needs. Even more than the choice of methodologies, it matters that the school adopt a single, consistent approach to the language that will be shared by all the students and encountered in many of the classes. The recent activity in the textbook market provides and promises to continue to provide a number of alternatives from which to choose.

One such methodology has proved extremely effective recently. It is a product of practicality, spawned not in the classroom but in the conference rooms of law firms, corporate legal departments, and government agencies across the country. Its four developers, functioning under the corporate name of Clearlines, Inc., are Joseph Williams, Gregory Colomb, and Frank Kinahan (all of the University of Chicago's English Department) and I. Some of the Clearlines methodology is currently available in print;[23] a textbook for law schools is forthcoming from Little, Brown & Co.[24]

There is not room enough here to present that methodology in detail, but its guiding concepts can be succinctly enough stated and have been introduced above. It has been discovered that readers expect certain things from the structure of any unit of discourse, be it a clause, a sentence, a paragraph, an essay, a memo, a brief, or a book. Readers also have a certain limited amount of energy they expect to have to use for each of those units of discourse. If writers can learn where readers expect to find the different components of the writer's substance, then the writer can manipulate that substance so that it appears where the reader expects to find it. The results: ambiguities decline, and readers are freed to use their energy for perceiving the writer's substance instead of expending most of it to untangle the writer's structure.[25]

To exemplify this concept briefly, I return to an example quoted near the beginning of this essay. Reconsider the following typically annoying bit of legal prose:

> Appellant's attempt to characterize the funds by the method of payment (reimbursement), rather than by the actual nature of the payment misses the mark.

This sentence is difficult, I suggest, not simply because it is "too long" or "wordy" or "awkward" or "unclear." It may be all those things to the reader, but not to the writer. It fails, instead, because it frustrates certain reader expectations of sentence structure, most particularly the expectation that a subject will be followed almost immediately by its verb. Here the subject ("attempt") is separated from its verb ("misses") by 19 words, almost 80 percent of the sentence. While the reader waits for the verbal shoe to drop, the reader is not free to concentrate on what seems to be interruptive material. As it turns out, the "interruption" was the whole shooting match. The reader discovers that only in retrospect. Solution: put the subject and verb together, and the structure reveals itself:

> Appellant misses the mark in her attempt to characterize the funds by the method of payment (reimbursement), rather than by the actual nature of the payment.

We are now free to see that the important substance of this sentence is the contrasting of the words "method" and "nature." We are also free to be clear-minded enough to complain that "nature" lacks the helpful example that accompanied "method"; the sentence needs a parallel to "reimbursement" in order to be clear in itself.

I have used the Clearlines methodology since 1984 in an elective course for second- and third-year students at the Harvard Law School. The course has been well received, enrolling 125 to 140 students yearly. Students who take the course one year are eligible to apply for teaching assistantships in the course for the following year. The Moot

Court board and the Legal Methods staff also have been exposed to some of the materials. As a result, there are now at Harvard several hundred students who can talk the same language to each other about language and who have had similar experiences in revising their own prose and editing the prose of others.

Law school is an appropriate place for students to encounter particular methods for handling the particularly complex rhetorical tasks they will be faced with as professionals; but until faculty and students alike cease being embarrassed that this "skill" has not been developed at earlier stages, little that is effective will be accomplished. The writing process is part of the thinking process. Students come to law school "to learn to think like a lawyer"; they should also have the opportunity to learn there how best to express those new and complicated thoughts. This calls for far more than the possession of some remedial "skill" or the knowledge of public rhetorical manners. Until recently, most efforts have been limited to learning how to *sound* like a lawyer; current stirrings in legal education lead us to hope that help is on the way.

Work in Related Fields

The ties between Law and Sociology, Psychology, Psychiatry, Business, Economics, and History have long been acknowledged and studied; but a new interest in Law *as* language has generated some fascinating work in the relatively new fields of Law and Literature, and Law and Language. As yet, the relationships between these fields and Composition have not been explored; those efforts should produce some meaningful and interesting ideas.

The godfather of Law and Literature is Benjamin Cardozo, whose essays and utterances are the most often quoted in contemporary articles in the field.

> We find a kindred phenomenon in literature, alike in poetry and in prose. The search is for the just word, the happy phrase, that will give expression to the thought, but somehow the thought itself is transfigured by the phrase when found. There is emancipation in our very bonds. The restraints of rhyme or metre, the exigencies of period balance, liberate at times the thought which they confine, and in imprisoning release.[26]

The law/literature movement has found a guide out of the wilderness in the person of Richard Weisberg, who for many years has organized and chaired Law and Literature sessions at Modern Language Association meetings, has helped to found the Law and Humanities Institute, and has written much that is interesting in the field. His article "Literature and Law" offers both a summary view of new developments and a helpful bibliography.[27]

For the decade from the mid-seventies to the mid-eighties, much of literary criticism concerned itself with critical theory. Influenced by the work of Jacques Derrida and others, the critics sought new concepts of signification and new methods of interpretation. The resultant playing with words and contexts, which curiously resembles Talmudic exegesis, reinforced a reader-response theory of literature — that no text exists without the context of the perception of a particular reader. Ears of law professors across the country must have started to burn. Was not that concept essential to the way law is made, taught, and interpreted? Result: the controversial movement called Critical Legal Studies was born. One of its main concerns is to demonstrate how the manipulative interpretation of legal texts can keep people in power who have always been in power, without regard for the welfare of the populace at large. If this sounds familiar, it should: It is much the same complaint made about legal writing several pages back. (See the section entitled The Lure of Money and Power.) And here it is, I suggest, that good work can be done in meaningfully bringing law, literature, and composition studies together. All the concerns of structural stylistics — the manipulation of reader expectations, the creation of context, the control of ambiguity — are of equal interest to lawyers, to literary people, and to all kinds of writers.[28]

A completely different set of people are drawing near the same meeting ground from a completely different direction. They are linguists and social scientists (especially sociologists and cultural anthropologists), and they are studying language and the law in order to understand how tools of communication actually determine legal relationships between people. They work primarily with oral language, but work on the written word is starting to increase. The potential here seems to me unlimited. For an overview of what is now being done in that regard, see Brenda Danet's excellent and lengthy article, "Language in the Legal Process,"[29] and the work of sociologist William M. O'Barr[30] and linguist Judith N. Levi.[31]

In summary, then, the abuse of the language in law, intentional or otherwise, exists and has existed for hundreds of years. What is new is a growing consciousness of that abuse and a will to do something about it. New structures for writing programs, combined with new structural methods of teaching writing, offer a great deal of hope that we will not long continue to pass the problem onward and upward.

Continuing legal education programs seem interested in developing rhetoric as a topic for serious study. Legislative willingness to enact statutes that demand rhetorical reforms are increasing in number and are already taking effect. Critical theorists, literary interpreters, rhetoricians, law professors, social scientists, and linguists are all becoming increasingly fascinated with the effects that words have on audiences. Things are happening, and for the first time in our history, legal writing has become a topic of great interest, depth, and variety.

Notes

1. Urban A. Lavery, "The Language of the Law: Defects in the Written Style of Lawyers, Some Illustrations, the Reasons Therefor, and Certain Suggestions as to Improvement." *Journal of Law & Education* 7 (1921): 277.

2. Robert W. Benson, "The End of Legalese: The Game Is Over," *New York University Review of Law & Social Change* 13 (1985): 519–73 at 531. Also see his footnote 58.

3. Steven Stark, "Why Lawyers Can't Write," *Harvard Law Review* 97 (1984): 1391.

4. Stark, 1392–93. "Standing": a legal term of art indicating the boundaries of a person's rights to be involved with a court suit. In general, if one has not suffered harm as a result of the actions to be contested in court, then one has no "standing" to bring the case.

5. Lavery, 277.

6. Fred Rodell, *Woe unto You, Lawyers!* (New York: Berkley Publishing, 1939, 1980), 3. Also quoted by Benson, 531.

7. Benson, "The End of Legalese," 530.

8. William Shakespeare, *Henry VI, Part 2*, IV, ii, 70.

9. For an excellent essay on the Bills in Eyre and an interesting selection of them, see W. C. Bolland, ed., *Select Bills in Eyre, AD 1292–1333*, (London: Selden Society, 1914).

10. *Milward v. Welden*, 21 Eng. Rep. 136 (1566).

11. Jeremy Bentham, *Works*, 260, 236, Bowring ed. (Edinburgh: W. Tait, 1843).

12. Arizona, Arkansas, Connecticut, Delaware, Florida, Maine, Maryland, Massachusetts, Minnesota, Nebraska, New Jersey, North Carolina, Ohio, Oregon, Rhode Island, South Carolina, Texas, Virginia, Washington, and Wisconsin.

13. Arkansas, California, Connecticut, Hawaii, Kentucky, Maine, Minnesota, Montana, New Jersey, New York, Oregon, and West Virginia.

14. Information from the Document Design Center, American Institutes for Research, Washington, D.C.

15. George H. Hathaway, "An Overview of the Plain English Movement for Lawyers," *Michigan Bar Journal*, 62 (1983): 945.

16. I wonder, for example, how the courts will handle the cases of conflicts of laws arising from Plain English Statutes. What is to be done when the same J. C. Penney layaway plan is deemed "plain English" by a court in Ohio but "Legalese" by a court in Arizona? On whom will the courts call? And what will be the consequences for future drafters?

17. I do not by any means intend by this simplification to deny totally the worth and interest of the work done with readability formulas. But the final products of their numbers can be used abusively by a reformer who has not taken the time to explore all the ramifications of the studies. For an intriguing summary of the applicability of these formulas to the problem of legalese, see Benson, "The End of Legalese," 547–58.

18. Although not written expressly for lawyers, Joseph Williams's *Style: Ten Lessons in Clarity and Grace*, 2d ed. (Chicago: Scott Foresman 1985) remains the single best text for lawyers to read. Its methodology is ideally suited to the kinds of complexities spawned by legal problems.

19. George D. Gopen, "An Advanced Composition Course for Pre-Law Students," *Journal of Law & Education* 29 (1978): 222–31; Kate Ferguson Hirsch, "Writing about the Law: A Composition Course for Pre-Law Students," *Journal of Basic Writing* (1980): 82–94; Norman Brand and John O. White, "Composition for the Pre-Professional: Focus on Legal Writing," *College Composition and Communication* 27 (1976): 41–46.

20. See George D. Gopen, *Writing from a Legal Perspective* (St. Paul: West Publishing Company, 1981). A writing text that can be adapted for an undergraduate course is Norman Brand and John O. White, *Legal Writing: The Strategy of Persuasion* (New York: St. Martin's Press, 1976). A fascinating text, though significantly harder to adapt to such a writing course, is James Boyd White, *The Legal Imagination: Studies in the Nature of Legal Thought and Expression* (Boston: Little, Brown, 1973).

21. Professor Baruch Brody, telephone conversation with author, June 19, 1986.

22. See Allen Boyer, "Legal Writing Programs Reviewed: Merits, Flaws, Costs, and Essentials," *Chicago-Kent Law Review* 62 (1985): 23–51; and Mary Ellen Gale, "Legal Writing: The Impossible Takes a Little Longer," *Albany Law Review* 44 (1980): 298–343.

23. Joseph M. Williams, *Style: Ten Lessons in Clarity and Grace*, 2d ed. (Chicago: Scott Foresman, 1985); George D. Gopen, "Perceiving Structure: Teaching Writing at Law Schools," *Harvard Law School Bulletin*, Summer/Fall (1984): 27–29.

24. The same publishers will also be releasing in the near future Veda Charrow's *Clear and Effective Legal Writing* and Richard Weisberg's *When Lawyers Write*, aimed primarily at practitioners. Other books of great interest that are currently in print include Richard Lanham's two books, *Revising Prose* and *Revising Business Prose*, and David Mellinkoff's two books, *The Language of the Law* and *Legal Writing: Sense and Nonsense*.

25. These discoveries have been independently confirmed by a great deal of recent work in psycholinguistics and cognitive psychology.

26. See Benjamin Cardozo, "Law and Literature," *Selected Writings of Benjamin Nathan Cardozo*, ed. Margaret E. Hall (New York: Bender, 1947).

27. Richard Weisberg and Jean-Pierre Barricelli, "Literature and Law," *Interrelations of Literature,* ed. Jean-Pierre Barricelli and Joseph Gibaldi (New York: MLA, 1982), 150–75.

28. For those who wish to investigate these issues, two law review issues will serve well. The *Texas Law Review,* 60, 3 (March 1982) printed a symposium on "Law and Literature." Particularly representative is the match between Ronald Dworkin ("Law as Interpretation") and Stanley Fish ("Working on the Chain Gang: Interpretation in Law and Literature"). (Professor Fish now holds a joint appointment between the English Department and the Law School at Duke University, thus personifying the new connection between the fields.) For a symposium on Critical Legal Studies, see the double issue of the *Stanford Law Review* 36; 1, 2 (January 1984).

29. Brenda Danet, "Language in the Legal Process," *Law and Society Review* 14 (1980): 445–564.

30. See especially William M. O'Barr, *Linguistic Evidence: Language, Power, and Strategy in the Courtroom* (New York: Academic Press, 1982).

31. "Linguistics, Language, and Law: A Topical Bibliography" (1983) is available directly from Professor Levi, c/o Department of Linguistics, Northwestern University, Evanston, Ill. 60201.

8 Writing by Academic Professionals

Dan Dieterich
University of Wisconsin–Stevens Point

We in the English teaching profession have written dozens of articles and books describing ways to improve the writing of college students. It is unfortunate that we have not devoted more attention to ways of improving the writing of their teachers and the other professionals in American colleges and universities. Who are academics? What do we write? How well do we write it? What should we do in order to make our writing more successful? These are the questions I will respond to in this article, although I can't claim to be able to answer any of them. The fact is, this is one of the most neglected areas of professional writing. A great deal of research needs to be done in it. I hope this article will spur academics to undertake that research.

The Academic Professional

Before looking at the writing of academic professionals, let's look at the writers themselves. People in academe are a strange breed. Many tend to be workaholics, often putting in 60 to 80 hours a week on their profession. Although often highly independent, they are passionately committed to a field of study. They tend to read a great deal in this field and related fields, so they often have sizable vocabularies.

As a result of their interest in discovering new information about their field of study, some academics also do research; in so doing, they learn how to handle data objectively. Most academics received their first training on how to do this in graduate school while working on advanced degrees. At the same time, they learned how to write reports on their research in a manner which would bring their readers to view the authors as dispassionate observers, unconcerned about either the outcome of their research or the reader's reaction to that outcome.

Most academics are teachers. They not only study a given discipline but share with others what they learn about it. However, unlike their fellow teachers in the elementary and secondary schools, most have not been taught how to teach. Although some love informing students about their subjects, others may view teaching as the price they pay in order to conduct their scholarly pursuits; and whether or not they view teaching as their primary role, they may fail to give their students the respect which they deserve.

Some academics are administrators either instead of being teachers or in addition to being teachers. The case could be made that these are the best-educated managers in America today. Many hold a doctoral degree and have had the benefit of extensive advanced education. And who are the worst-educated managers in America today? Again, the case could be made that they are college and university administrators. Most have had little or no education designed specifically to help them succeed as managers. Few have ever attended a business writing course. Few have learned in college how to write effective memos, letters, proposals, and reports. Most receive little or no on-the-job training to help them improve their business writing and other managerial skills.

The Writing of Academics

The writing done in colleges and universities is professional writing. As such, it is similar, if not identical, to that done by writers in government, business, and other professions. Education is a large and sophisticated service industry, despite the reluctance of many academics to view matters in this way. Within any given college or university, just as in any large corporation, people write an enormous number of memos, letters, proposals, and reports. The problems which academics face in doing so are similar to those which accountants and attorneys face in doing this same sort of writing.

In other words, the difference between the writing of academics and that of other professionals is subtle. For example, publish-or-perish academics write scholarly articles for publication in professional journals. But so do nurses, physicians, attorneys, accountants, and other professionals. It's true that some academics do far more of this sort of writing than some nurses, physicians, attorneys, and accountants do. It's equally true that other academics don't do any of it at all.

While some academics write many letters of recommendation, some business executives write just as many of them. Even curriculum materials are not the exclusive concern of academics; those involved in training and development in business, industry, and government write these as well. It is difficult to identify any type of writing which is unique to those in academe. It is, however, quite clear that we in academe do many of the same types of writing as do other professionals.

How well do we write? I base my answer to that question on my experience as an academic writer these past fifteen years, on the writing which my colleagues have sent me, on writing consulting which I have done for other academic institutions, and on the writing submitted by participants in an Administrative Writing Program which I established four years ago for my own institution's administrators. That's a limited data base to draw from; but from that base I can only conclude that we write no better and no worse than the other professionals I've worked with over the years in my consulting practice.

We academics have a great deal of classroom writing experience before we reach our academic posts. This may, however, work against us as well as in our favor, if in our academic writing we follow the same models which we used as college students in writing term papers and theses. Often, such models make us, as authors, appear pompous and cold. This, in turn, can reduce our effectiveness and damage our image, both within our institutions and with our institutions' clients.

Writing Processes

Many academic writers give little thought to the processes they employ when they write. Yet each of us employs specific strategies in accomplishing our writing. Some of us undertake elaborate planning before conducting a scientific study, yet in writing the report on that study we pay little attention to our readers' needs. Others spend a great deal of time writing a proposal or letter, yet never bother to carry out the proofreading necessary to ensure that the finished product is correct. Many need to learn that, just as they employ various reading processes in reading various kinds of material, so they should vary their writing processes according to the kind of writing they are doing.

For many academics, the model of academic writing is the scholarly article. Since this model wields an influence on academic writing far greater than we might expect (given the relatively small amount of it which academics produce), let's examine the writing processes involved in producing a scholarly article.

First and foremost, those writing scholarly articles spend a great deal of time thinking about a limited topic. As a result of this, they may develop theories about their topic, conduct empirical studies of it, or both. They also read others' thoughts and research on the same topic and topics related to it in order to establish the place of the new insight or finding in the body of knowledge on the topic.

Although those writing scholarly articles plan their writing extensively, it is a unique kind of planning. It focuses, not on the piece of writing itself (the message to be conveyed) or on those who will read it, but on the thoughts of the writer and the quality of the evidence which supports those thoughts.

In actually setting words to paper, those writing scholarly articles often take a formulaic approach, although the formula varies somewhat from field to field and from journal to journal within each field. Most use an objective, reportorial style and avoid the use of first-person singular pronouns. They highlight evidence and let their facts and ideas "speak for themselves." Since they are writing to fellow professionals, they freely use the jargon of their profession and devote relatively little effort to defining terms and explaining concepts.

Although the postwriting stage varies substantially among academics, many devote a great deal of energy to rewriting, editing, and proofreading scholarly articles they have written. However, they devote much of this attention to accuracy, correctness, and projection of a scholarly image. They seem less concerned about increasing the clarity of what they write or adapting their writing to meet the needs of their readers.

We find the products of this process in every scholarly journal. Here is one sentence from a recent article in *Publications of the Modern Language Association of America (PMLA)* by Joseph A. Boone:

> Given the reflecting levels of marital "structure" and social "Structure" noted by Tanner, it should not be surprising to find that the ideological precepts informing the romantic marital ideal were also encoded in the dominant narrative structures of nineteenth-century English and American fiction.[1]

A second sentence taken from the same article reads:

> Two varieties of ambiguity, thus, are promulgated in increasing proportion throughout book 2 of *The Golden Bowl*: a vertical probing into internal motivations and attitudes, which only unearths deeper ambiguities of character, and a linear multiplication of implicit and explicit plot lines and perspectival structures, which only complicates the reader's task of determining the objective truth of any reported incident of action.[2]

In both the first (44-word) sentence and the second (62-word) sentence Boone establishes that he is an extremely intelligent person.

He must be, in order to correctly use such sophisticated vocabulary and sentence structure. And he must establish that he's extremely intelligent in order to get his article accepted by the editors of *PMLA*.

But, while readers may respect the author's intelligence, his sophisticated vocabulary and sentence structure complicate the readers' task of determining what he means. In both sentences, the author focuses on things rather than people (e.g., "precepts," "structures," "ambiguity," and "multiplication"). He uses obscure technical terms without defining them, and he stacks them atop one another in complex passive constructions.

When writing scholarly articles, we academics often focus solely on our message. We write in order to present data and create an image of objectivity, not to communicate clearly and concisely with our readers. We simply assume that our readers — motivated by professional self-interest — will shoulder the burden of making sense from what we say.

When we turn from scholarly writing to the other writing tasks we academics engage in, we may well follow the same writing philosophy, and produce written products singularly ineffective at accomplishing our objectives.

Planning to Write

Despite the extensive planning many of us put into writing scholarly articles, we too often plunge into writing memos and letters with little or no planning or preparation. We begin writing without really deciding what we want to accomplish in the specific piece of writing we are working on. We pay for this by spending far more time than we need to on second, third, and fourth drafts of routine pieces of correspondence. We also pay for it with wordy, indirect, disorganized, ineffective writing.

To see the results of this lack of planning, we need only look at the beginnings of our letters and memos. The same teacher who urges students to be clear and direct may well take a roundabout approach in her or his own writing.

Often, we begin our memos and letters by talking about ourselves (e.g., "Earlier this week I received a telephone call from the Business Office of the [Name] School District." or "I am in receipt of your request for faculty contract information."). A busy reader may well respond, "So what?" to such egocentric openings.

At other times, we start by focusing attention on the piece of paper we are sending (e.g., "This memorandum is to confirm the meeting between the following persons: . . . ." or "This letter is in response to your letter addressed to [Name]."). Or, we focus on other things (e.g., "Your attention is brought to [topic]." or "Consideration is being given to readjusting summer salary rates."). Such openings are both indirect and impersonal.

By carefully planning our correspondence, we can make it far more effective. Before writing, we should first determine why we are writing. If it's to seek action, we should usually begin with our request. If it's to inform or query our reader, we should usually start with the most important information or question. And, since we accomplish our purpose through our readers, we should usually focus our opening requests, statements and questions on "you," the reader. By doing so, we save our readers' and our own time and energy, while increasing the likelihood that we accomplish whatever objective we have set for ourselves when we decide to write.

Reader Sensitivity

Effective professional writers have one quality in common: the ability to demonstrate their concern for others. In their writing, therefore, they usually concentrate their attention on the person or people involved in what they are writing about. Some academics instead dehumanize what they write. Perhaps believing that it makes them appear scholarly and scientific, they deal with things instead of people. As a result, they write sentences such as this one:

> The document sought to raise issues of concern as well as posit recommendations which could serve as benchmark questions at the institutional level regarding policy and procedural decision making for the evolution of this matter.

While this sentence is grammatically correct, it renders writer as well as reader invisible, and it places both in a world where things, not people, are at center stage.

Here's a second example of a lack of reader sensitivity. In this case the writer, representing a university placement service, makes the readers visible but also casts them in a subservient role.

> Those candidates who wish to utilize our services and desire assistance in their career plans are *required* to attend one group meeting offered under GROUP A; those interested in careers in Education are *required* to attend one group meeting offered under GROUP B.

Writers in other professions are prone to write the same sort of depersonalized sentences. We in academe, however, seem particularly prone to do so. When we write in this way, we distance ourselves from our readers and present an image of ourselves and of our institutions which is unflattering at best.

Self-Image

As English teachers, most of us have had the experience of telling someone what our profession is and then hearing the other person say, "Oh, then I'd better watch my language when I talk to you." Although the experience is not particularly pleasant, it does reveal that the general public views us as models of accuracy in speech and writing.

The view is inaccurate. English teachers, and all other academics, make mistakes. And, even though we may be good at identifying mechanical errors in the writing of students, we may be far less efficient in catching and correcting the mistakes we ourselves make. Spelling errors, punctuation errors, and typographical errors appear frequently in the reports, proposals, letters, and memos of academics.

Such errors can be especially damaging to the image of academic professionals, since we are held to higher standards in such matters than is the general public or even other professionals. For this reason, we academics must learn effective proofreading strategies which enable us to identify and eliminate our mechanical errors.

Our image is also shaped by the tone we take in dealing with our readers. By using sexist language or adopting a dehumanizing writing style, we can also convey an image of ourselves which damages our personal and professional reputations.

A colleague of mine uses the following passage from a memo to department chairs in his discussion of the impact of tone:

> Some recent events have persuaded me that it's time for me to remind each of you, gently, of the rules which apply to reimbursements for candidate expenses. I beg your willing and graceful conformance (because it saves me unseemly moments and high decibel levels in our office).
> 1) I don't sign the documents which bring candidates in; I APPROVE THEM. Approval requires adequate foreknowledge, some negotiation, and a little thought. Hence it takes time. If you give me no time, the result is predictable.

Organization

Most of us in academe have received a great deal of training in how to organize prose. We can list the Aristotelian topoi, make a Harvard outline, describe a chronological sequence, narrate a cause and effect process, and organize information in terms of general to specific.

What we need is the flexibility to determine the most effective organizational strategy for a given situation and audience. We are often limited to a narrow spectrum of logical approaches to organizing data, when in fact we need to learn to see a broad spectrum of psychologically sound organizational strategies.

Take, for example, the college catalog. The one I have before me now begins with a section on "The Student's Responsibility." Here are the first two sentences of that section:

> All colleges and universities establish certain requirements which must be met before a degree is granted. These requirements concern such things as courses, majors and minors, and residence.

It then goes on to explain how the student is to meet these requirements at the institution. This is certainly a textbook example of logical "general to specific" organization. However, is it the best organizational strategy to use in this section? And, in terms of its impact on present or prospective students, is this the best section with which to begin the catalog?

We all receive a great many memos which begin by narrating the history of a problem on campus and only later, much later, do they get around to telling us what the writer wants us to do to solve the problem. Again, this is a logical organizing pattern. But is it a wise one to use with a busy audience of academic professionals?

Writing Productivity

Writers, as well as readers, are busy people. Since writing is an important part of our professional lives, we should use our writing time efficiently. We usually don't, however. Perhaps because writing teachers over the years have urged us to write several drafts of every document we produce, perhaps because we are accustomed to sacrificing speed for accuracy in our research, many academics take far longer to write than is necessary.

We also waste time by selecting inefficient means of putting words to paper. Afraid of dictation and word processing equipment, many of us forfeit the time-saving benefits which such equipment provides. Unwilling to manage our writing time efficiently, many of us not only take twice as long as we should to produce our correspondence, but also force our readers to take twice as long to read it.

I wrote this article using a microcomputer. Had I done it using a standard typewriter, I conservatively estimate that it would have taken me three times as long to write it. There's also no doubt in my mind that the finished product would have been a much worse piece of writing. I wouldn't have revised it nearly as much as I did. Academics who disdain computers — and there are many who do — pay a price for their attitude.

Conciseness

Most college teachers evaluate their students' writing in order to determine whether the authors are intelligent. How can writing reveal that? One way is by demonstrating whether the writer has a sizable vocabulary and can use it to construct long and complex linguistic structures. We academics believe that people who write in this way are smart people. Since we academics place a high value on "smarts," we usually attempt to demonstrate our own intelligence by using the same strategy.

There are, of course, other ways to demonstrate our intelligence. For example, we can do it by demonstrating, through our writing, our awareness of, and sensitivity to, the needs of our intended audience. We can do it through the honesty, clarity, or precision of our expression. We can do it through the substance of our ideas themselves. However, each of these alternative approaches is hard work; the easiest way for us to show we're smart is by using big words in big sentences. And that's just the way that many of us do it.

As a result, reading memos, letters, and reports by academics is often about as much fun as doing the breaststroke in saltwater taffy. Big words — sometimes in English, sometimes not — abound, many of them unnecessarily. Phrases, especially prepositional phrases, appear where single words would suffice. Linking verbs and passive constructions outnumber action verbs and active constructions.

Some examples:

"If requirements have not been met, the degree will be refused until such time as they have been met."

"With regard to the hiring of faculty, an area of concern must be our use of adjunct faculty, which in some ways seems excessive."

"Services are numerous in number. The attempt is to utilize all available information on each student to provide for more effective learning."

"All questions about Financial Aid may be referred to the Financial Aid Office."

"All academic fee payments are refundable provided the Registrar is notified in writing prior to the first day of classes that the registration is being cancelled."

Readers may or may not view the academic writers of this sort of prose as smart. But they definitely view them as verbose and probably pompous — if they persevere in reading it.

Design

Many of us academics consider ourselves to be "word people." We pay a great deal of attention to selecting words accurately and to designing appropriate linguistic structures. We may well forget that there is more to writing than the words alone. When we write, we create a *visual* document. The effective use of white space, headings, underlining, various type styles and sizes, bullets, as well as charts and graphs can dramatically increase the visual impact of our writing.

The Document Design Center [American Institutes for Research, 1055 Thomas Jefferson Street, NW, Washington, D.C. 20007] has many fine publications on both the verbal and nonverbal aspects of design. If (like me) you lack a background in design, you'll learn a great deal from these materials.

How to Improve Academic Writing

As I said at the outset, the writing of academics — like the writing of most professionals — is a long way from perfect. This is not news to anyone who has spent any time on a college or university campus. The question is, "What can we do about it?"

One step we can take is to persuade our academic colleagues that they are indeed professional writers. Too often, they view professional writing as a concern only for attorneys, executives, and government bureaucrats — certainly not for academics. This is a curious view, especially in light of the prodigious number of memos, letters, reports, and proposals which we in academe generate each year.

Another step we can take is to help our academic colleagues to improve their writing skills. One way I do this at my own institution is through an Administrative Writing Program which I have established. Administrators have the option of signing up for fifteen-hour workshops, each one involving six 2½-hour sessions. Our text in these workshops is the writing done on the job by the administrators themselves. Our whole group (eight to fifteen people) discusses samples of typical pieces of their writing, concentrating on both their writing successes and their opportunities for improvement. How do participants respond to the program? At my institution, the responses have been uniformly favorable. Here are excerpts from the evaluations of the program by a half dozen of the participants:

> You taught and I learned more about my skills in administrative writing in your program than in the sum of all previous courses I have taken. Much better informed, I now enjoy practicing to improve my writing skills.

> I felt very inadequate with my writing skills prior to this workshop. Now I feel I can be more effective in planning and organizing my writing, thus saving myself and the reader valuable time.

> I have changed my writing style significantly as a result of what you presented and I learned.

> Through participation in the workshop I learned how to be a more efficient and effective writer. . . . I am now better equipped to critique my own writing.

> I am a more effective communicator as a result of my participation in the Administrative Writing Program.

> I learned new ways to make what I write more effective and understandable. . . . Most important, with continuing work on my own, applying what I learned, I believe my writing will continue to improve.

Conclusion

Academic writing may or may not differ qualitatively from the writing done by other professionals. Be that as it may, it is an important area of professional writing and deserves every bit as much of our attention as the writing of executives, attorneys, and government bureaucrats.

We in academe have cast far afield in our efforts to find opportunities to help professionals to improve their writing skills. We need never have left our own campuses.

Notes

1. Joseph A. Boone, "Modernist Maneuverings in the Marriage Plot: Breaking Ideologies of Gender and Genre in James's *The Golden Bowl*," *PMLA* 101 (1986): 378.
2. Boone, 384.

III Teaching Professional Writing

9 Use of the Case Method in Teaching Business Communication

John L. DiGaetani
Hofstra University

The case method includes many advantages for the teaching of business communication, both on the undergraduate and the graduate levels. A definition of terms is in order at the beginning: The case method is a way of teaching that begins with a case, or a description of a business problem, which should generate class discussion, as well as speaking and writing assignments.

The case method began in this country as far back as the nineteenth century in law schools, where the method was used to teach law students the complexities of the law, with a particular legal case to exemplify a legal problem or principle.[1] The rationale for the case method in law was to present students with what practicing attorneys confront: an actual legal problem that a client brings to a lawyer. The lawyer would then have to analyze all of the information presented in the case, do research into the law and possible legal principles and precedents, and then advise the client about what legal recourse or options he or she might have. From the classrooms of law schools, the case method spread to other educational areas.

The Harvard Law School, one of the earliest law schools in the country, used this method. When Harvard University began its school of business in 1908, it followed the precedent of the law school and decided to use the case method exclusively.[2] In fact, the Harvard Business School was the first to use the method for the graduate study of business, to the exclusion of all other methods.[3] The first dean of the Harvard Business School, Edwin F. Gay, encouraged the use of the case method, in part for political reasons, to ensure that the school would become as respectable and reputable as the law school.[4] In the business school, business communication is taught with the case method, as are all courses in the school. The class, as a result, spends from one to two weeks, depending on the complexity of a particular case, discussing and analyzing a case and speaking and writing on the communication problems in it.

187

So the Harvard Business School uses the case method exclusively to teach Management Communication, as the course is called there. The class studies cases that have already been written — generally by the Management Communication Department's faculty or other faculty in the school of business — for the study of communication problems, communication issues, and solutions to these problems. The cases also provide examples of possible assignments: topics for in-class speeches, for in-class writing, and more frequently for out-of-class writing. The speaking topics include role-playing of the various factions in the cases or a discussion of the communication issues for the case in question. The writing assignments include written analyses of the communication problems in the case, as well as letters, memos, or reports that could solve the communication problems raised in the case or in class discussions of it.

Advantages of the Case Method

The case method has numerous advantages for the teaching of business communication, especially with graduate students who have had some management experience. The first, and in many ways the main, advantage is what the method does to improve students' reading skills. It demands careful and critical reading; students must read the cases very carefully, taking notes and analyzing what the case presents. Such intensive reading and the development of analytical reading skills will surely help students in their business careers. Reading memos and company reports carefully — with a view to communication problems, a search for the major issues, and suggestions about solutions — provides excellent training for a career in business. This type of reading involves both words and numbers, thinking about the facts and opinions presented, analyzing where the communication issues and problems are, and what possible solutions exist for the problems presented in the case. This of course reflects how a manager would analyze communication problems in the world of business.

The case method also improves the student's ability to analyze problems. While a chapter in a text provides theory and practice in business communication, the case method provides no theory. Instead, the student must locate the problems in the case, analyze them, and suggest solutions. This method also confronts the students with a real-life business problem that has no clear-cut answers. While a typical noncase textbook presents a theory and then problems with solutions, the case method avoids all theory in favor of the real-life situation of a communication problem in business. Recent cases have presented problems at General Electric, Bristol–Myers, Chesebrough–Pond's, and the Humana Corporation. The student has to read carefully, discover the problems, suggest workable solutions to the class, and convince the class that the solutions would be effective.[5]

One of the best aspects of the case method is that the solutions often remain ambiguous. Where are the problems? Where are the solutions? Which is the best solution? In the case method these questions all remain debatable. There are various ways of explicating the case, and this process has the ring of real life to it. The practicing executive must locate the problems and then decide what solutions, if any, are possible, given the situation.

In addition, the case method usually presents the political realities of a business situation. While the root of the problem may be a particular executive, that executive's powers may be such that the student will have to work around that situation. Once again, this is a realistic communication problem in business rather than a textbook problem. The best solutions may not be available in a particular case, and the student must decide which solutions are possible, given the corporate realities in the case. The root of a communication problem might be the owner of a company, so the student must propose solutions that are possible, given the realities presented.

An advantage of the case method from some teachers' point of view is its similarities to the analysis of fiction, especially a short story. Because many teachers of business communication began as English teachers and had extensive graduate training in literary criticism, they are comfortable with the analysis of a text. The case method allows them to use those skills in a course in business communication.

The case method stimulates dialectical class discussion. A case should generate heated argument in class, sparking student interest in realistic business situations. To do so, the cases should be as current as possible,[6] presenting problems that students have been reading about in newspapers, problems that have been in the news. Serious business students want to know about and analyze business problems; the case method gives them examples from real life. The students must then suggest solutions that will work and must also persuade other class members that the solutions will correct the problems in the case. Students will develop analytical and communication skills as they critique each other's contributions to solving the problems.

The case method generates several kinds of assignments. Role-plays allow students to make speeches in class about some aspect of a case, in the role of an executive, for example. Or the method can generate class debates about where the real problems in the case occur and what solutions would work best. In addition, the case method enables the teacher to give many writing assignments: memos that analyze the communication problems in the case, letters and memos that arise from the case itself. As a result, students become aware of a specific audience for their business communication; they are not writing only for the teacher.

Disadvantages of the Case Method

Since the case method emphasizes real and current business problems, there is no room for theory. For teachers who like to provide a theoretical basis for much of what they do in class, the case method may prove frustrating if it is used exclusively and without other essays and lectures. If teachers like to discuss the nature of communication and how it gets entangled in "noise" or "improper channeling," those concepts will not arise easily from a case. In addition, the teacher is not supposed to dominate the discussion or even direct it. The students must analyze the case, which might not lead to the solution the teacher thinks is best. The teacher's main power is in picking the cases, not in solving them. The students must do this.[7]

For professors who like to lecture on research methods and give assignments involving research in libraries, the case method can prove frustrating. One solution is not to use the case method exclusively. Another, more subtle solution is to generate assignments from cases that will force students to do library research. For example, a case can raise a problem with advertising budgets, and the teacher can assign a paper requiring some research on patterns of advertising budgets. A case can present a problem in procedures for terminating employees, and the teacher can assign a paper requiring research on the various methods of termination. A case can reflect a particular personnel problem in middle management, and the teacher can assign a paper requiring the students to discover what three specific experts in this area would recommend.

Another disadvantage of the case method involves the required background for students. I have found that the case method as it is practiced at Harvard works best with graduate students, especially those who have had actual management experience. For undergraduates, especially those who have had few business courses, the more complex cases may be difficult to teach because few if any of the students will understand the problems in the case and the options available. On the other hand, some students may be able to do this, and they can generate a useful class discussion of the case. Much depends, of course, on the cases used. Some are simple while others are complex; a teacher's judicious choice can guarantee that most of the students can handle the cases to be discussed. Cases can be obtained in textbooks or anthologies of cases or through the HBS Case Services, Harvard Business School, Boston, Massachusetts 02163.

Pedagogy of the Case Method

For actual classroom use, the case method requires a certain pedagogical approach. The students teach each other, but the teacher can of course subtly direct the conversation by the nature of his or her questions and by picking productive and provocative cases. The more current the case and the more problems presented, the better. Once it has been picked, the teacher must trust the students to discuss and analyze it, although the teacher must understand what the case presents.

Since inductive reasoning remains at the core of the case method, the teacher's behavior must indicate trust in the inductive process, which necessitates student participation.[8] If students try to "discover" only what the teacher wants to hear, they are not analyzing the case itself.

But how can the teacher ensure enough class participation? First, the teacher should make it clear that participation will be a big determinant of the final grade. Class participation should count for at least half of the final grade in the course. This will communicate to the students that class participation remains the single most important factor in their grade. The teacher must also create an atmosphere that will encourage the students to speak. For one thing, the teacher must be a good listener. Using body language and a sensitive approach, the teacher must indicate that students' comments are important and that the success of the class depends on student involvement and inter-pretations of the cases. The teacher must be provocative and encouraging but not judgmental. If a student suggests a naïve solution to the case, the teacher must hope that another student disagrees with the first one. What the class finally concludes is less important than the process of case analysis.

The teacher should make intelligent speaking and writing assign-ments from the cases so that the importance of the class work creates an intellectual challenge for the students. With the right teacher and students, the case method can enlighten students about how com-munication problems in business occur and how they are solved.

Let us now look at an actual Harvard Business School case:

ST. MARK'S LTD.[9]

St. Mark's is one of the largest and most successful retail chains in Britain. In 1978 the 253 U.K. stores had sales of nearly £1,200 million, an increase of 19% over the previous year. The company had expanded abroad with 54 stores in Canada, 2 in Paris, 1 in Brussels, and 1 in Lyon. Exports to other countries totaled £35.1 million, an increase of 32% over the previous year. In 1977 St. Mark's received the Queen's award for export achievement. Sales in both the textile and food divisions continued to grow in real terms despite inflation and the recession.

St. Mark's merchandise — clothing, footwear, household furnishings, and food — was internationally famous for quality and good value. St. Mark's store was often the first stop for foreign visitors on a shopping spree. The quality was emphatically British. St. Mark's management made it a point of pride that 93% of the nonperishable goods were manufactured in Britain.

The company had a good record on civic responsibility. Its directors sponsored projects to create new jobs and supported the national policy of rehabilitating urban areas. In 1978 a sum of £638,000 was donated to national and local charities, with the emphasis on social well-being, the arts, education, and health.

The company also had a reputation for enlightened staff policies and harmonious relations with its employees. The average weekly number of employees in St. Mark's U.K. stores was 43,257 in 1978, including 25,426 part-timers. Nearly 40% of the staff had been with St. Mark's for more than five years. In addition to generous wages, the company offered its employees benefits such as a noncontributory pension scheme, subsidized cafeterias, and preventative health services, including dental inspections and cervical cytology examinations for female employees and wives of male staff.

St. Mark's position as a leader in the British business world meant its policies had a considerable impact on other firms. The decision, in 1973, to inaugurate a profit-sharing scheme for employees was significant: St. Mark's was one of the first large-scale employers in the country to introduce this form of worker participation.

The Profit-Sharing Scheme

St. Mark's profit-sharing scheme was initiated by the company directors and approved by an extraordinary shareholders' meeting on July 14, 1973. Any employee with five years of unbroken service received a present of company shares paid for out of pre-tax profits. Each year the Board decided, in the light of the profits achieved, how much money to make available for the purchase of staff shares. The number of shares each employee received depended on how much he or she earned. In 1978 shares equalled 4% of earnings.

The staff learned about the profit-sharing scheme through the August 1973 issue of the St. Mark's newsletter (Exhibit 1). Those eligible for shares also received a brochure entitled "Summary of the Main Features of the St. Mark's Limited Profit-Sharing Scheme," which set out to explain the various facets of the scheme (Exhibit 2). Many employees were ignorant of the workings of the stock market, and the share certificates they received the following June were often their first encounter with investment capitalism.

News of the scheme was well received by employees. They seemed pleased to earn another bonus and were appreciative of management's concern to involve them in the ownership of the company. There appeared to be little confusion about the principles of shareholding, and management assumed its explanatory booklet answered all questions.

St. Mark's increasing profits and the company's expansion meant new shares were issued every year and more employees became eligible to receive them. In 1973–74, 1.4% of the pre-tax profit was allocated to buy staff shares, an average of 65.77 shares per employee (Exhibit 3). By 1978 the share allocation per employee had risen to £115.87, due to increased company profits and a larger Board allowance — 1.7% of pre-tax profits.

The Board was satisfied with the operation of the profit-sharing scheme and, given the increasingly generous share handout and mounting dividend rate, the Board assumed employees were also satisfied with the profit-sharing scheme. During the course of 1978, however, the Board became worried by a growing trend among shareholding staff: an investigation conducted in the early summer of 1978 showed that nearly one-third of the 17,300 staff shareholders had sold their investments.

At a specially convened meeting in July, the Board discussed possible faults in the profit-sharing scheme. Some members wondered whether the shareholding idea had been explained sufficiently in the booklet. They suggested trying to elicit some feedback from staff about why stock was being sold; they suggested that clearer information about the benefits of shareholding might solve the problem. Other members were more pessimistic and were worried that the whole scheme was being undermined. The purpose of the scheme, they argued, was to involve staff more thoroughly in the operation of the business. As they saw it, employees were literally selling out. St. Mark's had not intended that the new shares be sold to the general buyer on the open stock market. It had also not intended to give its employees merely another cash bonus.

The Board decided to limit staff shareholders' ability to dispose of their stock. It decided to disallow staff from selling their shares until they had held them for at least three years, or until they left the employ of St. Mark's — whichever came first. At the end of the three-year time limit, St. Mark's had to be given first right of refusal to buy back the stock. The price paid by St. Mark's would not be affected by fluctuations on the stock exchange. It

would be fixed at the average middle market price for the 20
dealing days, ending March 31, that immediately precede the
announcement of the year's profits. The stockholders met and
approved the Board's measure.

Exhibit 1
ST. MARK'S LTD.

St. Mark's News   Issued August 1973
Sharing in Our Success

This year, for the first time, staff with five years' unbroken
service will reap an extra benefit — our new profit-sharing scheme.
Over £1 million has been set aside to buy you St. Mark's
shares, and the certificates will be issued by the end of June.

How many shares you get depends on what you earn, but they
are yours and you'll have the same rights as any other shareholder.
You'll become a part owner of St. Mark's, and you'll get dividends
on your shares. You can, of course, sell them if you want, but
saved and added to throughout your career with St. Mark's, they'll
build into a useful nest egg.

The scheme is designed as another reward for the loyalty and
work that have put our company where it is today. You already
enjoy the security, good pay, and benefits that only a successful
company can give — but now you'll be getting a stake in the
ownership, too.

The Board has decided that the amount you will get this year
will be 3p for every £1 of salary you earned last year. Tax has to
be paid on that, but it's all done for you and what's left is used
to buy your shares. The shares cost about £1.10 each at the
moment, so you can work out roughly how many to expect.

Profit-sharing is a benefit in addition to pay, bonus, and noncontributory pensions. It will not affect pay increases or other
improvements the company may wish to provide.

Many of you do not qualify this year for profit shares. But if
you stay with St. Mark's and clock up five years' unbroken service,
you will qualify for any future shares. Each year the Board will
decide whether the company has done well enough to enable
further shares to be issued.

And that depends on all of us continuing to work together for
the growth of the business.

Exhibit 2

ST. MARK'S LTD.

Summary of the Main Features of the St. Mark's Limited
Profit-Sharing Scheme

1. Introduction

The purpose of the Scheme is to enable the Company to issue to
Qualifying Employees ordinary shares of the Company paid up
out of pre-tax profits of the Company.

2. Qualifying Employees

If the Board in its discretion so decides in the light of the profits
achieved in any year, shares will be issued to United Kingdom
employees who have completed five years of continuous service
on or before the end of the accounting period to which the profits
refer. Both full-time and part-time employees will be entitled to
participate, except for temporary seasonal and casual staff.

3. Amount Available for Issue

The amount to be applied in paying for shares under the Scheme
will be determined by the Board at its discretion, taking into
account all the relevant circumstances, particularly the profits for
the year. The announcement of the amount will be made at the
same time as the announcement of the Company's results for the
year.

No amount will be made available for the purposes of the Scheme
unless the U.K. pre-tax profits earned in the year in question
exceed £75,000,000. . . .

Exhibit 3

ST. MARK'S LTD.

Five-Year Record

(Year ending March 31st)

	1974 £'000	1975 £'000	1976 £'000	1977 £'000	1978 £'000
Turnover (excluding sales tax)	571,650	721,252	900,923	1,064,837	1,254,055
Profit before taxation	79,208	81,906	83,774	102,445	117,915
Taxation	34,600	39,750	40,540	49,357	53,736
Profit after taxation attributable to the Company	44,608	42,156	43,242	54,668	64,535
Ordinary share capital and reserves	301,467	366,933	381,881	411,662	448,551

Commentary on the St. Mark's Case

The St. Mark's case is a story of good intentions gone awry. This British company started a profit-sharing stock plan to benefit all employees, but became disturbed when some employees decided to sell the stock, thereby deflating its market value. The board of directors of the company determined to alter the plan to eliminate this problem; management's problem is how to communicate the change to the employees. The situation is complicated because management, employees, and unions are all involved. As a result, the case lends itself to many speaking and writing situations.

Topics for Discussion in Class

1. What are the major issues in this case? Certainly communicating with employees is the major issue here, especially because management has some bad news for them. The board's decision to change the profit-sharing plan puts upper management in the position of having to communicate this change, which means bad news for most of the employees. The case also indicates something of the class system in England. On the one hand, the case presents upper management and the board, who are most probably upper middle-class people and, on the other hand, the employees, who are trying to make a living on their salaries. Selling those shares was a valuable means of income for some of them, and that is now being eliminated. But how should upper management communicate this bad news to the employees? In what progression? In a letter to all employees? In a union meeting? Orally via each employee's manager? Each method has advantages and disadvantages.

2. What errors did management make in this case? The original letter clearly did not foresee the problems that developed, but they were predictable at the time. The profit-sharing plan should have been thought through more clearly before it was established. Also, the tone of the original letter is paternalistic and condescending to the employees. That should have been changed before the letter went out.

3. What did management do correctly? The idea of a profit-sharing plan is certainly a generous one that has gained much company loyalty for St. Mark's. While that loyalty will be diminished because of the changes, those changes can be explained so that most employees see why they were necessary and why the altered plan remains a good deal for them. The board and upper management deserve credit for

initiating a significant benefit for all employees of the company. But would most employees have preferred a raise instead of profit sharing? Were employees ever consulted about what benefits they would like?

4. How should management communicate the board's decision to St. Mark's employees? Orally? In writing? Both? Students will have several options here, but the discussion will probably conclude that a combination of methods is best. An initial letter from the board announcing the plan can be followed by a meeting with upper management or individual managers to explain the changes and why they are necessary. Upper management cannot hope to satisfy all employees on this issue, but most will see the need for the change. Upper management should also beware of too many meetings on this issue, because they could easily become a forum for general complaining. Management needs to emphasize the value of the profit-sharing plan to the employees; the plan is valuable to them even with the new limitations. And some employees, as stockholders, probably approve of the change themselves, because deflated stock values affect them.

5. Is the problem that the employees of St. Mark's are not being paid enough? Is that the real reason they are selling their profit-sharing stocks? If this is the case, what should the company do about the situation? These questions could easily lead to an interesting discussion of the class system in England and the United States and its implications for management. How management faces these issues can be basic to its treatment of employees in other situations. Management's options are clearly limited here by the realities of its society, but being aware of the problem and its economic consequences is useful for students.

Writing Topics for St. Mark's

1. Write an analysis of the writing problems in the first letter announcing the plan to the employees. Where are the communication errors?

2. Write a consultant's position paper on how management should communicate the board's changes in the profit-sharing plan to the employees. The purpose here is to avoid as many problems as possible.

3. Write a new letter to the employees, announcing the board's changes in the profit-sharing plan. Justify the changes to the employees, and emphasize the value of the new plan.

Student Speakers' Topics for St. Mark's

1. A representative from the employees' union states the workers' case against any change in the profit-sharing plan.

2. A representative from a left-wing radical fragment of the employees' union states his or her position about the inadequate wages at St. Mark's.

3. A representative from management announces the board's changes in the profit-sharing plan to a group of St. Mark's employees. The representative would have to defend the changed plan against hostile questioning from the audience.

4. An outside consultant makes recommendations to upper management on how it should communicate the changed plan to the employees. He or she would present a model letter to be sent to the employees, defending the letter against possible criticism.

Clearly, then, the St. Mark's case — if properly used — will generate several interesting classes and useful speaking and writing assignments.

New Directions in Using Cases: The Rhetorical Case

Traditional case writing involved doing extensive research on a managerial communication problem or set of problems in a particular company, but more recent developments in the use of cases involve rhetorical cases. These differ from traditional ones in that they focus on communication rather than on managerial problems, and they are simulations rather than actual business cases.[10] The simulation has the advantage of allowing the teacher to create a new case or to use a simulated case from a textbook, although these have the disadvantage of being less realistic than an actual business case based on the experiences of a real corporation.

The Cleary Real Estate Case, which I wrote with a colleague, Rochelle Cleary, for use in undergraduate business communication classes at Hofstra University, was designed to address issues of persuasion, writing for a specific audience, ecological problems, and the ethics of business communication. All these topics need to be discussed in class after the case has been read.

The Case of Cleary Real Estate

You are Mrs. R. Cleary and have formed a corporation to develop 100 acres of land in central Florida as a model retirement community. The land is in a very isolated area of Florida, without phone or electric lines, but its location about 15 miles from Disney World is attractive. The area is very marshy in spots and contains some nonpoisonous snakes, but much of it is beautiful and pastoral as well. The nearest town is six miles away and contains only a post office, a 7-Eleven store, and an airport rental company which offers some hunting guides. In addition, many rare and beautiful birds make the abundant foliage their home; so you envision this land as a wonderful place to make many retired people happy for the remainder of their lives.

Therefore you have formed your corporation, hired a lawyer and an architect, and drawn up plans for a series of small retirement homes with plenty of land around each home. You also want to provide large parks and small lakes to preserve the beauty of the land as well as to create recreational areas for the retirees.

However, the Florida Audubon Society has gotten wind of your plans and remains adamantly opposed to any plans to develop the land. The President of the Society, Mr. William Byrd, has called you to argue that many rare birds and other animals rely on that swampland to survive, that land development in Florida has already destroyed the Everglades and other fertile swamplands, and that these animals might well become extinct without their natural habitat. You have argued that you will keep the land as natural as possible, and that parklands and large lots are part of the planned development, but Mr. Byrd insists that the development will still destroy the natural habitat of the land, and that the natural habitat supports an ecological system that cannot be replaced.

The conflict of land development for people versus animals' rights groups falls squarely in the lap of Mrs. Cleary. She feels that compromises are possible and wants to build a retirement community for retirees within a beautiful natural setting. In addition, she wants to make a substantial profit from the development.

Discussion Questions and Writing Assignments

1. Fully discuss the case in class. What are the conflicting issues in the case? Who is right? Who is wrong? Is compromise possible here? What are the communication issues?

2. Mrs. Cleary has received a list of about 200 people who have retired from a large corporation in New York within the last two years. Write a one-page sales letter selling the land as Sunshine City, a retirement community. To be legal, your letter cannot lie, but it may contain omissions or positive interpretations of the truth. The letter will be addressed to a senior on the list Mrs. Cleary has gotten, trying to persuade him or her to come to Florida to look at the land or to call or to write for a brochure with more specific information and prices.

3. You are Mr. William Byrd, the president of the Florida Audubon Society, seeking to prevent the building of Sunshine City. Write

a letter to your congressman using the same data and urging him to stop the project, with a copy to the local newspaper.

4. You are Mrs. Cleary, the developer, and have read the Audubon Society's letter in the local newspaper objecting to the project. Write a letter to the newspaper defending your project and convincing its readers that the project will help Florida and should not be stopped.

5. Imagine that you are one of the buyer–retirees and very dissatisfied because the project has not been finished on time. Write a letter to the developer complaining about the delay in the completion of the project and asking for a 20% discount on the site as compensation for a six-month delay.

6. As Mrs. Cleary, answer the letter in Question #5, and offer instead, as compensation, free landscaping for the front of the house — and provide reasons to defend the fairness of your proposal.

Commentary on the Cleary Real Estate Case

This rhetorical case, while not based on research into a communication problem in an actual company, does present the student with interesting issues and valid speaking and writing assignments. The case presents problems involving the ecology, the morality of land development, and possible techniques for successful persuasion. The case has generated interesting discussions in my classes, plus persuasive speeches both for and against the real estate development. These heated speeches have then become letters in support of the project, trying to persuade customers to buy into the project, and letters of protest to stop the project.

Although not as realistic as the historical, researched case, the simulated case is easier to find or create on one's own and can succeed in making students aware of important issues in business communication classes. This type of case has been used for computer problems, research problems, and writing and speaking assignments.[11] And certainly the issues in the case have stimulated student interest in real business communication issues and in the idea that successful communication can help persuade people, make students better entrepreneurs, and give them real power to develop their own professional careers.

Conclusion

Whether an actual case or a rhetorical case is used, the case method can enliven business communication courses and provide an outlet for teachers' own creativity through writing their own cases. The case method can be used exclusively in a course or as a unit in it. Cases can be interspersed with lectures and readings on communication theory. While the theoretical aspects of the field are ignored in the case method, the practical, real-life aspects of business communication become clear through use of the case method. The actual method of analyzing real business communication problems and suggesting and creating solutions to those problems — the core skills that the case method offers — will prepare students for handling communication problems successfully.

Notes

1. Melvin T. Copeland, *And Mark an Era, The Story of the Harvard Business School* (Boston: Little, Brown and Co., 1958), 27.
2. Copeland, 27.
3. E. Raymond Corey, "Case Method Teaching," *Harvard Business School Case Services,* 1980, 4.
4. Corey, 4.
5. Corey, 5–7.
6. Michiel R. Leenders and James A. Erskine, *Case Research: The Case Writing Process* (London, Canada: School of Business Administration, the University of Western Ontario, 1973), 2–5.
7. Corey, 3.
8. Corey, 5–8.
9. This case was prepared by Alison Eadie, under the direction of Thomas J. Raymond, as the basis for class discussion rather than to illustrate either effective or ineffective handling of an administrative situation. Copyright © 1978 by the President and Fellows of Harvard College. Reprinted by permission of the Harvard Business School.
10. Linda S. Flower, "Communication Strategy in Professional Writing: Teaching a Rhetorical Case," in *Courses, Components, and Exercises in Technical Communication* (Urbana, Ill.: National Council of Teachers of English, 1981), 37–39.
11. Michael Orth and Carl R. V. Brown, "Computer Generated Rhetorical Simulations for Business and Report Writing Courses," *Journal of Technical Writing and Communication* 14 (1984): 29–31.

10 Building Ethos: Field Research in a Business Communication Course

David Lauerman
Canisius College

During an interview, a social worker responded to the researcher's questions about one of her clinical reports by explaining some of the reasons behind her writing:

> *Researcher:* Let's look at the first whole paragraph of this report. The paragraph begins: "B. remained there for approximately a year. His adjustment was very poor." These strike me as fairly general statements. After that we get into more specific points, "bed wetting," "extremely labile," "bursts of sporadic energy," "climbing walls and furniture," "dancing, acting," and we even get some quotes — "acting crazy" — which I assume were picked up from some other document. Am I reading that right?
>
> *Social worker:* I think that's what's going on: I'm trying to capture behavioral realities for this patient.
>
> *Researcher:* I know what answer I'm going to get when I suggest deleting those details, but I'll ask anyway. Would you be willing to delete them?
>
> *Social worker:* No. Especially since this is clinical material.
>
> *Researcher:* What I really want to hear is your explanation.
>
> *Social worker:* Because this is a clinical assessment of an individual, it is extremely important that you are exact and descriptive in behavioral reactions of the client you're working with.
>
> *Researcher:* Why is this detail so important in a clinical summary?
>
> *Social worker:* That is how you begin to put into definite frameworks certain types of personalities. You do it because of definite patterns that come out behaviorally and so it is very important to describe those behavioral patterns because that can give you insight into the type of personality pattern that you are working with. It also tells the professionals who read it what type of personality pattern that you're working with. So the description of the behavior is very important. It is far more important to describe the behavior than to give your perception of what you thought you saw.

This interview, which occurred six years ago, was one of about 150 conducted by a team of Canisius College English teachers working on a course development project. For three years we were guided by Lee Odell and Dixie Goswami and were funded by a Title III grant. During the project we did field research interviews, collected writing samples, worked with groups of college faculty and field professionals, then set to work designing senior-level writing courses for students majoring in business, in social science, in humanities, in science, and in education — five courses in all. The keystone of this work is English 389, Business Writing, a course popular with our students and with the dean of our business school.[1] Best of all, we like teaching it, mainly because it is something different:

> It really is a writing course, in which students have the sort of authorial control they might expect in "Creative Writing" or in a writing group.

> We teachers have learned several valuable lessons, some of which have changed the way we teach.

We are very proud of the outcomes from our project. English 389 has been taught every semester and every summer since 1981 to an eager clientele. While this is a free elective course with a heavy workload, we have enrolled business majors, English and communication majors, and M.B.A.'s, as well as college staff members. The business dean has now decided to require English 389 for all of his students.

To create English 389 we had to learn to do field research and to look at writing in a way new to us, and we found that our field observations changed the way we looked at writers and at writing. We even have a new motto — "Writing for the job is doing the job." Our students profit from our new enthusiasm, and our English department has profited, too, from increased enrollments. In fact, we are building a new image on our campus as a writing department.

But can other teachers and departments replicate our experience? Grant money is scarce these days, budgets are tight, and who has the time to do the field research, much less the course development work?

I will answer those questions by offering an overview of our project: goals, assumptions, support needed, research procedures, course design, and outcomes. After that, I will describe our course design and a sample assignment. Finally, I will reveal our best discovery: Our students can replicate our field research and in doing so consolidate their learning, validate their growing sense of how writing works, and add to our growing "hoard" of new material for writing assignments.

Field Work: A Conversation with Joe

When Canisius College applied for a Title III grant in 1979, I laid out a course development activity (labeled "Writing Across the Curriculum") that would generate five new writing courses for our seniors. All were electives aimed at writing in the career areas our graduates had chosen. We already had a business writing course, but I never felt that my textbook materials and assignments matched the complexity of real-world writing tasks.

The first time I taught the course, I ordered a textbook (one recommended by a colleague) and followed along from Memos to Letters to Reports to Proposals to Graphics. Luckily, it was a good text: clearly written, with attractive samples and workable exercises that included cases. Nevertheless, I was restless. Here I was, grading memos for the same features required in freshman themes. Furthermore, I did not know the territory (a territory many of my adult students worked in every day!). Clear, readable text is important; so is tone of voice; so is detail. But which tone works best and how much detail is needed? I needed more context for evaluating tone and detail; my students did too.

My goal in developing a new business writing course was simply to find, or create, a better match between instruction and application. This meant that I had to get off-campus and see writing at work. I had not come to this awareness without help.

Our inspiration in this project came from Lee Odell and Dixie Goswami, who at that time were setting out on an NIE-funded research project called "Writing in Non-academic Settings." They agreed to guide our research efforts, and our work with them soon made clear to me the research assumption on which our work is based: Writers in the work world deal with complex rhetorical and intellectual issues. Whereas this complexity — this demand for decision making — seems absent from textbook activities, it is a powerful presence in the workplace. As we began, this was more an intuition than an ordered concept or hypothesis.

I designed our course development project principally to measure school writing against writing in the professions. Given grant support for released time, clerical help, and guidance from consultants, our research team set out to contact and interview people working in jobs our business graduates are headed for: to collect and study samples of their writing and to probe their tacit knowledge of writing by asking them to reenact specific rhetorical decisions in individual pieces of text. From individual writers we collected portfolios (descriptions of tasks and approaches, writing samples, transcripts of taped interviews) that later yielded one- or two-page writing tasks for the course. (We call them "scenarios"; they could as easily be called "cases.") We also invited our interview subjects to a daylong workshop with business faculty, during which we reviewed procedures and research materials and asked for suggestions about course design. The last workshop activity was creating a list of goals to be addressed in the course.

We contacted our research subjects by several means, but mainly by networking. We told ourselves, "You are never more than three persons removed from the professional you wish to interview." We began with local alumni and friends. An English major with an M.B.A. in personnel put us in touch with twenty-five of our thirty business participants. All twenty-five of them worked in one division of a local manufacturing company. We also made contacts through colleagues in our school of business. We anticipated some difficulty getting access to our subjects' time and writing samples; to forestall these problems, we supplied our contacts with a letter outlining the purpose of our research and requesting two thirty- or forty-minute interviews. Later, in person, we promised to "sanitize" any writing samples we photocopied by whiting out all identifying references.

We spent our first half-hour interview getting to know each writer in his or her own milieu. To guide this interview, we used an informal survey form. The first page asked for a loose taxonomy of "usual" writing tasks to be described by mode, audience, and frequency. The second page asked for comments on his or her own attitudes and approaches to writing. This interview yielded a portrait of the professional as a writer; more importantly, it told us what writing samples to ask for and convinced the writers to trust the research team with copies of their work.

This interview gave us a representative writing sample — a portfolio containing at least one sample of each of the kinds of writing our subject usually generates (a hand-written note, a typed internal memo, a letter to someone outside the company, a monthly report, a travel report) and extra samples of whatever task the writer had described as "important" or "difficult." This added up to eight to twelve pieces and fifteen to thirty pages of text.

I did my first interview in the spring of 1979 with Joe M., in charge of marketing one of the graphite product lines at a local manufacturing plant. As product manager, he had no sales force but used "sales representatives," independent contractors who sold his product line on commission. His product line had been developed from recent and fast-changing technology. Joe, I learned, had to consult frequently with engineering and plant managers on special orders, quality control, and new products. He is not an engineer or a technician, but has had to learn some technical language and processes. Beneath all that, he is a salesman.

Joe said that, within his branch, he wrote memos and reports to superiors (branch manager, project manager, branch controller, sales director), to personnel and customer service departments, and to his own sales engineer. He wrote letters to his sales representatives. Moreover, he often provided copies of his memos to various departments and to corporate offices. Outside the branch, he wrote letters to prospective sales representatives and proposals and product data sheets to customers; he also retained a research consultant. For three days, Joe had been working on his annual self-appraisal — a task he did not enjoy. He also produced annually a Strategic Plan and a Business Plan — large management-by-objective documents. I guessed that he spent about half of his workweek writing; he agreed and noted that, while writing is extremely important in his job, it gives him some trouble. Writing takes much of his time. He has trouble controlling tone and projecting the desired persona; answering technical questions can be difficult; the rhetorical purpose of the company's annual Strategic Plan seemed unclear, making the document difficult to produce. Luckily, Joe could articulate a clear sense of how he composed these various kinds of text ("a week to gather the information, a minute to write it up"), and he had at least one friend (not a supervisor) he turned to for help. He uses some secretaries to "clean up" text, as well; others are "robots," useless for this purpose.

This was my first interview. It opened my eyes to the volume of writing Joe produced and to the variety of modes he had internalized. I was also impressed by his awareness of audience, persona, and tone and his awareness of the writing process. Beyond his desk, I began to see how the paper trail follows reporting lines within the company and affects Joe's image among his co-workers. Indeed, few college teachers could probably match Joe's writing load for volume or for complexity.

Joe photocopied eleven samples of his writing for me. He expressed no reluctance about showing me his work — largely, I think, because he felt he had something to learn about writing from our conversation. (I believe he did learn, not from my rather bland responses, but because describing his tasks and performance created a perspective and suggested a kind of control that he found helpful.) Only one person among the twenty-five we interviewed in this branch said he could not show us any of his writing (all of which he said was "highly confidential'') even in a sanitized version. Indeed, he expressed some surprise that others were giving us samples. Luckily, his refusal was the only one we encountered.

Joe's portfolio contained three letters, two of them addressed to a new sales representative; the third was a blind sales letter announcing a new product and addressed to select customers. There were four memos. One requested approval of travel plans; one requested that another office change its procedures for handling product literature; a third requested that Joe's new sales representative be given a territory code so that he could be credited with new orders written in his territory; a fourth specified details of this arrangement. Joe also gave me the first quarterly sales report he had written three years earlier; a job description for a new position; a set of typed notes for a two-hour talk on marketing strategies he was giving at a staff meeting; and a copy of his own résumé, newly revised.

This modest sample reinforced my first impression: Joe writes on a wide range of subjects, in a variety of modes, to audiences nearby and remote, including superiors, peers, and subordinates. His writing world is complex and demanding. This is the first lesson that our field research offered me as a teacher.

I then chose six samples — three memos, two letters, and the sales report — to work up for our second interview. The first five seemed typical tasks; the sixth Joe had identified as important. Guided by Odell and Goswami, I set out to explore Joe's experience as a writer (his tacit knowledge of practical discourse) by focusing on specific places in these six texts where Joe appeared to have made choices and to ask him to reenact his decisions for me. One of the letters — a cover letter accompanying the contract mailed to the new sales representative — will illustrate the question protocol.

27 September 1979

Mr. Ronald P. Bunch
Marketing Corporation
100 Southward Island
Clearwater, Florida 33500

Subject: Sales Representative Contract

Dear Ron:

Pursuant to our conversation over the past few months and in line with our desire and need for professional sales coverage in Florida, I am happy to report that you have been chosen to represent the PDS portion of the Amalgamated product line.

As a result, I have enclosed two copies of our sales representative agreement covering Amalgamated products. This agreement has an 11/1/79 effective date and you will receive 5% commission on the listed products for all invoices dated 11/1/79 and beyond. This, of course, includes all new orders received on or after this date plus all orders presently in house.

Please sign both copies of this contract and return one to us for our records.

Ron, it is indeed a pleasure to have you as part of our sales team and I am excited about the prospects for the future.

I am looking forward to a long and mutually beneficial relationship.

If there should be any questions in this matter, please call me.

Sincerely,

J. F. Moon
Product Manager

JFM/ds
Enc.

Joe's letter will serve to illustrate our interview strategy. We designed the interview questions to pose possible alternatives, to ask first for a choice and then for reasons for that choice, and thus to find access to the writer's tacit knowledge of such situations.

I modified Joe's cover letter at five points, each time offering a choice between the original text and an alternative formulation I felt Joe might have chosen. As can be seen in the reprinted letter, at three points I offered alternative forms for addressing his sales representative, Ron Bunch (#1); asking Ron to sign the contract (#4); and referring to himself (#5).

At two other points, I asked Joe to consider deleting a context-setting statement (#2) and a passage that elaborates some details of the accompanying contract (#3).

Joe's letter, modified to show him the choices I wanted him to consider in our second interview, now looked like this:

27 September 1979

Mr. Ronald P. Bunch
Marketing Corporation
100 Southward Island
Clearwater, Florida 33500

Subject: Sales Representative Contract

1.   Dear Ron:

            Dear Mr. Bunch:
2.   Pursuant to our conversation over the past few
(delete?)   months and in line with our desire and need for
            professional sales coverage in Florida, I am happy to
            report that you have been chosen to represent the
            PDS portion of the Amalgamated line.

As a result, I have enclosed two copies of our sales representative agreement covering PDS products. This agreement has an 11/1/79 effective date and you will

3. receive 5% commission on the listed products for all
(delete?) invoices dated 11/1/79 and beyond. This, of course, includes all new orders received on or after this date plus all orders presently in house.

You must now sign . . .

4. It is imperative that you sign . . .

Please sign . . .

both copies of this contract and return one to us for our records.

Ron, it is indeed a pleasure to have you as part of our sales team and I am excited about the prospects for the future.

I am looking forward to . . .

5. We are looking forward to . . .

Amalgamated Products is looking forward to . . . a long and mutually beneficial relationship.

If there should be any questions in this matter, please call me.

Sincerely,

J. F. Moon
Product Manager

JFM/ds
Enc.

To explore Joe's tacit knowledge of these issues, I put my questions in the following form and sequence: You address him as "Dear Ron." Elsewhere, you refer to other addressees as "Dear Mr. X." Would you be willing to change "Dear Ron" to "Dear Mr. Bunch"? Joe said he could possibly use "Dear Mr. Bunch," but in this letter he would not.

My next question: What basis do you have for preferring "Dear Ron" to "Dear Mr. Bunch"? Joe explained that he had talked to Ron a number of times and felt they were "on a personal basis. It's a business letter but I didn't want to make it so stiff." Clearly Joe had chosen this form of address to establish a personal tone, and his response made it clear that his working relationship with Ron was the primary factor in this decision. In this case, Joe had told me that he was aware of the conventions of the cover letter, but that his personal relationship with Ron overrode such conventions.

Joe's other responses supported my growing sense that writing for him was a decision-making activity. He rejected my request that he delete the context-setting introduction (#2) for two reasons. He wanted to remind Ron that Ron had sought the account — had "chased the daylights out of me." Further, Joe wanted to use that reminder as a motivating factor "in such a subtle way as to further make him do the job." Here again, Joe's choice is conditioned by a working relationship that is just beginning.

Joe rejected the request to delete the terms stated in the contract (#3). My classroom strictures against "redundancy" were never mentioned: "The important part of any relationship is the beginning, and I don't want anything inferred or assumed." There was a second reason: Ron was to receive his 5 percent commission on orders already received — ones he had not written. This very generous arrangement (referred to again in Joe's memo to the controller) was a second motivational strategy, one I would have overlooked without Joe's explanation.

My attempt to offer Joe alternatives that would modulate the tone of his request to "please sign" the contract (#4) earned me a scolding. Joe seized upon the second alternative ("It is imperative") and called it "too strong. We're supposed to be professionals." This alternative was not a possible choice for him. His reason was clear: the phrase projects an undesirably authoritarian persona and would make Ron uneasy.

Joe responded in two stages when I focused on his way of referring to himself (#5). At first he accepted my alternatives as ways of correcting an error he had made: "Absolutely correct. That is a mistake on my part, using 'I.' " Joe had not forgotten about the teacher's red pen I carry. "You should basically stay away from too much of 'I, I, I' in a business type of letter. That's a mistake. That's almost like he's dealing one to one with me, as opposed to me as a representative of Amalgamated Products as a whole." Joe had quietly shifted ground; he had begun by citing a rule governing pronouns in business letters, but in the last sentence he had offered a rhetorical reason, had cited the persona he intended to project. Thus, given a moment's thought, he could go beyond rules to reasons for choices he had made in this letter.

The interview lasted about forty-five minutes. I asked Joe to look at twenty-five or thirty decisions I had found in his writing samples. He saw the pattern of my questions and moved ahead intently, excited in his discoveries about himself as a writer. The reasons he offered varied with the situation but consistently circled back to the basics — subject, audience, ethos (the image or voice he wished to project).[2] For example, his reasons for elaborating (providing detail) varied from sample to sample, having to do here with the reader's need for background, there with the importance of the details provided. The same is true of the other features we looked at — form of address, reference to self, form of request, and use of a context-setting introduction. I saw clearly that Joe's responses made me believe that as a writer he made rhetorical choices; he rarely cited external rules. Furthermore, Joe's decisions are complex, often based on projections about a reader's response, an awareness of self-image, a sense of the inherent importance of certain information, and a sense of the way things are done at Amalgamated Products. In a case study based on his experience as advisor to a New York consulting agency, C. H. Knoblauch observed a similar complexity in the "operational" decisions of writers he worked with.[3]

This is not to say that Joe is a gifted writer. By his own description, he works slowly and often needs help. Indeed, I find the letter to Ron Bunch at one point stodgy ("Pursuant to our conversation . . .") and elsewhere self-consciously effusive ("Ron, it is indeed . . ."). While I might have offered to edit some of Joe's text, I did not do so.

Before leaving my experience with Joe behind, let me summarize the outcomes of our field research as reflected in the materials we used in designing English 389 and in broader terms as well.

As we began the work of designing English 389 and the other "writing for the professions" courses that grew out of our project, it was clear that our ideas about teaching and writing had been changed. Writers like Joe had made it clear to us that writing is bound up in decision making: it affects decisions, and it reflects decisions. Writers like Joe appear to have learned from experience to "think about audience" and to "project an ethos" appropriate to the situation. Thus we had to let go of some of our graduate school biases about text: there appeared to be more than one workable approach to a situation, more than one text that would do the job. The central, crucial activity in our writing course would not be producing an approximation of an ideal text (Joe's original letter, or my improved version of his letter), but should be producing text that represents the young writer's attempt to address the situation as Joe had, *with his own resources*. In short, we must be willing to give our young writers some measure of authorial control, within constraints imposed by the situation as we presented it.[4] This conviction, and our research orientation, led us in designing our courses to

Provide *contexts*, such as we had observed

Focus on *decision making* about the discourse to be attempted

Indicate *constraints* that the situation (and our reenactment) imposed

Sequence *tasks* in order of increasing complexity[5]

For this, our research interviews and our portfolios of writing samples provided us with a rich fund of material for assignments.

From Field Work to Class Work

The syllabus for English 389 states a set of course goals articulated in May 1980 and based on our research. We ask students

To become aware of what happens when you write and to learn to use writing as a way to discover and learn

To improve your ability to formulate ideas and to condense and summarize the ideas of others

To learn to collaborate with other writers

To attempt the kinds of writing tasks common in the world of business and recognize the special challenges in those tasks

To make your own firsthand observations of writing performance in the work world

This statement, followed up by our classroom activities, makes it clear that English 389 is a writing course. We write in every class; we use journals and we free-write early and often; prime classroom time is spent responding — talking and writing about formal tasks done outside of class.

The course enrolls twenty-five to thirty-five students and meets two or three times a week over our fifteen-week semester. A typical three-hour session begins with a free-write, usually keyed to the demands of the scenario just completed. The first half of the session is spent in peer review of the task, done in small groups. The talk-write-talk-write sequence helps me to create and support a workshop milieu. Over the first ten weeks of the course, these young writers repeatedly practice writing and responding. They try their hand at a writing task for homework; write about and discuss the demands of the task in class; read a sampling of the texts produced by their peers; create a list of performance criteria for the task in small groups; then, working solo, write a signed comment addressed to the author, who will then decide to revise her or his work or submit it for grading. After ten weeks of writing and responding (as well as some work on style, editing, the logic of reports, and so on), our students begin a field research project that recapitulates my encounter with Joe.

In the first week of English 389, I use the "Bunch letter" as I used it above, describing the research we did in designing the course. A brief discussion of individual choices confronting Joe in the letter — begun with a show of hands to indicate which alternatives my students would prefer — makes it clear at the start that, there being no overwhelming classroom voice to indicate a "correct" choice, Joe's choices were real ones. He might well have gone either way. Thus Joe's is not a "model" or an "ideal" letter for its circumstance, if indeed one exists. Our course is designed so that students may expect to learn as Joe has learned — by trying out various tones and voices and by anticipating varied responses from readers.

The Bunch letter shows students where their assignments came from and it illustrates the kinds of decisions they will have to make in writing the assignments. Further, it suggests that their letters will reflect their own decisions and that responses to their letters will reflect their readers' preconceptions. Our classroom milieu will thus have some of the complexity of Joe's writing world. The sample represents one writer's set of workable solutions to a complex set of problems. "In this course," it announces, "you will write out of yourself."

Let me now show how we designed writing tasks based on the material collected, incorporating the special qualities of our "scenarios" that make them different from "cases." After that, I will explain how we use these in class and how our use of them bears upon the issues of context, decision making, constraints, and sequence that seemed so important when I looked at Joe's writing world.

I will use another piece from Joe's portfolio, a blind sales letter, to illustrate our procedure for developing writing tasks. I have already described the setting in which Joe works as a writer, as well as the writing sample he gave me. Here is the letter:

Subject: Phosphorous Wafer Introduction

Dear

[1] Some time ago, you and your company expressed an interest in solid planar phosphorous wafers. We are pleased and excited
[5] to announce the development of P-10. This new dopant
[2] complements our existing dopants: BN 6, BN 12, and BN 24. Among the many advantages afforded to the users of this phos-
[4] phorous source are: elimination of damage and safety hazards from corrosive and toxic off-gasses, very low field oxide penetration, reduction of the amount of electrically inactive phosphorus, and the elimination of chlorine segregation in oxide layers.

P-10 wafers are presently tooled in two and three inch diameters, both .20 inches in thickness. Other sizes, such as four and five inch diameters can be tooled as warranted by user demands.

Preparations for full production of P-10 have already begun
and production lots of the material will be available during
the first quarter of next year.

We have enclosed copies of the data sheets and price lists for
P-10 to supplement the catalog in your possession.

If you should have any questions, please feel free to call on
us. We look forward to further serving you.

[3]   Very truly yours,

JFM:mm
Enc.

To create the writing task, I reviewed Joe's portfolio and reread the
transcript of our interview. I had identified five points in the letter
that I would ask him to discuss.

1. Joe's opening sentence referred to the customer's expressed
interest in phosphorous wafers as the context for his announcement.
Joe did not often take such pains to set context. I asked him to consider
deleting this sentence.

Joe replied: "Let me give you a little bit of history. Phosphorous
wafers are something we've introduced in the past unsuccessfully and
now we are really ready to introduce them. People have been absolutely,
up to this point, driving us crazy, asking for them and in some cases
they had asked — we kept track — they had been six months previous
in writing this letter. All I'm trying to do is have them remember that
they indeed did do that; I don't want it dealt with as an unsolicited
letter."

2. Joe's opening paragraph concluded with the list of other "dopants" (chemical additives) currently available. Joe had told me he
liked to shorten his letters. To explore his reasons for this elaboration,
I asked him to delete just the three items.

Joe's reply: "No. It is important because our competition doesn't
show that many different grades or choices, if you will. I try to get
the point across here, which I did later on in an ad, that we are a
full-line supplier."

3. I saw no request for orders in the letter, so I chose to read the
closing sentence as a very subtle solicitation; I asked him to delete
this line.

Joe completely missed the point of my questioning and indicated
that this was simply a formulaic close. There was no request stated in
the letter, only implied.

4. Focusing on the "advantages" listed in the second paragraph and
recalling that Joe sometimes presented such information in numbered

lists, I showed him this alternative format, to follow his colon in paragraph two:

1. Elimination of damage . . .
2. Very low oxide penetrations . . .
3. Reduction . . .
4. Elimination . . .

Joe immediately preferred the changed format "because they don't have to wade through four or five lines to get the important points."

5. Knowing that he often used the pronoun "I," I pointed to the consistent use of "we" and "us" in the text and asked Joe if he would substitute "I" and "me," beginning with "I am pleased to announce. . . ." He rejected this alternative. "This is Amalgamated. The company is pleased, and I'm part of that whole package."

Joe's responses suggested some of the demands of his writing task; I inferred some others. He had to establish a common frame of reference with his distant (even anonymous) readers; he had to establish an ethos that provided a conduit between the buyer and Amalgamated, a person who was well informed about both need and product; he had to provide the information buyers needed (product features and availability) to begin ordering. The presentation of his letter had to be attractive and easily readable. He did not, however, feel the need to directly request an order.

I laid out a writing task for English 389 with these demands in mind. Here is the scenario:

The Phosphorous Wafer Scenario

You are marketing director for one product line at a corporation that does manufacturing and research in non-ferrous materials for technical applications.

Two years ago, your company introduced a new product — solid phosphorous wafers for use in industrial processes. The phosphorus is used as a dopant — an impurity deliberately introduced into silicon to enhance its properties as a semi-conductor. Sad to say, that earlier product was unsuccessful; yet your customers continue to ask for phosphorous wafers.

Your research and production engineers have now come up with a product that works: it's called "P-10." They describe it as a "solid, planar phosphorous wafer." Your job is to write a letter announcing this new product.

The wafer has several desirable features. Earlier designs produced toxic, corrosive gases; these have been eliminated. They also contained large amounts of phosphorus which was electrically inactive — a bad feature in a semi-conductor; the level of inactive phosphorus has been reduced. Your engineers also boast of "very low field oxide penetration" and elimination of "chlorine segregation in oxide layers."

P-10 wafers will be produced in 2- and 3-inch diameters, .20 inch thick. Other diameters can be produced, on special order. Production has already begun; deliveries can begin in the first quarter of the coming year.

This new product complements your line of boron nitride dopants — BN 6, BN 12, and BN 24 — which are used in similar applications. You have a separate data sheet and price list, which you will send along with your letter.

You are not replying to recent correspondence, even though your letter is going to companies which have requested your new product over the past year. Yet you do not want your letter to be lost in a pile of unsolicited mail on the purchasing agent's desk. Your letter is unsolicited, but you believe it will be read eagerly by the right people.

My familiarity with the context and with the demands and some of the constraints associated with this writing task guides my directives to students and my expectations. I ask them to write the letter as homework; to review and articulate in class the demands of the task; to review in small groups the performance of this task by other writers, and to reflect on the various approaches to the task, including their own, which they have become aware of.

Our peer review session begins with a free-write triggered by "The hardest part of writing the phosphorous wafer letter is _____." Immediately thereafter, students working in small groups swap papers across groups, read the full set of letters they have received, and pick one that everyone feels is well done. They review the task by writing up a list of criteria, using a formula such as this: "A good phosphorous wafer letter does the following _____." We review this list together; the consensus list should include those demands I had identified, and some others as well. Using these criteria as points of reference, peer reviewers write individual, signed responses to one another's work on separate pieces of paper; these are folded so that each subsequent reviewer is blind to previous reviews. I like to provide each writer with at least three independent reviews, not including my own.

I have elaborated this fairly ordinary peer review procedure to make this further point: Reading one another's work carefully enough to produce a written review, our young writers cannot help but take note of approaches and choices somewhat different from their own. Aside from adding to their repertoire of strategies — tones of voice, motivational devices, turns of phrase, formats — this observation of a range of workable approaches (and a few unworkable ones) brings us back to the basics of Joe's writing scenario: projecting an audience, creating an ethos, selecting and arranging subject matter. Each writer assumes full authorial control in making these decisions and, like Joe, is reluctant to alter his or her work at more than one or two points. I believe this is because the letter is written out of the writer's self — those experiences and resources that can be brought to bear on the creative work at hand. The audience imagined arises from audiences one has known; the ethos created arises from "possible selves" one can recall; arrangements of language and format arise in a similar way. This belief — that writing the phosphorous wafer letter is a creative act — is what prompts me to describe the task as a "scenario." The assignment sheet stands in relation to the completed letter in a way similar to the relationship between a script and a play — it wants an ethos to make it real.

For this reason, I think it is useful that our young writers study and respond to and respect a variety of approaches to the phosphorous wafer letter, especially as they bear on ethos. The young writer, busy creating a self to write out of, finds it helpful to have a look at other personae, including ones that appear inappropriate or unacceptable. The presence of adult students experienced in the work world is particularly helpful at this point. Younger students may describe another writer's letter as "too bossy" or "wimpy." But they may later try that same voice themselves. For similar reasons, I want to accept the ethos offered me (so long as I can imagine that it might work) as the best persona that our young writer can discover, for the moment, but also as one manifestation of a growing personality. For help in this, I need only recall that Joe's letter was not at all an "ideal" text, and not very much like the ones I write. Yet it worked. Joe had filled the role.

These work-world tasks gave us the assignments that fill out two-thirds of our course syllabus and that dispense with the need for a business writing textbook.[6] The assignments are rhetorically and intellectually demanding. To do them, a writer must make decisions — visualize audiences, discover an ethos, recognize constraints, be clear about purpose. In formulating these tasks, we English teachers had to put aside "the assignment habit" and to visualize our own audience, purpose, and ethos — a practice we are now learning to apply to our assignments in literature courses as well.

The creation of writing tasks out of work-world situations is not a new thing. Our scenarios become different mainly because with them we teachers recall the work-world milieu and the writer's decisions that generated them, and we try to give our young writers some measure of the authorial control that our work-world writers asserted when we interviewed them. This control is, I believe, essential to the discovery of ethos.

Back to the Field

My interviews with Joe yielded two pieces of material for use in English 389, out of a total of six to eight pieces that I usually assign along with other work in the first ten weeks of a semester.[7] The other pieces were ones collected by Mel Schroeder and by other members of our team. It is clear to me that a business writing teacher does not need a grant or released time to begin collecting one's own material. Indeed, our students learn the procedures quickly.

To consolidate classroom experience, we send students out to do field research on their own. We feel that they should have a chance to learn as we learned — by firsthand observation. We lay the groundwork early in the semester, with a "Futures Invention" exercise, asking for a description of the job each expects to be doing five years hence. (The immediate products of this exercise are a letter of application and a résumé written for this projected job.) The student researchers are directed to recapitulate our procedures, namely, to locate (networking, again) two persons working in that field and to arrange for two interviews and a writing sample. My four- to five-week timetable for the project specifies certain outputs: a progress report, an oral report, and a final written report.

To capture some of the push that collaborative work demands in many jobs, we provide team and solo options. We also provide the questionnaire for the first interview. I supply materials, practice, and models (the Bunch letter, again) for developing question protocols from the writing samples. The job of designing the final report is the occasion for the most challenging decisions a young writer makes in our course; the voice of the researcher, proud of the work outcomes and modest about the tiny scope of the observations, can be a thrilling one for our students to discover.

At three points in this research, students are especially anxious. First, we all know that bankers and accountants and lawyers are busy people, so how can the researchers persuade them to give over time for an interview, not to mention writing samples? These students have already done three interviewing projects: a portrait of a classmate; a job interview (role-playing) based on the letter of application; and a portrait of a student as writer. We now spend time talking about sources of motivation and searching for a usable researcher's persona to give heart to our young researchers. The first students who report successful interviews to the class — the pathfinders — finally convince their fellows that the job can be done.

Students become anxious again when they look through a folder containing eight or ten pieces of writing: "What can I ask this banker without being rude?" Armed with a set of specific questions about specific pieces (and forewarned about gaucheries: "Don't mention spelling or punctuation."), they feel less vulnerable. Again, first reports of success in the field give heart to the timid.

The third anxious moment comes when it is time to design the final report. We have done several reports by this time. Recalling that Joe had had the chance to look for models in the office files, we set out an array of reports written by forerunners in the course. Each team finally must make its own decisions, create its own presentation.

I offer this description of our course and of my students' research project in order to make some final points.

I decided some time ago that as a writing teacher I must be able to foresee a "payoff" (Dixie Goswami's word) for each writing task. A payoff to the writer, that is. A grade is one sort of reward, but this field research offers some others:

1. Most important to me as teacher is the young writer's firsthand observation, which students tell me *validates the course* for them. What I have told students about, they now see for themselves.

2. Student writers are in control of their own research. Their observations are unique; peers and teachers can give advice, but not directions. The *decisions* are the students'.

3. Each writer must present herself or himself — in person and in writing — in such a way as to elicit help from older writers and collaboration from peers. This "dealing with people" is a powerful *stimulus to maturity* in basic rhetorical functions such as "projecting audience" and "discovering an ethos." Even adult students can be naïve about how they come across; each person on our research team talks about how the field research changed us as writers.

4. Each writer *makes contact* with persons in her or his chosen career world. These contacts sometimes provide offers of jobs or internships for our students and sometimes prompt changes in career paths, equally valuable as outcomes.

We have written elsewhere about the value of this experience for ourselves as teachers, and I have reiterated this above. One dimension of this changed attitude needs repeating. When my students are doing these tasks, I can recall how complex are the demands they struggle with. I have been there myself. When these young researchers express anxiety before an interview, I recall the feeling. The sources of my own learning are recent and vivid, and so I feel better able to make my own learning strategies available to young writers.

There are other payoffs for teachers, besides this one:

1. Today, my students bring me portfolios and case studies from their own field research. Their reports give us an occasion to share our excitement over the writing worlds we have discovered, and they occasionally provide me with materials for new scenarios.

2. Our practice in creating writing situations for English 389 has affected our practice in creating writing tasks for students in our literature courses. These tasks begin to look like our scenarios.

3. Our research has given us occasion to begin some private consulting at local firms — including Joe's. Not only is this work exciting, but it also permits us to continue our observations.

The final lesson is this: If these youngsters can get their nerve up to ask working professionals for a look into their writing worlds, so can we teachers. The payoffs that await us are no smaller than those awaiting our students.

Let me return at last to my initial question: Is this sort of excursion and retraining readily available to English faculty? Here at Canisius we had a rich supply of local alumni willing to help us; we had the direction and advice of innovative researchers, Odell and Goswami; and we had some of the luxuries of grant support — clerical help, released time, and team support. Few teachers have such advantages.

However, Canisius today is not a research institution; we have heavy teaching loads; we currently have no graduate students to help in research; our English department includes no one who, when hired, had a background in rhetorical theory or research. Could we at Canisius have managed this undertaking without help? I believe that, aided by an account of our experiences and procedures as well as by the published work of Odell and Goswami, we could.

Field research by Odell and Goswami, by Knoblauch, and by our own team at Canisius tells us that writers in nonacademic settings balance complex issues of audience, ethos, and subject in their rhetorical decision making. Our experience in applying these observations shows that some of the complexity of this decision making can be recapitulated

in writing done in our classrooms, especially in matters of ethos. We
believe that this practice helps our young writers to mature.

Notes

1. The primary design work for English 389 was done by Melvin Schroeder;
   other members of the team were Kenneth Sroka, Roger Stephenson,
   Joseph Sandman, Candalene McCombs, Lucella Dumpert, and Maire
   Courtney. Some aspects of our work are reported in Schroeder and
   Sroka, "The Canisius Project: From Field-work to Classroom," *Journal
   of Advanced Composition* II (1981): 127–37; and in Lauerman, Schroeder,
   Sroka, and Stephenson, "Workplace and Classroom: Principles for
   Designing Writing Courses," in Lee Odell and Dixie Goswami, *Writing
   in Non-Academic Settings* (New York: Guilford Press, 1986), 427–50.

2. Edward P. J. Corbett, "What Classical Rhetoric Has to Offer the Teacher
   and the Student of Business and Professional Writing" (this volume)
   uses the phrase "the personal character of the speaker or writer."

3. C. H. Knoblauch, "Intentionality in the Writing Process: A Case Study,"
   College Composition and Communication 31 (May 1980): 153–58.

4. We always impose at least one constraint on the writer's decision
   making: we ask for "perfect copy" — typed, edited, error-free text.

5. See our essay in Odell and Goswami.

6. As I pointed out earlier, my colleague Mel Schroeder designed this
   course and created most of the assignments and materials. Everyone
   teaching the course creates an individual syllabus based on his work,
   and we share our work. Thus the syllabus has become a collaborative
   effort.

7. Descriptions of some other materials prepared for English 389 and other
   courses in writing for the professions are available in the publications
   cited earlier. See also the course syllabus and cases in Goswami et al.,
   Writing in the Professions (Washington, D.C.: American Institutes for
   Research, 1981).

11 A Critique of the Rhetorical and Organizational World of Business Communications Texts

Brian Gallagher
LaGuardia Community College

> "I go about my business, like any
> good citizen — that's all."
> "And what *is* your business?"
> "The spectacle of the world."
> — Gabriel Nash and Nick Dormer
> in Henry James, *The Tragic Muse*

Even a cursory look through recent issues of *College English* or *College Composition and Communication* or any of a dozen other journals devoted to the theory and practice of teaching writing will quickly establish that business writing has received scant attention, and little significant analysis, from those most regularly concerned with teaching writing in American colleges and universities. During the years in which writing finally established itself as a subject worthy of the rigorous academic scrutiny long given literature, courses in business writing essentially remained what composition courses had for so long been: an unacknowledged, unexplored, unexamined segment of the English curriculum.

This general neglect of business writing is, I think, traceable to two attitudes, contradictory but ultimately complementary, which dominate American thinking on business. On the one hand, there is the notion that, as Tocqueville put it a century and a half ago, "In democracies nothing is greater or more brilliant than commerce; it attracts the attention of the public and fills the imagination of the multitudes; all energetic persons are directed toward it."[1] Because of this exalted view, as Santayana shrewdly noted, Americans often revere business virtually as an end itself, rather than as the ultimate medium of expression for that evident materialism which pervades our culture:

> It is sometimes said that the ruling passion in America is the love of money. That seems to me a complete mistake. The ruling

passion is the love of *business,* which is something quite different. . . . The lover of business . . . [finds] his joy . . . in that business itself and in its further operation, in making it greater and better organized and a mightier engine of the general life.[2]

On the other hand, there is in America the notion that business — which, we should recall, is a disyllabic reduction of the trisyllabic *busyness,* whose most obvious opposite is *idleness* — is seen as a morally uplifting activity, the one and only fully valid expression of the Protestant work ethic. As such, it must necessarily be a compendium of tedious, boring tasks, the faithful performance of which not only safely produces a regular salary, but also conveys some secular measure of that righteousness the adolescent Christ exhibited in his scrupulous disputations with the doctors in the temple, where he professed himself to be "about my Father's business" (Luke 2:49). Common phrases such as "to mean business" and "to get down to business" derive from this vague but powerful cultural equation of *business* with *seriousness* and its opposition to some of the sweeter things of life: pleasure, contemplation, speculation, dalliance.

These two visions, business as a risky, compelling adventure and business as a dull, righteous duty, are epitomized by two common cultural images: the robber baron and the workaday drudge. Neither image, it appears, holds much appeal for most composition teachers, at least that majority of the professedly humanist stripe. As a result, many have foresworn, sometimes with condescension and smugness, the business world on which the academy borders and from which it has long taken much of its revenue and, increasingly, its direction.[3]

Because of this general neglect, courses that deal with writing in business situations are now frequently taught under the aegis of "business communications," whether by business departments or more commonly by English departments, which simply adopt one of the many large business communications texts on the market and cut out a business writing course from it, often none too effectively. In either case, two problems exist. First, since all of these texts apply a similarly rigid and semantically based version of communications theory, *business* writing must inevitably be taught as a narrow subactivity of a larger activity, *business* communication. Second, and probably more importantly, these texts make very few connections, either explicit or implicit, between business *writing* and the kinds of writing that students have done and are doing in other courses or between the text's approach to writing and those evolved through the intensive writing, linguistic, and literary research of the last three decades.

The purpose of this essay is to analyze the rhetorical and organizational world of "business communications" as it is depicted in some current textbooks, including several relatively new to the market, as well as in some standard works now in a fourth, fifth, or sixth edition. In conclusion, I briefly suggest why and how approaches to teaching business communications need to change. Much of the critique scores the indicative failings and limitations of these texts before moving on to their various virtues, which include a wealth of exercises and assignments from which to choose. Let it be said at the outset, however, that these texts represent some of the best that are now available and that any writing teacher of talent could certainly make good use of them through a careful selection and a thorough reworking of their materials. Still, the very fact that using them successfully demands such extensive adaptation bespeaks the very problematical pedagogical status of writing for business and the professions at the moment.

Textual Paradigms and Reader Management

> Rhetoric may be defined as the
> faculty of observing in any
> given case the available means
> of persuasion.
>
> — Aristotle, *Rhetoric*

Two things are immediately obvious about all of these business communications texts: they are big and full, running five hundred to eight hundred pages in small print and large-sized formats, and they are very much more conditioned by the workaday drudge image of business than by its opposite. These are heavy tomes, both to carry and to read.

In their attempt to be comprehensive, the authors of many of these texts stretch what could easily be a single chapter (for example, on similar kinds of business letters) into two or three, or turn what might be an effective prefatory section (for example, on basic communication principles) into detailed treatises, sometimes consuming more than a quarter of the text. These expanded sections usually do little more than prove over and over that "your success in your career . . . will depend to a great extent upon your ability to communicate, perhaps more than any other ability."[4] Often *communication* is defined so broadly — "Members of management spend about 90 percent of their working days communicating"[5] — that it covers almost every activity in the business day, save for trips to the water cooler and toilet.

In their desire to be inclusive, the authors of many texts lack *form* ⟩ (
in the specific sense Kenneth Burke describes it in his "Lexicon '
Rhetoricae": "A work has form in so far as one part of it leads the
reader to anticipate another part, to be gratified by the sequence."[6]
About the only kind of anticipation these works create is directive:
readers know they will be told, usually in excruciatingly mundane
detail, exactly how to write a report, compose a memo, give a speech,
or even just how to go about their reading. Consider, for instance, the
implication of the pseudo-directives, even to the colors for coding, in
the following passage:

> The speech should be typed in large print. (Very large-sized
> type — often referred to by typewriter manufacturers as "orator
> style" — is available.) It is also a good idea to leave plenty of
> space on the paper between lines and paragraphs. Key ideas can
> be underlined in red to remind the speaker to give those points
> emphasis. Green marks can be noted here and there in the margins
> to remind the speaker to look up and at the audience. At
> appropriate places, the marginal note *smile* may be written.[7]

Communication in business ultimately exists to produce profit and
not just to pass information, a fact that makes business communication
necessarily narrower and less disinterested than many other forms of
communication. Rather than trying to establish a limited number of
clear, valid principles for the use of language in the system of business,
these texts inundate readers with the minutiae of business formats
and procedures, with long lists of information, flowcharts, diagrams,
and checklists, as if the learners were incapable of imaginative application of general principles to any specific situation.

Akin to the penchant for reducing information to flowcharts and
diagrams is an overreliance on classification — as a pedagogical tool
and even an epistemological principle — in most of these texts. One
author, for instance, classifies reports by "Time Intervals," "Authori-
zation," "Degree of Formality," and six other factors,[8] but fails to
illuminate the important distinctions (and decisions) a business writer
must make concerning these overlapping factors. Too often the authors
of these texts prefer a neat solution, whether it be a clear diagram or
a rigid classification system, to an exploration of the many norms,
often ambiguous and sometimes conflicting, that govern even the
simplest varieties of business communications.

Ultimately, such organizational thinking imposes a too neat rigidity
on material that otherwise is quite sound and sensible. For instance,
one text reduces business communications principles to the "7 C's"
(completeness, conciseness, consideration, concreteness, clarity, cour-

tesy, and correctness), to which the authors devote two chapters and produce in summary form on the inside cover.[9] Another text dutifully lists "objectives" for each part, but does not distinguish between vague aims like "develop[ing] an understanding of the communications process and related behavior" (which covers the better part of human existence) and concrete, useful goals like "compil[ing] an effective personal résumé."[10]

What too often gets stressed, precisely because they are tangible and explicit, are the appearance and format of various kinds of documents, usually at the expense of understanding the content and deeper purposes.[11] Most authors start their chapters on business letters with a detailed discussion of format and layout. One text even begins with a discussion of the "quality, color and size" of the stationery.[12] Many lay heavy stress on format editing, urging, as does *Communicating in Business*,[13] the use of short paragraphs, topic headings, wide margins, graphic aids, and other devices (which can easily become gimmicks if they have no essential relation to the text being arranged through them). By contrast, little is said about the content of such messages and even less about the integral use of messages in business.

Often similar kinds of letters, which might be simply and better explained as very like those kinds already discussed except in a few particulars, receive a whole section or even a whole chapter of their own. Are "sales letters" so very different from "persuasive requests" that they demand an additional sixteen pages in a following chapter?[14] Or are "neutral," "good news," and "bad news" messages so difficult and different from one another that they need two chapters and more than seventy pages of explanation?[15]

Many of these texts in their attempt to be inclusive extend themselves into basic writing and reading skills. One author at least is honest enough to assert, "I believe the major thrust of a business communications text should be toward the improvement of basic writing skills and toward the application of those skills to business writing situations" and to include a good deal of basic writing instruction in her chapters on "Basic Writing Principles."[16] Others make passing reference to basic writing skills in the text and relegate the better part of the issue to an appendix called "A Guide to Correctness in Writing"[17] or "A Brief Guide to English Usage."[18] Obviously, most of these authors envision their student readers as still needing help with the rudiments of writing. Unfortunately, though, basic writing instruction is almost entirely confined to prescriptive grammar and usage rules, making writing seem chiefly a matter of obeying rather than discovering, of regularizing rather than expressing. Years after composition teachers have abandoned, on very solid evidence, a grammar-based approach to teaching writing, these texts still take such an approach.

Several of these texts also concern themselves at length with reading, which usually means some application of the Gunning Fog index to what students are reading and will be writing. (In addition, one text opens by heavily stressing speed reading.)[19] While the application of such quantifiable indices is debatable in many situations, it is especially problematic in business situations. As Walker Gibson has noted in the clearest analysis of one kind of business writing, advertising, "We don't want to be brief, we only want to appear brief, we want to *seem* businesslike."[20] "An adwriter," he asserts, "is inconceivable without modification; his product has got to be *best-selling, delightfully different, finest, all brand-new.*"[21] Similarly, in other business situations, it will not always be in the interest of the business writer to avoid those polysyllabic and jargon words, those neologisms, and those longer-than-average sentences that most readability indices score as ineffective. For instance, any plan you are advocating will appear better as "cost-effective" rather than "cheap," and that plan will likely be better received if it can be tied to certain jargon words current in the institution. "To impact" is an atrocious verb, but if your supervisor asks you how a certain measure is likely "to impact on" the company, you would do better to answer the question than to dispute the verbal sense. And when writers in business are forced to advocate measures about which they are unsure, putting their decision in long sentences with several qualifying phrases not only allows them to indicate their uncertainty, but it also provides some evidence of their negative impressions should that decision prove unwise in future. The fact is that in business one does not always want to be read too easily or too unequivocally.[22]

One reason for the sameness of these texts is the sameness of the sources upon which they rely. The works of S. I. Hayakawa are frequently referenced, if usually just to stress that "we must consciously be concerned with problems of semantics," as one text reminds us.[23] Alfred Korzybski is also regularly invoked for his scientifically oriented idea of "general semantics," a concept seemingly important to many of these authors, but one they typically define and apply in a manner little different from "ordinary" semantics; for example, Treece describes general semantics as "basically concerned with the way language affects our thought and behavior."[24] Still, despite their reliance on semantics, these texts really make few specific applications of its ideas, such as using the notion of "semantic overload" to explain why "bureaucratese" or sentences that contain too many embedded clauses do not readily convey meaning.

A third expert frequently cited is the psychologist Abraham Maslow, whose "need hierarchy," ranging from the physiological needs (food, shelter, rest) up to "self-actualization" needs (achieving one's "fullest potential"), is employed to make the point that business situations typically deal with the possibility of fulfilling the "higher" needs, an observation that the writers of the more persistently directive texts might have done better to bear in mind. Several texts also employ, rather dubiously, the ideas of "transactional analysis," derived from works such as Berne's *Games People Play* and Harris's *I'm OK — You're OK*.[25]

Beyond this very limited range of sources — almost all the other nonbusiness works cited are also in semantics — these texts rely for support exclusively on works in business management, analysis, and communication. One text, for instance, takes half a page and cites eighteen sources, *all from business-oriented publications*, to support the idea that "business communications skills significantly influence . . . advancement to executive positions."[26] With so much matter that might be brought to bear interestingly and enlighteningly on business communication and business writing — for example, structural linguistics, sociolinguistics, psycholinguistics, writing theory, semiotics, history, sociology, literary theory, even deconstruction and Marxism[27] — this severe restriction seems unnecessary, unwarranted, unfair. These texts are formulated within a closed system, and they attempt to confine their readers imaginatively within that system.

In 1922 one contributor to a volume on *Civilization in the United States: An Inquiry by Thirty Americans* averred, with a mixture of admiration and revulsion, that "modern business derives from three passions in this order, namely: the passion for things, the passion for personal grandeur and the passion for power."[28] Over time this rapacious vision of American business has been displaced — perhaps most noticeably in the present onto grandiose television soap operas like *Dallas* and *Dynasty* — by a vision of business as the inevitable American fate, by the idea that, as Calvin Coolidge blandly but truly put it, "the business of America is business." Compare the heroic, if adversary, stance evident in Garrett's critique of the business mentality with the timid, diffident tone found in these texts. There is little wonder then that one author expresses in passing what so many others clearly imply, namely, "Most of us consider writing something of a chore."[29]

Textual Fantasies and Business Realities

> "The question is," said Alice,
> "whether you *can* make words
> mean so many different things."
> "The question is," said Humpty
> Dumpty, "which is to be master
> — that's all."
>
> — Lewis Carroll,
> *Through the Looking-Glass*

One text seems rather to give the game away in a pithy assignment: " 'One cannot not communicate.' Discuss."[30] If communication includes virtually every activity in business — and a number of these texts have extensive sections on nonverbal communication — then it is impossible to separate in any meaningful pedagogical way "business acts" from "communication acts." As a result of this underlying confusion, these texts are replete with overly general, and so specifically unhelpful, pronouncements about the way language is employed in business. Such pronouncements fall into two categories. The first deals with obvious facts about communication. That "our world is filled with words"[31] and that we "live in a world of communications, which influence our actions"[32] and that "our minds serve as storehouses of information"[33] are statements that really do not inform the reader. The second kind of pronouncements offers supposed advice for specific business situations, but just restates commonsense maxims: for example, "Always prepare for an interview before you go to it."[34]

And although many of these texts urge "conciseness" as one of the primary virtues of business writing, they are none of them concise. Wordy passive constructions are common, as are phrasings that suggest the readers are destined either to be autonomous functionaries ("Select proper listening mode")[35] or grammatical victims in the business world ("Do not be tripped into putting a comma between the subject and verb").[36] Even when texts attempt to be helpful on writing matters, they are often wrongheaded or outdated. One writer laments, "Unfortunately, too many of us know too little about the conventional rules of English grammar,"[37] implying that such rules need be learned (and so must be taught), a stance that directly contradicts more than fifty years of writing research, supported by linguistic research, that shows no direct correlation between learning grammar and the improvement of writing skills. As Chomsky succinctly puts it, "Language is not taught, for the most part. Rather, it is learned, by mere exposure to the data."[38] Yet the language data to which students are exposed in these texts would likely make them into plodding, sometimes careless, and almost always dull writers.

On no single point are these texts so simplistic as when giving advice about just what kind of language to use and in what size units. One text, for example, lists as the final of its (mostly questionable) ten "Principles for Effective Writing" the admonition "Write to Express and Not to Impress,"[39] a directive that would be especially unhelpful in a business world where one *must* often impress as well as inform one's superiors to achieve any measure of success. (Business writers would do better, I think, to attend to what Roland Barthes, writing in another context, intriguingly terms "the morale of the discourse,"[40] which is maintained through a balance of information, attitude, and shared knowledge.) It is likewise an article of faith among all these authors "to prefer the short to the long word"[41] and "to avoid too many big words,"[42] points that often have dubious value in business situations. In many situations, business favors polysyllabic words (*negligible* for *small*, *supercede* for *replace*, even *communicate* for *tell*), as well as awkward sounding compounds (*throughput, interface, can-do*). Not to employ these locutions in appropriate contexts is to make one's business writing appear too simple, too uninitiated, too stylistically fussy.

Most of these texts do not look at the real and complex way language functions in American business. Therefore, much of the advice they offer on matters like vocabulary is unhelpful at best, dead wrong at worst. One text, for example, offers a list of "colorful words" one might substitute for "drab ones," but any business writer who switches *snoop* for *investigate*, *pocket* for *receive*, or *wicked* for *bad* (especially modifying *idea*) is not likely to remain a business writer for long.[43] These so-called colorful words represent, in almost all cases, violations of linguistic business decorum, which demands, in the main, that discourse maintain a dispassionate, factual, positive tone on the part of its implied writer. (The real writer can be angry, vexed, or ecstatic as long as these stronger emotions do not show through.)

Of a piece with the advice to use short words is the usual advice to "keep your sentences short on average."[44] Unfortunately, this admonition would deprive the future business writer of what can be a very useful weapon in the necessarily competitive world of business, namely, the qualified statement. In many business writing situations, and particularly with internal messages, it is crucial to indicate contexts for and make reservations about observations. Besides, the ability to contextualize and qualify descriptions is a useful self-protective mechanism when matters do not turn out well and people are looking back to see who might take the blame.

Although these texts sometimes suggest that they are meant "even for executives,"[45] the fact is that they are really written for potential middle-management personnel — *and* that they are written to keep middle-managers forever in their place. Despite their repeated stress on the centrality of communication to business and on communication as the quintessential business act, these texts more than occasionally posit an implicit split between writing and success in business. In asserting, "As you move up the executive ladder in business, probably you will spend more and more of your time writing,"[46] the author is guilty of begging, or at least obscuring, the question. The fact of the matter is that writing is more cause than effect: those who write effectively, who manipulate the language of business best, are very often the persons who *are* moved to higher positions, precisely because the higher positions allow them the opportunity to do more of what they do well, namely, to write effective business prose. Yet the stress of virtually all these texts is on writing as a service function, as a means of accomplishing one's present task, thereby ignoring the fact that the most successful business writing is self-serving as well as other-serving. Although these texts have a wealth of information on communications flow (up, down, across, in and out) in business institutions, not one of them really speaks to the question of language and power in a capitalist society.

While it has become a linguistic (and semiotic) commonplace that "knowing a language as an instrument of communication is to be able to understand its principal subcodes and to know how to use them in appropriate situations,"[47] none of these texts makes any consistent effort to explicate the complex but definitive subcodes that go to make business writing. And it is this failure that ultimately means their users will not be sufficiently empowered to use language to their greatest advantage in a business environment. As John Searle observes, "Every institutional fact is underlain by a (system of) rule(s) of the form 'X counts as Y in context C'" — and it is precisely the entire dependence of the relation of "X and Y" on context that distinguishes "institutional fact" from "brute fact."[48] For a simple example, it would be proper if perhaps callous to speak of "deadly diseases" in terms of "costs" and "profits" in the context of a pharmaceutical company or a hospital, but anyone who agreed to care for a relative dying of one of these diseases "on spec" (that is, balancing actual costs against a possible inheritance) would be improper to the point of immorality within a family context. And when we consider the contextual implications of phrasings like these two sentences on a sample résumé in one text — "Completed four-year degree in two years and nine months of un- interrupted study" and "No absence from school or work because of illness in past three years"[49] — we can see that many of these business communication texts are being, at best, disingenuous. What these assertions "count as" in the context of business is the willing admission of subservience and bought loyalty to any employing institution: these writers are presenting themselves as the kind of persons who would willingly make any sacrifice to serve.

There are, of course, balancing mentions in these texts of how power in business comes to be exercised both on the small and the large scale. One text, for instance, stresses how "eye gaze relates to power,"[50] but often, as in this case, these observations are cast more in terms of surviving the imposition of power than in terms of asserting it within the specific context of business. Some of these texts are quite specific about avoiding the use of the generic male pronoun, making it clear how its habitual use necessarily predisposes readers to accept — and so hierarchize — various business functions by sex. Other texts, though, seem less cognizant of just how male-dominated American business imagery is. One text, for example, opens with an analysis of an ordinary communications scenario, in which male workers converse on the way to work: "There is a joke or two, some comments about politics, a few words about the coming football game, and some raves about the new woman at the company switchboard"[51] — the "raves," we can assume, are not about her telephonic skills. Many of these texts, understandably, find it difficult to choose between a realistic reflection of sexist or racist discourse in the workplace — undoubtedly Lesikar's scenario is a basically accurate reflection of the conversations of many male workers — and the imposition of a glaringly false vision of sexual and racial equality in business. One text, in sketching out its "dilemmas" for solution, makes a particular point of including many with identifiably ethnic names — "Becky Trujillo," "Raj Singh," and "Roosevelt Jackson"[52] — in positions of some importance, but it is doubtful that any but the most unobservant students would take these as reflecting the real distribution of power and authority in business. What is lacking in all of these maneuvers is a real sense of how, in an admittedly conservative, male-dominated business envi- ronment, *all* potential workers can employ language to gain, maintain, and extend their power.

The manner in which these texts (mis)handle one point, the "you attitude," and virtually ignore another, the significant impact of word processing on written business communication, epitomizes their inability to cast themselves as the students' advocate rather than as the representative of the business institutions for which these students will come to work. According to the standardized concept, "The you attitude speaks to the reader and makes the reader's problem your concern,"[53] and it "project[s] the benefits the product or service will bring to the readers — not the writer."[54] As such, it should be seen as very much a piece of artifice, an exaggerated and self-conscious rhetorical masking of the reader's only real function in a business situation, namely, to consume, whether a product or a service. Unfortunately, most of these texts do not treat the "you attitude" as a rhetorical device, one dependent on the recognition of some pretense by both the writer and reader (encoder and decoder), but rather insist that it means "treating people the way they like to be treated,"[55] and even that "the you-attitude is sincere" and as such it is part of "a sound and workable system of communication . . . based on openness and honesty."[56] By urging the simplicity and sincerity of the "you attitude," these texts do students a considerable disservice. If, as Raymond Williams puts it, "Language . . . is not a medium; it is a constitutive element of material social practice . . . meaning is always *produced*; it is never simply expressed,"[57] then the business writing students should be told, if not specifically taught, how the "you attitude" produces meaning quite apart from having to express any sincere concern for the recipient–buyer. The pedagogical point is not whether the "you attitude" is manipulative — for, *parti pris*, it is — but rather how it works as manipulation, how its decoders are, within the confines of a capitalist system, manipulated even though they recognize the encoder's attempt to manipulate.

With one partial exception (see below), none of these texts follows up on the obvious fact that, as one author notes in passing, "the potential contribution of the word-processing concept is staggering."[58] As I have argued elsewhere, word processing is a great break with all previous ways of producing written products:

> Word processing is a *very efficient* electronic system for recording, formatting, editing, storing, retrieving, combining, and printing documents. The key difference between a word processed document and one produced by even the fanciest electronic typewriter is that the entire word processed document is first and foremost an electronic entity. As such, it is always and everywhere subject to instantaneous alteration. The production of a material text — i.e., characters imprinted on a piece of paper — is very much a discrete act, a material realization of the latest electronically created version of the document. With a word processor, one is never limited by the relative immutability of words in a typewritten or

handwritten document. Even in draft versions, these will allow
only a certain amount of correction, revision, and alteration; then
they must be retyped or rewritten. *With a word processor, however,
one need type only a single version of any document.*[59]

What this shift from materially fixed to electronically alterable
documents means in a business setting is almost incalculable. Basically,
it means that documents can be reproduced in endless variations, from
simple letters in a thousand personalized forms to lengthy documents
that pull in sections from another dozen, or even another hundred,
documents. For business, word processing is not so much a time saver
as a time redistributor. More time can be put into creating the basic
version of a text simply because so much less time is needed to produce
each individualized version of it. Similarly, reports can often be edited
and rearranged within minutes to create different versions for the
different audiences receiving them. Also, standard formats — which
are certainly important to business, but which most business communications texts now make the chief focus of their instruction — can
be electronically stored, a procedure that not only saves time in
constructing reports, but also provides a ready-made structure into
which information can be set. Moreover, word processing encourages
a more exploratory, discovery-oriented form of writing, since additions,
deletions, and rearrangements are so quickly made and remade. In
future, the most efficient executives may well be those willing to sit
before the computer keyboard, creating and reworking their own
documents.

It is just the present generation of students who could profit most
from being thoroughly introduced to the business possibilities of word
processing, since they might well have the chance to implement uses
of the new technology in an environment where many of their veteran
co-workers are suspicious of, and so reluctant to take advantage of,
computers. In ignoring the impact of word processing on business
writing, these texts deprive their users of the one area of new knowledge
that might provide them with a significant edge in moving into many
business positions.

The fact that certain sections, such as those on the "you attitude,"
could profitably be deleted from these business communication texts
and replaced with others, such as one on the business implications of
word processing, should not obscure the fact that all of these texts are
already too long and too prosy. Cyril Connolly once fancifully observed,
"Imprisoned in every fat man a thin man is wildly signalling to be let
out."[60] So it is with these oversized business communications texts:
inside them is a lean, brief "rhetoric of business" — perhaps something

akin to a business version of Strunk and White's *The Elements of Style* — wildly signalling to be let out. This business rhetoric would substitute general guidelines for endless instances and directives, and would derive from classical rhetorical premises, such as Aristotle's assertion that "a statement is persuasive and credible either because it is directly self-evident or because it appears to be proved from other statements that are so,"[61] *combined with* modern understandings of how "persuasiveness itself is a profoundly conventional notion, a reflection of cultural and historical attitudes."[62] What Jonathan Culler writes about literary texts, "To understand the language of a text is to recognize the world to which it refers,"[63] is no less true for texts that derive from and refer to the language construct that is the "world of business." And it is just the ability to maneuver within such a construct — which differs substantially from the construct of everyday language — that these business communications texts fail to impart to students, for all their hundreds of pages of material on language in business.

Using Current Texts

> For *true* and *false* are attri-
> butes of speech, not of things.
>
> — Thomas Hobbes, *Leviathan*

Since matters concerning business writing and business communications texts are not, unhappily, likely to change dramatically in the near future, it will continue to be the task of effective business writing teachers to excerpt and amplify a rhetoric of business from whatever text they are using. Fortunately, most texts do contain valuable, accurate sections on writing that can form the basis for such a task. Haggblade, for instance, lays out and elaborates on "two basic truths about writing," points on which there can be little dispute: "To write well, or even to write at all for that matter, one has to have something to say," and "Unclear writing generally reflects unclear thinking."[64] More specifically, Treece rightfully stresses the need to avoid a "doubtful tone" in virtually all business documents, and goes on to specify common words that almost always signal doubt to the reader.[65] Himstreet and Baty provide a very helpful list of "frequently misused words," with clear explanations of the particular difficulties they can cause in business communication: for example, "*You*. Do not use *you* to mean 'I' or 'people in general.' . . . Such misuses can make a reader think his or her abilities have been underestimated."[66] A number of texts, such as

Effective Business Communications,[67] stress the use of "action words,"
which reflect the primary reality that business is first and foremost a
world of actions rather than of contemplations. Some texts (for example,
Communicating in Business)[68] suggest verbal strategies for "selling
yourself" through résumés, letters, and other documents, an approach
that contrasts favorably and realistically with the overly sincere and
straightforward tone they adopt in many other sections. Much of what
they say about overtly selling oneself might also be translated into
means of covertly selling oneself — as qualified for promotions, new
positions, even jobs with other companies — through the language
one employs in handling a job on a daily basis.

Concerning the communication act itself, several of these authors
provide good, sound insights. Haggblade lays out clearly and rationally
the major advantages and disadvantages of communicating "in written
form" as opposed to other forms.[69] Lesikar introduces and makes
intermittent use of the notion of "encoding" and "decoding" messages,
an idea that can be used to get to the concept of specific "business
subcodes," which must necessarily be involved in such a process.[70]
Even more to the point, Himstreet and Baty early on introduce a key
idea (but do not apply it to the specific kind of business documents
they discuss): "Information is the property of a signal or message
enabling it to convey something a recipient finds both unpredictable
and meaningful."[71]

Several of these texts also, if more through repeated practice than
sustained explanation, make it clear that much business writing can
effectively become a routine matter *without* losing for its recipient the
requisite degree of unpredictability and meaningfulness Himstreet and
Baty characterize as the essence of communication. As Dorothy Augustine notes, "Reading is not simply the inverse of writing"[72] — and
a number of these authors do make it clear that roteness, if intelligently
applied, in the preparation of a message does not mean roteness in
its reception. A business writer can, for instance, develop a knack for
encoding (and almost endlessly recoding) sales messages that will
produce the desired response from their decoders: that is, readers will
buy the product or service. And there are, in such circumstances,
standard inducements — "free" gifts, trial usage periods, the option
to pay by credit card — that will continue, if properly phrased, to
entice buyers even though they have been similarly enticed before.
As Aristotle put it (and that icon of American business, Benjamin
Franklin, heartily concurred), "Habits also are pleasant; for as soon as
a thing has become habitual, it is virtually natural."[73] It is one of the
chief virtues of a number of these texts that students are shown how

"habitual" ways of constructing many kinds of business documents result in a saving of both time and intellectual energy that can be better spent on *sui generis* pieces of business writing. (Too often, though, these texts stress the habitual as more a matter of format and surface organization than of tone, rhetorical stance, persuasive phrasing, and so forth.) As Richard Lloyd-Jones has observed, "Most of what we call creation is really adeptness in handling conventions of language and social situations."[74] These business communications texts do work hard, if not always efficiently or interestingly, to give students such adeptness with the conventions of business language.

Other strong points of these textbooks are their hundreds of realistic, useful, business writing assignments and the factual information they provide, such as Seigle's detailed appendix on "Library Sources for Business Research"[75] and Treece's discussion of the different kinds of research resources, both secondary and primary, with her evaluation of the advantages and disadvantages of each.[76] Lesikar gives a fine sample "long, formal report," which probably conveys more information about how to construct such a document than the many pages of directives this and other textbooks contain.[77]

Sigband and Bateman's *Communicating in Business* is a notable exception to the general neglect of word processing in these texts. Although the authors do not take their analysis far enough, they are absolutely correct in stressing how important it is to see word processing as a "system" that links various personnel (initiator of communication, supervisor, administrative assistant, and others) and is backed by a "secretarial support system."[78] And one suspects that other authors will soon realize that word processing is not "just another tool" for producing written messages but a substantially new way of controlling all of the written material within one's business domain.

Still and all, these business communications textbooks would be much more useful if they were reconceptualized and made rather more different from one another in the process. This reconceptualization should stem from a stronger recognition of the great differences between written and other forms of communication, both within and without business. And reconceptualization should derive from the perception that the creation of business documents, which often seems too simply routine, is by no means an uninteresting act, for subtle and important manipulations of language within a narrow context can be a challenging activity. The aim of these textbooks, as primers on writing in the capitalist system, should be to make their users always just a little better communicators than the co-workers with whom they will inevitably be in some kind of competition for advancement. As a first step toward achieving this aim, writers of business communication and business writing texts might enact what Thomas Kuhn would term a "paradigm shift"[79] — instead of considering their users as essentially dullards who learn chiefly through linguistic drill and practice, they might consider them as learners capable of absorbing and applying the basic linguistic principles of American capitalism and also capable of having some linguistic fun in the process.

Envisioning New Texts

> Languages differ from one
> another in the way they divide
> objects into categories.
>
> — James Britton, *Language and Learning*

If, following Wittgenstein,[80] we think of language as both a set of social practices and a set of instruments, it becomes apparent that there is a real need for business writing (and business communication) textbooks that are at once more radical and more practical than those available at present. By admitting to and incorporating within them something of the typically competitive, occasionally avaricious, and always profit-oriented aspect of business, these new texts would not only become less uncritical of the business world whose language they expound, but they would also become more interesting and more enlightening thereby.

Such texts might, for instance, be sufficiently radical to start their discussion of résumés by asking students to probe Dorothy Parker's gibing little poem:

Résumé

Razors pain you;
Rivers are damp;
Acids stain you;
And drugs cause cramp.
Guns aren't lawful;
Nooses give;
Gas smells awful;
You might as well live.[81]

Because Parker's satire is predicated on the reader's precise foreknowledge of just what a résumé is (namely, a detailed, interconnected statement of professional accomplishments and qualifications), *and* because students immediately grasp the intended conflict between the mock-logical list of reasons for eschewing suicide and a genuine résumé, the poem serves well to initiate a discussion of just how functionally specialized and linguistically limited a document a résumé is.[82] Were the poem untitled or alternately titled (say, "Conclusion"), its effect would be quite different. But as is, it *implicates* our business-oriented culture, and it becomes the reader's task, in a sense, to "deconstruct" the title by removing the diacritical marks and turning the title into a command: "Resume!" In so doing, business writing students might well learn something about the résumé as a social practice that pages of prescriptive (and proscriptive) writing fail to convey.

From a practical point of view, two kinds of textbooks, perhaps combinable into one, are needed to help students utilize business language as a set of instruments: the short, elegant business rhetoric mentioned above and a textbook built around an *interconnected, complex* set of written problem-solving exercises. In fact, at least one model for this second kind of text already exists, *Managerial Communication*, which comes out of the M.B.A. program at the Harvard Business School.[83]

This textbook approaches business communication as essentially a rhetorical problem, and it parallels some of the best general work being done in the field of composition. For instance, the authors ignore semantics in favor of Kenneth Burke's "dramatistic" approach to the writing act, specifically applying his "pentad" of agent, act, scene, agency, and purpose to business writing situations: for example, "An act-centered perspective is common in operating manuals, instructional kits, and managerial 'action plans,' but rare elsewhere."[84] That Burke's theory has been one of the most important influences in shaping the composition textbooks of the last two decades is very much to the point: *Managerial Communication* is clearly concerned with adapting to business writing contexts the best set of writing instruments available, and not with perpetuating a set of business writing formats as business writing formulas.

When *Managerial Communication* does become directive it is almost always with reason and right to the rhetorical point, as in these comments on *tone* from a chapter on "giving and receiving feedback":

> *Strive for a matter-of-fact tone.* Most people try to avoid a harsh or hypercritical tone in discussing another's work, but other undesirable tones often creep into their responses as a result. Both praise and criticism can be rejected if the tone is exaggerated, coy, or condescending. . . . To maintain a matter-of-fact tone, use superlatives sparingly and exclamation points not at all. Keep yourself out of the picture.[85]

Managerial Communication is both analytic and logical in assessing various kinds of business documents. It explains and justifies whenever it can. And it gives regular due to the profit motive that underlies, and ultimately should explain, every communicative act in a business context:

> Communications to and from employees are probably the most pervasive form of management communication. . . . One reason for the growing importance of employee communication is the interdependence of tasks assigned to a rapidly changing work force that brings new skills and expectations to the work place: these factors generate new kinds of information that companies *want* to communicate to their people. . . . Aside from these specific motives, however, careful attention to employee communication is a principle of efficient and responsible management. From management's point of view, such communications contain substantial potential rewards.[86]

In terms of giving students practice in writing for the business professions, probably the most valuable aspect of *Managerial Communication* is the extensive "Case Study" and accompanying assignments at the end of each chapter. Students must first digest and analyze pages of information and then present their conclusions in documents written from several different organizational perspectives (for example, manager at corporate headquarters, assistant to the CEO). Without ever having to make the point explicit, such complex, realistically indeterminate assignments make students aware of the necessarily somewhat conflicting points of view in any business situation and that it is not so much the absolutely right view that prevails as it is the most persuasively presented and most calculatingly argued. Therefore, when students are asked, "Given the concerns and informational needs you see as important for your target audience, what style, tone, and argumentation are appropriate in a communication explaining the planned change?"[87] they are being asked a highly relevant question about language usage in a very specific business context — and they *must* apply the principles of business rhetoric if they are to answer these demands in the document they are preparing.

Of course, something like *Managerial Communication* is too dense, complex, and advanced a textbook to use with undergraduates, but it is not at all inappropriate as a model. Properly scaled down, its rhetorical stance and multisided case study method would vastly improve the teaching of business communication to the several million undergraduates studying it every year. Instead of being stuck with a large business communication textbook that does little more than inundate them with endless production details about business documents, they would have a briefer book to inform them about and require them to apply the principles of business rhetoric in realistically complex situations.[88]

The ultimate issue here is one of freedom and power: Should undergraduate business majors be educated in a manner that virtually ensures they will be forever stuck as middle managers, or should they be educated in and given practice applying rhetorical techniques that allow them access to real power in business contexts? If we want the latter, we will first have to start producing undergraduate business communications textbooks adequate to the task.

Notes

1. Alexis de Tocqueville, *Democracy in America*, trans. Henry Reeve et al. (New York: Vintage, 1945), II, 64.

2. George Santayana, "Tradition and Practice," *George Santayana's America: Essays on Literature and Culture*, ed. James Ballowe (Urbana: University of Illinois Press, 1967), 117.

3. This direction is constituted more and more within the institution as well as from without, most specifically in terms of what students demand be taught them. A recent study by the Higher Education Research Institute of the University of California, Los Angeles, "found that 23.9 percent of the students [entering in September 1985] — all-time high — intended to major in business. As recently as 1972, the figure was only 10.5 percent, and college admissions officers say those students were generally not as talented as the undergraduates studying business today." (See Gene I. Maeroff, "Reading Balance Sheets Instead of Poetry," *New York Times*, 26 Jan. 1986, sec. 4, 22E.)

4. Marla Treece, *Communication for Business and the Professions*, 2d ed. (Boston: Allyn and Bacon, 1983), 4.

5. Herta A. Murphy and Herbert W. Hildebrandt, *Effective Business Communications*, 4th ed. (New York: McGraw-Hill, 1984), 7.

6. Kenneth Burke, *Counter-Statement* (Berkeley: University of California Press, 1968), 124.

7. Norman B. Sigband and David N. Bateman, *Communicating in Business* (Glenview, Ill.: Scott, Foresman and Co., 1981), 329.

8. Treece, 283–90.

9. Murphy and Hildebrandt, 37–93.

10. William C. Himstreet and Wayne Murlin Baty, *Business Communications: Principles and Methods*, 6th ed. (Boston: Kent Publishing Co., 1981), 1, 217.

11. Unfortunately, this emphasis on format over content plays right into the weaknesses many poor writers have. As Linda Flower and John Hayes observe in an important research report on the composing process, "Good writers respond to *all* aspects of the rhetorical problem. As they compose, they build a unique representation not only of their audience

and assignment, but also of their goals involving the audience, their own *persona*, and the text. By contrast, the problem representations of poor writers were concerned primarily with the features and conventions of a written text, such as number of pages or magazine format" ("The Cognition of Discovery: Defining a Rhetorical Problem," *College Composition and Communication* 31 [Feb. 1980]: 29).

12. Murphy and Hildebrandt, 115ff.

13. Sigband and Bateman, 64ff.

14. Raymond V. Lesikar, *Business Communication: Theory and Practice*, 5th ed. (Homewood, Ill.: Richard D. Irwin, 1984), 254–69.

15. Bobbye Sorrels Persing, *Business Communication Dynamics* (Columbus: Charles E. Merrill, 1981), 257–327.

16. Berle Haggblade, *Business Communication* (St. Paul: West Publishing Co., 1982), xiii, 67–123.

17. Lesikar, 541–48.

18. Treece, 615–48.

19. Treece, 3–29.

20. Walker Gibson, "Sweet Talk: The Rhetoric of Advertising," *Tough, Sweet and Stuffy* (Bloomington: Indiana University Press, 1966), 78.

21. Gibson, 77.

22. What Gerald Prince, writing specifically about narrative texts, says about "legibility" might be borne in mind by business writers in circumstances where they do *not* want to be read too simply or singlemindedly: "To determine how legible a given text is, we would have to determine how many questions one must ask in order to arrive at an answer, how complicated they have to be, how different they are one from another, how they are answered or could be answered, and even whether they can be answered at all" ("Questions, Answers and Narrative Legibility: A Structuralist Heuristic," *Rhetoric and Change*, eds. William E. Tanner and J. Dean Bishop [Mesquite, Texas: Ide House, 1982], 167). Prince goes on to argue — and it is a point that is often obscured by the stress on absolute "clarity" in many business communications textbooks — that writing can be too legible: "A text may be so legible that it becomes unreadable. Too much homogeneity, too much redundancy, too much explicitness may result in a lack of interest and a lack of pleasure" (175).

23. Himstreet and Baty, 15.

24. Treece, 36.

25. A significantly more substantial and productive alternative to these popularized treatments would be the often brilliant studies of Erving Goffman, from *The Presentation of the Self in Everyday Life* (Garden City, N.Y.: Doubleday Anchor, 1959) and *Interaction Ritual* (Garden City, N.Y.: Doubleday Anchor, 1967) onward.

26. Murphy and Hildebrandt, 9.

27. A useful, if for business necessarily an unsettling and provocative, discussion of these last two is Michael Ryan's *Marxism and Deconstruc-*

tion: A Critical Articulation (Baltimore: Johns Hopkins University Press, 1981).

28. Garet Garrett, "Business," *Civilization in the United States: An Enquiry by Thirty Americans*, ed. Harold Stearns (New York: Harcourt, Brace Co., 1922), 397.
29. Lesikar, 86.
30. Lesikar, 14.
31. Treece, 29.
32. Sigband and Bateman, v.
33. Lesikar, 42.
34. Murphy and Hildebrandt, 378.
35. Persing, 37.
36. Lesikar, 545.
37. Lesikar, 105.
38. Noam Chomsky, *Reflections on Language* (New York: Pantheon, 1975), 161.
39. Sigband and Bateman, 40.
40. Roland Barthes, *S/Z*, trans. Richard Miller (New York: Hill and Wang, 1974), 32.
41. Lesikar, 89.
42. Natalie R. Seigle, *Dynamics of Business Communications* (Columbus: Grid Publishing Co., 1984), 259.
43. Persing, 206ff.
44. Sigband and Bateman, 36.
45. Seigle, xii.
46. Lesikar, 112.
47. Eddy Roulet, *Linguistic Theory, Linguistic Description and Language Teaching*, trans. Christopher N. Chandlin (London: Longman, 1975), 74.
48. John Searle, *Speech Acts: An Essay in the Philosophy of Language* (Cambridge: Cambridge University Press, 1968), 51–52.
49. Treece, 492, 493.
50. Persing, 56.
51. Lesikar, 5.
52. Sigband and Bateman, 35 passim.
53. Seigle, 82.
54. Sigband and Bateman, 44.
55. Lesikar, 117–18.
56. Treece, 78, 96.
57. Raymond Williams, *Marxism and Literature* (Oxford: Oxford University Press, 1977), 165–66.
58. Persing, 219. It is significant that this observation occurs in one of the earlier texts (or editions) considered here. While these works — some completed more than half a decade ago — cannot be faulted for lacking a precise delineation of how thoroughly computers are now integrated

into the production of business documents, they can be faulted for a lack of foresight concerning word processors and writing. Since at least 1980, it was apparent that computers would become a central instrument in the production of business documents — and that the whole "writing for business" process would be markedly changed thereby.

59. Brian Gallagher, *Microcomputers and Word Processing Programs: An Analysis and Critique*, Research Monograph Series, Report No. 9 (New York: CUNY Instructional Resource Center, 1985), 2.

60. Cyril Connolly, *The Unquiet Grave: A Word Cycle by Palinarus* (New York: Harper and Row, 1973), 61.

61. Aristotle, *Rhetoric and Poetics*, trans. W. Rhys Roberts and Ingram Bywater (New York: Modern Library, 1954), 27.

62. Seymour Chatman, *Story and Discourse: Narrative Structure in Fiction and Film* (Ithaca: Cornell University Press, 1978), 265.

63. Jonathan Culler, *Structuralist Poetics: Structuralism, Linguistics and the Study of Literature* (London: Routledge and Kegan Paul, 1975), 135.

64. Haggblade, 55–56.

65. Treece, 89ff.

66. Himstreet and Baty, 35–45.

67. Murphy and Hildebrandt, 353.

68. Sigband and Bateman, 429ff.

69. Haggblade, 53ff.

70. Lesikar, 26 passim.

71. Himstreet and Baty, 94.

72. Dorothy Augustine, "Geometrics and Words: Linguistics and Philosophy: A Model of the Composing Process," *College English*, 43 (March 1981): 224.

73. Aristotle, 67.

74. Richard Lloyd-Jones, "Ex Nihilo . . ." *College English*, 40 (Oct. 1978): 150.

75. Seigle, 479–82.

76. Treece, 333ff.

77. Lesikar, 335–52.

78. Sigband and Bateman, 204ff.

79. See Thomas Kuhn, *The Structure of Scientific Revolutions*, 2d ed. (Chicago: University of Chicago Press, 1970).

80. See Ludwig Wittgenstein, *Philosophical Investigations*, trans. G. E. M. Anscombe (New York: Macmillan, 1953).

81. Dorothy Parker, *The Collected Poetry of Dorothy Parker* (New York: Modern Library, 1936), 50.

82. Another poem that works well in connection with business writing, although in a less document-specific way, is W. H. Auden's "The Fall of Rome," which conflates the decay of Rome and the disintegration of British society during the Depression, setting both "de-civilizing" processes against the indifferent persistence of nature. What makes the poem particularly relevant in a business context is Auden's ironic vision

of how a bureaucratic mentality remains dull and dutiful even in the face of social chaos and personal distress:

> Caesar's double-bed is warm
> As an unimportant clerk
> Writes I DO NOT LIKE MY WORK
> On a pink official form.

From *Selected Poetry of W. H. Auden* (New York: Modern Library, 1958), 122.

83. Linda McJ. Micheli, Frank V. Cespedes, Donald Byker, and Thomas J. C. Raymond, *Managerial Communication* (Glenview, Ill.: Scott, Foresman and Co., 1984).

84. Micheli et al., 23.

85. Micheli et al., 113.

86. Micheli et al., 231.

87. Micheli et al., 229.

88. Such a textbook would also avoid a nagging problem in many current business communication textbooks, namely, the running, wholehearted endorsement of the value system of American business. By presenting business rhetoric as a set of instruments for use in a specific context, this new kind of textbook would clarify the values on which business language rests, while also making students aware of the context-specific nature of those values. As Paul Taylor points out in *Normative Discourse* (Englewood Cliffs, N.J.: Prentice–Hall, 1961, 151ff.), it is possible for two value systems to be relevant and not in conflict because one will always logically take precedence in a given situation. In other words, students might see they can work according to one set of values and live by another, somewhat different set.

12 The Teaching and Practice of "Professional Writing"

C. H. Knoblauch
SUNY at Albany

The composition business has quickly discovered what other businesses have long recognized: the link between prosperity and diversification, the value of new markets, half perceived and half created, to ensure future growth. Hence, the introduction of specialty product lines over the past several decades, basic writing, advanced expository writing, practical writing, personal writing, creative writing, business writing, journalistic writing, technical writing, writing in the disciplines, writing on computer, all in a range of models (even "basic" writing has "beginning" and "advanced" versions) and all bearing a potential for further expansion as long as economic indicators are bullish on literacy instruction. There is even some talk, as its market share grows, that composition studies will force out its principal competition, the English literature business, and subsume its territory.

In the midst of such exhilarating growth, raising intellectual questions, as I propose shortly to do, about the school concept of "professional writing" or about the teaching of "practical" writing courses is, in a sense, to miss the point: like wondering whether the latest cologne can really deliver on its promise to make people irresistible; or whether the health of women, aged thirty-five to sixty-five, truly depends on a new, individually paced, multilevel, medically approved, aerobic fitness and exercise program. The cologne and the new fitness program are valuable largely because they exist, accompanied by energetic campaigns of validation that have "explained" their necessity. Within limits they achieve their ends (the gratification of needs that the products themselves, and the contexts of their production, have partly created) so that no one seriously wonders about why they are needed or what they are actually worth. At the same time, however, successful product managers understand the interdependence of their company's success, the quality of their merchandise, and the subtlety, not to say accuracy, of their advertising. My questions about the teaching of "professional writing" are not designed to challenge the pertinence of the enterprise — for the market and product have already been created; prosperity is at hand. But they do address, let's say from the vantage point of a consumer advocate, the sophistication of both the product and its presentation.

The commercial analogy is not merely mischievous, nor do I intend anything disproportionately cynical about the manner in which the "discipline" of composition is at present constructing itself as a social formation. Bowles and Gintis, among others, have pointed out that resemblances between the organization of schools, including personnel, departments, and curricula, and the organization of (other) managerial hierarchies and labor specializations in the capitalist workplace are far from coincidental. The former is both a reflection of the latter and a contributor to its maintenance.[1]

Still more broadly based work, such as that by Berger and Luckmann, has clarified the processes by which social formations emerge, shape themselves, express their rationales, consolidate influence, and ensure their perpetuation.[2] The structures and practices of academic institutions too obviously parallel those of the workplace generally in the United States to require extensive demonstration here. But what follows from that fact for a discussion of the emergence of particular forms of curricula, together with the kinds of theoretical argument designed to validate them, is important and I want to insist on it for a moment. "Composition studies" is currently in the process of asserting its disciplinary legitimacy,[3] a process entailing the search for venerable precursors (such as classical rhetoric[4]), intellectual prestige (through the establishing of research agendas and methodologies[5]) and, of course, a share of political authority and institutional resources.[6]

Legitimacy in American universities requires both a successful demonstration of public demand for a product — in the case of composition programs a call for improved literacy as well as for practical pre-professional training in schools — and also a dignifying intellectual rationale for disciplinary status, such as a need to understand the writing process, the nature of discourse, the history of thinking about discourse, and the means of teaching literacy. Manifestations of success include, then, a growing market for services, which can be stimulated advantageously by offering new or more specialized courses, and a growing body of research arguments that not only enlarge the lore of the new discipline, but also justify the focuses of instruction and the diversity of courses (for instance, by constituting unusually needy populations such as "remedial" writers). Accompanying this growth is the formation of a disciplinary hierarchy, with theorists, researchers, and program administrators at various levels of authority on top and large numbers of teachers — service personnel — at the bottom, as in any managerial context.

Seen from this vantage point, the concept of *professional writing* (or *writing in the workplace*) and the subdiscipline rapidly growing up around it stand in a revealing light. They represent an expansion of market as well as a diversification of the research enterprise in the interest of legitimizing and solidifying the power of composition studies as a university institution. Efforts to accomplish these ends appear likely to succeed, but the road to success crosses some challenging terrain that specialists in the field are only now beginning to traverse.[7] The journey will eventually constitute an interesting story about the construction of a discipline; but all I hope to do here is sketch some complications in its plot.

I have in mind three potentially troublesome disjunctions within the subfield, the first concerning what textbooks say about professional writing as opposed to what writers in the workplace do; the second concerning what research characterizations are trying to suggest in the face of rather obstinate workplace realities; the third concerning the phenomenal world of workplace writing as opposed to the phenomenal world of school writing, and the attendant struggle in research and teaching alike to bring those worlds closer together so that plausible claims can be made for the situating of preprofessional training within schools. Let me take them up somewhat in turn, though they are in fact complexly interwoven.

Textbook bashing is a joyless exercise, reminiscent of punching that inflated, bottom-heavy "Joe Palooka" dummy of yesteryear: every time one hit it, no matter how hard, it quickly righted itself as though no blow had been struck. But there are some interesting characteristics of textbooks devoted to professional writing that bear investigation in the context of an argument about the primarily school-sponsored, rather than workplace-sponsored, nature of business and technical writing courses. One awkward but probably inevitable feature of the emergence of professional writing, so far, is that the expansion of market and the growth of new products to meet its demands have been more rapid than the development of the research enterprise designed in part to validate it. The best indicator of that fact is surely the disparity between vast numbers of textbooks in the supposedly various domains of professional writing, all devoted to supporting the emergence of curricula, and the scanty amount of academic research affirming the reality of the concept, distinguishing the forms of professional writing, asserting the characteristics of each form, observing professional writers, and — not least — authorizing the statements that textbook writers make with such considerable assurance yet with rather little support from experiences of the workplace itself.

A consequence has been that the "principles" of technical communication have evolved with only haphazard regard for what practitioners actually do and for what sorts of knowledge constitute their sense of normal discursive practice. The textbook argument about writing in the workplace has focused primarily on *formats* (and the strategies that enable their realization in practical circumstances), as though the Memo, the Report, or the Proposal exists as a model, the practicing of which in school will prepare students for composing within essentially the same structure in professional life.[8] The advantage of this view is, of course, that it offers teachers something concrete to teach, not just the formats themselves but also a set of valued assumptions about the order, clarity, truthfulness, and efficiency that they embody. The disadvantage, however, is that the formats are school-sponsored abstractions bearing only marginal pertinence to the activities of the workplace, while the values, stable enough within a current American myth about literacy, have chiefly the force of conventional moral exhortations, not necessarily a practical relationship to professional discourse.

The first text on technical writing that I happen to pull from my shelf, one chosen for no other reason than its proximity, offers the following list of features that "all useful technical documents share": (1) each is the product of a writer who fully understands the subject; (2) each focuses purely on the subject, *not* on the writer; (3) each conveys *one* meaning, allowing one interpretation; (4) each is selective about the information it offers, tailoring its message to the specific needs of an audience; (5) each is written at a level of technicality that will be understood by the specified audience; and (6) each is efficient — every word advances the writer's meaning.[9] The values here are evident enough, and also evidently mythological: good professional writers possess absolute technical know-how, transmitting their unassailable knowledge through dispassionately objective prose that is clean, efficient, precise, no-nonsense, rigorous, persuasive (but without visible rhetorical coloring), and economical. There are no purposes to be served beyond factual matters at hand; narrators are translucent conduits of data; audiences are passive receptors.

Following these characterizations, the book proceeds to tactics: reader focus, paragraph design, and a range of operations that look suspiciously like those in any first-year composition text — summarizing, defining, describing, dividing, explaining a process, making an outline, doing research. The book then offers an array of formats, each with several subforms, to be learned and practiced (though with no mention of any context of use) — the Letter, the Short Report, the Proposal, the Formal Report, the Oral Report — and concludes with the obligatory overview of grammar, usage, and mechanics. The writer is a college teacher, I would wager from an English department, possibly with some consulting experience, although no mention is made of it. All of the book's reviewers, named in the preface, are also college teachers; all of the supportive individuals who helped prepare the text are either from colleges or from the house that published the book; of fifteen people mentioned, not one appeared to be from the business or technical workplaces for which the book claimed to be preparing students.

I do not single out this text as better or worse than others; indeed its typicality is what I want to emphasize. Glancing quickly at another one on my shelf, I note again a university-based author, this time with ten years of consulting experience, who thanks twenty individuals, all from colleges or publishing houses, none from another workplace, and whose book offers essentially the same information, though somewhat rearranged and distinguished by blue rather than black chapter headings.[10]

It would only try a reader's patience to chronicle all the obvious ways in which textbook reality differs from workplace reality. The point I prefer to make is that professional writing, insofar as textbooks define it, is altogether an academic conception, very much tied to school notions of literacy, language, and discourse, specifically those held among humanities faculty.[11] For that reason, business writing teachers are often inclined to exaggerate the glamorous persona of the austere technical professional, oversimplify the rich practical awareness of intention and audience in the concrete circumstances of professional life, reduce writing to the same uncontextualized skills and strategies they recognize from traditional undergraduate composition classes, and characterize professional communication as chiefly the management of prefabricated formats that "everyone uses." They lament the evils of nominal style, jargon, imprecision, passive voice, inelegant phrasing, and misplaced modifiers, as though the workplace could not possibly function effectively in the absence of clarity and grace, those supreme fictions of Higher Literacy. And they myopically imagine that writing is perceived as a central activity in the workplace, on a par with making money, winning a new client, engineering a better camera, and selling more automobiles, despite the fact that consulting fees for academic communication specialists are typically paid out of petty cash (compare them with the fees of a marketing consultant or a tax lawyer) and despite the atmosphere of disengaged indulgence that consultants regularly encounter in writing seminars that have been set up by eager personnel managers (who do not attend) for the enrichment of subordinates (who are thereby subtly shown their place within the hierarchy of a firm). Professional people *do* a lot of writing, to be sure, and may even insist occasionally that they (or more likely their subordinates) should learn to do it more effectively. But it is not an intrinsically interesting or even particularly visible activity for them, nor are they very reflective as a rule about its importance in their working lives.[12]

I recall a consulting job with a conglomerate, headquartered in New York, composed of stunningly unrelated businesses, including a barrel manufacturer in the Northeast (the parent company), a lingerie distributor in the Midwest, and a meatpacking company in Texas, among others. My task was to help the corporate headquarters reevaluate formats and procedures for the memo traffic between the main office and the subsidiary companies. As in many businesses, these formats were indeed important, a mark of belonging to a particular community of correspondents.[13] For that reason, they were eventually gathered into a loose-leaf folder and passed out to the staff as models to follow henceforward.

Several facts about these formats deserve mention. First, they were precisely tailored to conditions within that single corporation and to the sometimes whimsical desires of the corporate management. No writing teacher could have anticipated their features, many of which depended on the circumstance that very diverse business enterprises were obliged to communicate among themselves. Second, they had little to do with how well or how poorly different employees wrote. Learning the format was easy — it was there to follow in the loose-leaf folder. But saying what needed to be said was a different matter, depending on an individual's sociopolitical, no less than technical, understanding of that particular business environment. Third, the writing was, on the whole, dreadful by the standards of English teachers, yet colorfully functional as far as headquarters was concerned. I should add that the senior personnel in nearly all of the subsidiaries had high-school educations, although headquarters managers had college backgrounds.

The writing at the meatpacking plant, for instance, consisted mainly of quarterly reports and memo requests for material assistance. It was important to effective, orderly management, a principal vehicle for cost and profit projections, equipment requisitions, problem solving, and record keeping (but it was not as important as "moving meat"). The plant manager's prose was ungrammatical, disorganized though broadly clear, inventively Texan in its idioms, rather blustery, and occasionally obscene. It was more brusque than efficient, more dependent on a restricted code than economical. It was politically canny, keenly aware of the two or three executives in the New York office who would act on it, and therefore far from neutrally descriptive or explanatory. It invariably had many purposes to serve, since making a request for some new piece of equipment necessitated also dramatizing its importance to people who knew little about meatpacking and who received equally pressing requests from barrel manufacturers and lingerie distributors. That meant stroking the New York office no less than pleading a case. Headquarters had considerable tolerance, even a certain fondness, for the idiosyncracies of their employee's messages, which as a rule came distinctively, albeit ungracefully, across. And though the thought would be a source of considerable mirth to him, the manager was plainly a successful professional writer.

But how does the manager measure up in terms of textbook reality? He is far from the coolly rational, precisely organized, self-effacing, blandly competent technocrat heroically portrayed there. Furthermore, his memos would never qualify as illustration of the memo form. To be sure, he might be called a writer of *bad* memos, insufficiently attentive to matters of clarity and grace. I could even partly agree: there is no need to privilege his idiosyncracies or to insist extravagantly that they are normative in business practice. My point is only that he is an *actual* memo writer, knowledgeable about his work, perceived to be adequately effective in his company. Surely, we could learn more about workplace writing by asking why this writer would be regarded as successful than by lamenting his deficiencies. In any case, why privilege a textbook writer's theories about "good memos" unless as tacit demonstration of the fact that the idea of *professional writing* is a school concept, defined philosophically quite apart from the workplace and then applied retroactively, with all of the usual rules of academic decorum, to the writing that occurs there?

Given the disparity between textbook and workplace reality, it is not surprising that relations between professional writing programs and the professional world should be as peculiar as they are. There is no doubt that the movement to create such programs enjoys support from the now well-established public concern for literacy, an interest no less apparent within business and professional communities than elsewhere. But at the same time, it seems to be largely a school-sponsored curricular change, arising less from any organized or persistent demand from the workplace than from an internal economic realization that certain kinds of courses will attract large populations of students who have been socialized to expect a connection between their school preparation and their success in later careers. Consider the following points as evidence.

First, businesses and schools alike generally acknowledge that specific job skills relevant to professional life are largely acquired *in* professional life, not in classrooms, though the social preparation for that life is importantly carried out in school. Businesses did not initially, and by and large do not now, come to schools requesting courses in business writing, although they have long expected schools to provide for basic literacy. These days, some businesses like to see an introductory writing course on the résumés of young applicants, but they seldom if ever insist on a more specialized course, realizing how remote such training will surely be from anything employees are likely to encounter in specific workplaces. It is interesting how comparatively few business schools today offer such courses, as against a large number of English departments, despite their preprofessional relationship to the business community. At my university, the business school assumes that writing is wholly the concern of the English department, not a subject relevant to its own preparatory curriculum — and reasonably so since most of the pressure it has encountered to offer such courses has come from the English department, not from the business community it serves.

Second, in my experience, businesses that recognize some need to improve the writing of their employees hire consultants, sometimes inside but just as often outside the academic community, to assess their particular circumstances and offer recommendations. They do not send employees to school-based writing programs (as they sometimes do to management programs or specialized marketing or computer courses), nor do they exhibit much patience with academic consultants who come in with writing theories or writing tasks that reflect school reality (including generalized "professional situation" exercises) instead of an understanding of the organization's own concrete circumstances.

Third, there are comparatively few professional writing programs that have been able (or have even attempted) to establish useful connections with the particular kinds of workplace for which their training is intended — including cooperation with practitioners in the development of pertinent curricula. The Wayne State "Professional Writing Project" is a notable exception, and even that program was apparently initiated by Wayne State's English department.[14]

What all of this suggests is that the dramatic growth of business and technical communication courses has been distinctly the outcome of an energetic drive among composition programs, typically housed in English departments, to diversify their production — with only the most tentative support or encouragement from outside. It may be that the textbook generalizations at the heart of school-based professional writing programs (which continue, after all, to reflect those durable public myths about literacy), will be enough to sustain the growth of such programs even despite their disregard of workplace realities and their independence of specific demand from business and professional communities. But I would guess that their continuation must partly depend on proving their worth beyond school, which will surely mean that textbook generalizations must be supplemented at least, and perhaps supplanted, by practical understanding of the workplace if instruction is to have credibility in the specialized communities to which it hopes to appeal. If that turns out to be true, then the need for research — concrete observation of the workplace — to help alleviate the discrepancies between textbook pronouncements and professional practice is all the more imperative.

Such research is, of course, now substantially under way, though it is not itself free of some complicated difficulties. What makes it especially problematic is the current intellectual and political confrontation between different methodological perspectives in the field. Each perspective claims a special explanatory power, each wishes to connect its conclusions to instructional agendas, and each eventually runs into the limitations of its own assumptions. One perspective, which might be called "structuralist," emphasizes the depiction of genres of discourse, conceived to be systems of rules that more or less absolutely enclose the practices of writers. Another, which might be called "phenomenological," emphasizes the observation of those practices as richly contextualized social realities, lacking precise boundaries or formal rules, that appear (to practitioners no less than observers) at particular historical moments as normative conditions but that in fact ceaselessly evolve throughout the discursive activities of a given group of language users.[15]

The first, or structuralist, perspective is plainly more useful in the service of curricular agendas because its processes of observation eventually generate a body of (at least potentially) teachable concepts: a bounded idea of some particular genre, distinguished structurally from others, a range of specific, isolable constraints or rules for people to learn in order to use the genre, an array of explicit dos and don'ts in terms of which to define acceptable practice. Much theoretical work in "writing across the curriculum" has tended to advance this view, emphasizing the professional discourses of the academy, the features of which — social, political, rhetorical, linguistic — are presumed to be accessible to observation, objectively characterizable as models or sets of formal abstractions, and available as such for simulation in classroom writing assignments, all to the end of making students more familiar with the discursive constraints of one form of practical writing or another.[16] But however convenient structuralist representations may be for furthering curricular interests, a question arises about the plausibility of their implicit root assumption — that business writing or chemistry writing or any other professional discourse possesses an intrinsic formal "grammar" to which particular instances of composition inevitably subordinate themselves.

The issue here, obviously, is not whether there is writing in the workplace — a plain enough reality — but whether what happens there has a generic integrity that entitles us to distinguish it from writing elsewhere in terms of precise constraints, such as focusing mainly on the subject of discussion, or avoiding personal references and other marks of a visible narrator, or solving rhetorical problems through a particular kind of analysis and then representing the solution in a particular sequence, let's say synthetically arranged with the dominant conclusion first. If we cannot make such distinctions, then what exactly are we teaching when we teach professional writing? — never mind the subsequent question whether teaching it makes any difference to the development of professional writers.

Is there a space, somewhere between that broadly characterized ability to write that schools seek to nurture in ordinary writing classes and the specific practices of IBM regarding memos and reports, in which we might locate the *genre* of technical communication so that researchers and teachers alike can make statements about it? The structuralists may believe so, but they have not yet proven the case. I have encountered the problem in attempting to describe my own experience as an advisor for several years to a large New York-based consulting firm specializing in computer software packages for solving a variety of management problems.[17] Specifically, the more closely I studied the circumstances of this company's writing, the more localized (and hence less generic) my conclusions about it were forced to become. What I observed there were not rule-bound behaviors but rather *practices*, of the sort that phenomenological inquiry identifies, sufficiently visible as normal activity within the explicit conditions of that workplace to shape and interrelate individual writers, yet also sufficiently inexact, inarticulate, and transient to allow for considerable flexibility in the writing of different executives, depending on their own personalities, their positions within the organization, and their sense of the necessities of a given task. These practices were partly codified — for instance, the company had a published collection of formats including proposals, reports, and memos — but for the most part writers' performance depended on what Polanyi has called "tacit knowledge" of the firm's operating circumstances and expectations.[18]

Those circumstances are intriguingly subtle, confirming (to my mind) the intellectual superiority of a phenomenological viewpoint. They involve — often with regard to a *single* document — a range of purposes for writing (selling services, promoting products, solving technical problems, making contractual obligations); multiple audiences, both in-house and external; different degrees and dimensions of expertise; a variety of ready solutions to management problems, some the company's own, others copyrighted elsewhere, combined with a certain flexibility for troubleshooting and the subsequent development of new packages; degrees of tolerance for taking risks both technical and legal; a range of possible clients, from small businesses with no computer experience to large corporations; and an always changing economic as well as technological climate. The company features three personnel ranks, including staff, manager, and partner, so that sociopolitical relations among these divisions, including issues of competence, territorial prerogative, seniority, and promotion, invariably affect processes of communication — the more so since any proposal or report is initiated at staff level and then subjected to review at higher personnel levels, manager for technical soundness as a rule, and partner for contractual considerations. Moreover, employees come from different academic backgrounds, some from mathematics and computers, others from finance or accounting, some from business management, some with legal experience, a few from the humanities, yet all involved in preparing and reviewing documents as well as working (and communicating) with other members of the teams that undertake particular projects.

In the face of such complexity, the notion of practicing a proposal format in school (even if it were the company's own) as a means of learning to write in this business environment seems evidently inadequate. These employees all knew the format well but encountered fascinating problems, as one might expect, in using it on given occasions to accomplish their purposes. More important, they made myriad local judgments, sentence by sentence, document by document, on the basis of their language experience and feel for the demands of a particular situation, none of which seemed to me characterizable as a rule (and therefore transferrable to other writers or circumstances) without gross misrepresentation of the controlled arbitrariness, not to mention rhetorical delicacy and flexibility, of their actual practices.

To be sure, a structuralist might argue nonetheless that careful inquiry can still yield the system of constraints that constitutes this form of professional writing, perhaps turning my list of intentions, readers, and special conditions into a complicated but no less orderly model of the genre. The problem here is two opposed dispositions toward the object of attention, not something in the object itself that necessitates one view or the other. A "phenomenologist" would argue that no such "grammar" exists *within* the observed practice, but that it emerges only as a consequence of the researcher's decision to create it for explanatory purposes.[19] The tendency of phenomenological inquiry is to return the conclusions of observation to the life-world, which both produces them and sabotages their apparent solidity. It also implicitly challenges, therefore, the objectivist tendency to reify abstractions about genre, rule, and format by separating them from the human circumstances out of which they were formed.

The phenomenological research perspective seems to me intellectually more defensible than the structuralist, for it remains more self-conscious about the reductive tendencies of generalization. Its disadvantage, from the standpoint of curriculum, is not (for me) philosophical, not located in the kind of match it proposes between theory and the practices it intends to describe. Rather, its disadvantage is tactical, for it raises the awkward question whether so context-specific and complex an activity as writing in the workplace can be adequately represented, let alone taught, in schools. A phenomenological argument about professional writing, which will always maintain that workplace practices are embedded in additional layers of social reality and cannot be understood — or learned — apart from them, has potential to call into serious doubt the very idea of professional writing curricula.

Short of recreating the entire life-world enveloping the writers I have described in that New York consulting firm, what will a teacher do to help students "practice" this particular version of job-related discourse? Phenomenological research will have powerful value in future for actually depicting workplace writing — the narrative account of writing at Exxon ITD by Paradis, Dobrin, and Miller in the Odell and Goswami collection of articles on professional writing is an instance. But it is significant that this study offers little in the way of teaching implications beyond the observations that technical writing teachers tend not to be very familiar with the life-world of scientists or engineers and that schools "can hardly anticipate the full gamut of demands that industry makes on individuals."[20] Such assertions do not constitute a promising start toward devising curricula.

I have come to the third plot complication I wanted to consider in the story of "professional writing" instruction. Suppose, as seems likely, that research is able soon to offer more plausible images of workplace writing. To what extent can the improved understanding of that reality, even if it can be represented in generic terms, be transported to the context of school discourse? How fully and how usefully can the two worlds interrelate? These questions need answering as long as writing specialists want to insist that the place to develop professional writing skills is in the academic setting. Again, difficulties multiply. Schools are characterized by their discursive practices as richly and powerfully as any other social reality. The functions of school discourse are various, including the exploration and testing of new knowledge, the display of learning, and even the practicing of school formats (the term paper, the lab report) for its own sake. Ordinarily, school discourse presupposes a writer — the student — who is subordinate to, and under the scrutiny of, (teacher) readers. Even writing aimed supposedly at other students maintains, within the normal conditions of school reality, an evaluative function: other students will rarely be the only, or the principal, readers. Successful students understand these aspects of their rhetorical situation rather well; their tacit knowledge of their condition is precisely parallel, it would seem, to that of the writer in some (other) professional setting.

School performance, even within a writing-across-the-curriculum program supposedly devoted to learning the conventions of biology writing or sociology writing, is always shaped by the other social conditions of school life — the concern for preparing people who are not regarded as mature for the roles and tasks that post-school maturity will eventually make available to them, the concern for assimilating the values and beliefs of a community to which students seek adult entrance, including respect for authority, personal responsibility, discipline, reliability, and good habits or organization, all of which are signaled as much by decorous prose as by other forms of school performance. It is not accidental that even graduate dissertations, the last version of school discourse, are seldom published, as is, by academic presses: they are perceived to be school writing, the work of apprentices, not the sort of manuscript material submitted by professional scholars. Still less is the anthropology field report of an undergraduate regarded as an authentic contribution to the field of anthropology, not so much because of the quality of its statements as because of the *context* of its production. School writing has many advantages, but it does not seem to me to serve realistically as an introduction to the "academic discourses" of professional scholars.

Given the contextual richness of the school discursive setting, given especially the powerful reality of its agendas, purposes, writer roles, and reader roles, how plausibly can the competing reality of business writing, or legal writing, or technical writing, each with its own agendas, purposes, and roles, be introduced or simulated? The case approach which has lately come to prominence in professional writing courses, certainly aims to construct the desired social, political, rhetorical, and other circumstances that impinge on the choices writers make in practical settings, but the approach has two serious limitations. First, it cannot be as context-specific as normal professional (or other) writing situations are. It is inevitably schematic and artificial, typically with a teacher filling in social texture, as needed, by guesswork and unreliable make-believe. Second, its demands conflict with the prior and far more affecting demands of the school discursive world, where the teacher is the reader *as* teacher, not really as business manager, or lawyer's client, or politician, or engineer; where the teacher may have little experience of the business, technical, or professional world (aside from teaching) but considerable experience of the academy, with quite specific notions about acceptable student performance; and where the real school agenda controls writers' decisions, if they are smart and sensible, rather than the fictional agenda of the case.

Where does all of this leave teachers of "professional writing," whose textbooks convey a school-based fantasy about the workplace, whose knowledge does not as yet include a very clear sense of generic distinctions (if they exist) among forms of job-related discourse, whose own practical experience of the workplaces beyond schools may be severely limited, and whose school-reality effectively dominates and reshapes the dynamics of other nonschool discursive practices, assuming that they can be brought persuasively into the classroom in the first place? Well, some comfort can surely be derived from recalling that "professional writing" curricula are already healthy, growing realities in schools and are probably destined to bloom still more brilliantly in years to come as the field of literacy instruction continues to flourish. In short, all of the intellectual anguish of the preceding pages is largely irrelevant to the social facts that such curricula exist and that their validation is currently under way as one significant function of the research effort to characterize writing in the workplace.

If such teachers were simply to continue what they have been doing, they might not be conspicuously less successful in perpetuating their enterprise. But at the same time, the question surely deserves some serious thought if we are to make responsible promises to the students we intend to prepare and to the professional fields that will employ them. One answer is, of course, that we can teach, not the specific discursive practices of some workplace, but the general rhetorical competences that enable writers to respond effectively in a range of situations, including potentially those typical of their intended jobs. (Linda Flower's contribution to this collection makes such a case rather well.) As an intellectual position it seems eminently sound, but it may be politically awkward because it raises the question: Why introduce *professional* writing curricula when their goals — the practicing of rhetorical tactics — have already been anticipated in ordinary (not to mention advanced) composition classes?

I am not much driven to find a solution to this problem because the continued prosperity of technical writing courses (assured in any case) is not, for me, the most significant issue here. *Any* writing experience, presuming that it encourages the making of statements that matter, seems to me valuable wherever and however it can be made available. But at the same time I continue — happily — to teach "practical writing" courses, albeit without illusion about the economic interests served by their institutionalized presence in my English department. And I would attest that they can be especially rewarding because the juniors and seniors who typically take them believe, rightly or not, that they have value for future professional life and are therefore worth the trouble. So, let me offer a suggestion that may improve the credibility of "professional writing" instruction, if not from the standpoint of the committed theorist in its domain, then at least from that of a teacher who has found such courses beneficial.

Why not concede the richly layered and enveloping social reality of the school and allow it to be what it, in any case, is, namely, the professional context that students best understand, whose discursive practices are already familiar, whose political and rhetorical subtleties are partly known and available to additional analysis? Students have much to gain from acquiring a critical consciousness of their own situations within school life and could begin a professional writing course — in any school discipline — by working to develop it.

When I undertake a consulting project in some workplace, I start with ethnographic observation, inviting employees to talk about the kinds of writing they do, the time they must devote to it, the purposes it serves, the audiences it addresses, the importance it has (if any) in their professional lives, the forms and tactics on which they rely, the languages or expressive styles they use, the importance of writing for their social position and advancement, the demands of superiors regarding the features of their prose, the evaluative pressures they face. Typically, employees have only partial awareness of the implications of these questions and offer proportionately limited answers. But as the answers become fuller, through talk, writing, and reading, their awareness of their own professional practice expands and with it, seemingly, their sophistication in approaching new tasks, recognizing the rhetorical contexts in which the tasks are embedded and assessing their own as well as others' performance. Students, like these employees, can learn about the discursive practices that affect their school lives, including distinctive characteristics of biology writing, sociology writing, history writing, or literary critical writing, and through that learning come to an awareness of the *idea* of discursive practice, which they may take with them into other workplaces.

Students can then engage in their school writing, through the curriculum, with this altered awareness as support. Their writing in different disciplines for different purposes constitutes a part of their workplace reality. Their improvement as writers depends on continued application in the context of their knowledge of the demands, social, political, rhetorical, that school reality places on them. They are not simulating the writing of a biologist or historian, though they may well be working with the same materials and methods. Instead, they are responding with full rhetorical authenticity to the tasks and shaping circumstances characteristic of their environment.

I see no reason that the tasks should not include writing about business matters in a business course, or engineering matters in an engineering course, or about other professional concerns in the appropriate courses. But the writing (unavoidably) will achieve the ends of school discourse: learning the concepts, arguments, and modes of inquiry that distinguish those disciplines. It will not carry on the professional work of business or engineering, nor simulate carrying it on, nor even very adequately prepare people to carry it on (a preparation more effectively achieved on the job than in school). It can accomplish another end also, as any fully conscious discursive activity does: it can reveal the fact that writing-in-the-world never involves simple motives or simple effects, to my mind a more important realization about job-related writing than all of the formats and strategies, plans and invention heuristics, that occupy so much space in typical technical writing classes.

Professionals are effective as writers just in proportion to their knowing how to modulate all of the conditions that impinge on them — an art of appraising circumstances, balancing competing values and priorities, interpreting demands and expectations, telling the more important from the less, listening well to other voices in order to estimate the register of one's own, assessing the gains and losses of any rhetorical choice, anticipating reactions, judging myriad political, ethical, personal, and other consequences. Writing assignments that dramatize these abilities, explore them, and cause students to come consciously to terms with them are good assignments wherever they occur, preparing people as well as school can for the working world that demands the same feel, the same sensitivity, the same social intelligence.

One advantage of the case approach, its artificiality notwithstanding, is that, properly introduced, it invites writers to acknowledge just such a texture of competing values, intentions, and rhetorical possibilities so that they may acquire some subtlety in the practice of reading and responding to the world around them — an eminently practical ability. Curiously, many case presentations do not take themselves seriously enough to accomplish this end — they concede they are fictive by proposing fantastic situations (for instance, trying to persuade a community that a new chemical plant, one that promises to emit pungent black smoke, will be advantageous to the community's future), or inserting comic names of firms, people, or towns, or neglecting to include sufficient detail to prompt a willing suspension of disbelief. But the silliness of some cases need not indict them all, nor need the evident inadequacies of case assignments imply their inappropriateness as school exercises.

At the same time, the fact that students are discursively enveloped in their academic setting does not mean that they cannot inquire about other settings (for instance, by conducting ethnographic studies of businesses or professional organizations — including academic disciplines — to which they can gain access). Nor are they precluded from writing or discussing their own practical correspondence, employment letters, school applications, résumés, among other forms, within a composition class. If that class wishes to call itself "professional writing," as a sign to students that it seeks to prepare them for life outside school or as a sign to the academic world that a new industry is expanding its production, then, granting the beliefs that all writing opportunities are valuable and that those which students are inclined to take seriously are even more valuable, let it be so.

Notes

1. Samuel Bowles and Herbert Gintis, *Schooling in Capitalist America: Educational Reform and the Contradictions of Economic Life* (New York: Basic Books, Inc., 1976).

2. Peter L. Berger and Thomas Luckmann, *The Social Construction of Reality: A Treatise in the Sociology of Knowledge* (New York: Doubleday & Co., 1966).

3. See, for instance, Maxine Hairston, "The Winds of Change: Thomas Kuhn and the Revolution in the Teaching of Writing," in *Rhetoric and Composition: A Sourcebook for Teachers and Writers,* 2d ed., ed. Richard L. Graves (Upper Montclair, N.J.: Boynton/Cook, 1984), 14–26.

4. See, for instance, *Essays on Classical Rhetoric and Modern Discourse,* eds. Robert J. Connors, Lisa S. Ede, and Andrea A. Lunsford (Carbondale and Edwardsville, Ill.: Southern Illinois University Press, 1984).

5. See, for instance, "The Tacit Tradition: The Inevitability of a Multi-Disciplinary Approach to Writing Research," in Janet Emig, *The Web of Meaning: Essays on Writing, Teaching, Learning, and Thinking,* eds. Dixie Goswami and Maureen Butler (Upper Montclair, N.J.: Boynton/Cook, 1983), 146–58; or Carl Bereiter and Marlene Scardamalia, "Levels of Inquiry in Writing Research," in *Research on Writing: Principles and Methods,* eds. Peter Mosenthal, Lynne Tamor, and Sean A. Walmsley (New York and London: Longman, 1983), 3–25.

6. See, for instance, Maxine Hairston, "Breaking Our Bonds and Reaffirming Our Connections," *College Composition and Communication* 36 (Oct. 1985): 272–82; or Jay Robinson, "Literacy in the Department of English," *College English* 47 (Sept. 1985): 482–98.

7. Stephen M. North has revealingly demonstrated the intellectual and political complexities that writing researchers and teachers face in the process of legitimizing their "field." See *The Making of Knowledge in Composition: Portrait of an Emerging Field* (Upper Montclair, N.J.: Boynton/Cook, 1987).

8. Elizabeth Tebeaux has pointed out the typical features of various "professional writing" textbooks, although her conclusions about those features are more sanguine than mine. See "Redesigning Professional Writing Courses to Meet the Communication Needs of Writers in Business and Industry," *College Composition and Communication* 36 (Dec. 1985): 419–28.

9. John M. Lannon, *Technical Writing,* 3d ed. (Boston: Little, Brown, 1985).

10. Michael Markel, *Technical Writing: Situations and Strategies* (New York: St. Martin's, 1984).

11. This point is forcefully made by James Paradis, David Dobrin, and Richard Miller, "Writing at Exxon ITD: Notes on the Writing Environment of an R&D Organization," in *Writing in Nonacademic Settings,* eds. Lee Odell and Dixie Goswami (New York and London: The Guilford Press, 1985), 286ff.

12. It is this fact that gives such special urgency to recent pleas directed toward practical-writing teachers to get out of their classrooms and observe what professional writers actually do. See, for instance, Lee Odell, Dixie Goswami, Anne Herrington, and Doris Quick, "Studying Writing in Nonacademic Settings," in *New Essays in Technical and Scientific Communication: Research, Theory, Practice,* eds. Paul V. Anderson, R. John Brockmann, and Carolyn R. Miller (Farmingdale, N.Y.: Baywood Publishing Co., 1983).

13. Paul V. Anderson is surely correct in observing that formats are important in business and professional settings, but he concludes, mistakenly I think, that the very particular shapes and special relevance of formats within individual contexts are reliably generalized in school-sponsored fictions about "proposals" and "reports." See "What Survey Research Tells Us About Writing at Work," in *Writing in Nonacademic Settings*, 11–12.

14. See Barbara Couture, Jone Rymer Goldstein, Elizabeth L. Malone, Barbara Nelson, and Sharon Quiroz, "Building a Professional Writing Program Through a University–Industry Collaborative," in *Writing in Nonacademic Settings*, 391–426.

15. The distinction between "structuralists" and "phenomenologists" is theoretically plain in the contrasting arguments of Chomsky (in linguistics) or Lévi-Strauss (in anthropology), on the one hand, and Foucault (in "discourse theory") or Geertz (in anthropology) on the other. See, for instance, Noam Chomsky, *Aspects of the Theory of Syntax* (Cambridge, Mass.: MIT Press, 1965), or Claude Lévi-Strauss, *Structural Anthropology* (New York: Basic Books, 1967), as opposed to Michel Foucault, *The Archaeology of Knowledge* (New York: Harper & Row, 1972), or Clifford Geertz, *The Interpretation of Cultures* (New York: Basic Books, 1973).

16. See, for instance, Elaine Maimon and others, *Writing in the Arts and Sciences* (Cambridge, Mass.: Winthrop, 1981), or Anne J. Herrington, "Classrooms as Forums for Reasoning and Writing," *College Composition and Communication* 36 (Dec. 1985): 404–13.

17. C. H. Knoblauch, "Intentionality in the Writing Process: A Case Study," *College Composition and Communication* 31 (May 1980): 153–59.

18. For an interesting application of Polanyi's concept in professional writing research, see Lee Odell, Dixie Goswami, and Anne Herrington, "The Discourse-Based Interview: A Procedure for Exploring the Tacit Knowledge of Writers in Nonacademic Settings," in *Research on Writing*, 220–35.

19. For thorough explanations of the philosophical underpinnings of phenomenological research, see Elliot G. Mischler, "Meaning in Context: Is There Any Other Kind?" *Harvard Educational Review* 49 (1979): 1–19, and Kenneth J. Kantor, Dan R. Kirby, and Judith P. Goetz, "Research in Context: Ethnographic Studies in English Education," *Research in the Teaching of English* 15 (1981): 293–309.

20. Paradis, Dobrin, and Miller, 303–304.

IV Surveying Professional Writing Programs

13 What's Going On in Business and Management Communication Courses

Mary Munter
Dartmouth College

If you were to sign up for a course in Shakespearean tragedy, you would be assured that the main focus would not be on *Pride and Prejudice*. If you were to sign up for a course in Renaissance art, you would be assured that the main focus would not be on Jackson Pollock. If you were to sign up for a course in business communication, however, you would have no such assurances. Such a course might cover almost any subject related to business and vaguely related to communication. Such a course might include any subject from how to type (or, rather, how to "keyboard," as they call it these days) to how to restructure an entire corporation. My conclusions about what is being taught in various courses, then, are necessarily wide-ranging. What is being taught varies tremendously among different schools and among different teachers.

In my former life as a student of literature, I would probably have felt perfectly comfortable about making such generalizations based on personal experience. But after having spent the past decade teaching at two business schools (the Stanford Graduate School of Business and Dartmouth's Amos Tuck School of Business Administration) and at more than forty-five corporations, I find myself less comfortable about making generalizations without some kind of statistical evidence. Therefore, I give you fair warning: What follows are my subjective and prejudiced impressions. These impressions are based on interviews and conversations with twenty or thirty colleagues, and on what I have heard at fifteen or twenty conferences over the past ten years.

With that warning in mind, then, let us look at what is going on — in terms of students, faculty, and curriculum.

Students and Faculty

One thing we can say with assurance is that a great many students are studying business these days. In 1982–83, according to the most recent figures available from the American Assembly of Collegiate Schools of Business (AACSB), which is the accrediting institution for business schools, 23 percent of all 969,500 bachelor's degrees granted — or about 222,900 students — were in business. The same year, 22 percent of all 289,900 master's degrees — or about 63,700 students — were in business.

Twenty years earlier, in 1962–63, business students made up a much smaller piece of a much smaller pie. Then, only 13 percent of the 410,400 bachelor's degrees — or about 53,300 students — were in business. Only 6 percent of the 91,400 master's degrees — or about 5,400 students — were in business.[1]

Virtually all of these students take some kind of business communication course before they graduate. At the undergraduate level, one of the AACSB standards for accreditation is a breadth requirement including communication course work. Although it is not an AACSB standard at the graduate level, my best guess is that most M.B.A. programs have communication components. Every one of the following well-known graduate schools of business has a communication program: Carnegie-Mellon, Chicago, Columbia, Cornell (Johnson School), Dartmouth (Amos Tuck School), Duke (Fuqua School), Harvard, MIT (Sloan School), Michigan, Northwestern (Kellogg School), NYU, Stanford, Rutgers, UCLA, USC, Pennsylvania (Wharton School), and Virginia (Colgate Darden School).[2]

So, many business students are taking many different business communication courses. Furthermore, I feel that these students are increasingly motivated about learning to communicate better. They know that business people value communication. As long ago as 1964, *Harvard Business Review* readers placed "ability to communicate" as the top-ranked criterion for managerial success.[3] A decade later, the AACSB surveyed personnel managers, who also ranked communication number one in importance.[4] And in a more recent study, more than one thousand executives selected Business Communication as "very important" more often than any other course in the business school curriculum.[5] Students also know that as business people they will, in fact, spend most of their time at work communicating.[6] Finally, students know that the current trend toward "participative" (as opposed to "authoritarian") management makes communication more important than ever before.[7]

Increased emphasis on communication stems, I believe, from the business world's needs, not just from some students' remedial needs. Although we certainly see remedial students in business communication classes, it is a mistake to focus our courses too much on remediation.[8]

For one thing, such issues as spelling, punctuation, and placement of the inside address on a letter will soon be done routinely by computer. For another thing, the make-up of business students is changing. Over the past twenty years, the percentage of women — traditionally stronger communicators — has grown from 7.9 percent to 41.9 percent of the bachelor's degrees in business, and from 3.7 percent to about 28.8 percent of the M.B.A.'s.[9] Undergraduates who might have gone into humanities or social sciences twenty years ago are more likely to go into business today; M.B.A.'s are more likely to come from humanities and social science backgrounds now than they were twenty years ago. Finally, the very existence of communication programs at highly selective schools shows that, instead of teaching remedial spelling and punctuation, many such courses teach a brand-new and different expertise to students: how to communicate in the business world.

Although we may easily agree that there are a lot of business students out there, the matter of who is teaching them how to communicate is less clear. Professors' backgrounds vary tremendously; their degrees may be in management, communication, English, speech, or theater arts. On the one hand, this variety gives the profession a rich and diverse mix. Participants in panel discussions at professional conventions may be likely to quote anyone from Aristotle to Maria Callas to Lee Iacocca. On the other hand, this diversity can lead to bickering about the "right" background. I remember once being literally yelled at during an Academy of Management meeting for daring to teach at a business school when my training was in English. Not only do our backgrounds differ, but our departments differ. Most people teach in schools of business or management. But many others teach in departments of English.

My own feeling is that it is easier to train a good writing instructor about the ways of business than it is to train a good business person how to teach writing. For eight years I hired and trained writing and speaking consultants at the Stanford Graduate School of Business. Almost all of the more successful consultants whom I trained in business were people with English or humanities backgrounds. It was easier to teach the subtleties of the business world to language experts than it was to teach the subtleties of language to business experts.

On the other hand, people with English backgrounds often have a hard time establishing initial credibility with business students. Students can easily disregard comments from people they feel they can write off as "unbusinesslike." For this reason, people teaching in departments of English may have a much harder time establishing credibility than those teaching in departments of business or management.

General Curriculum

Business communication courses vary just as much as the backgrounds of those who teach them. Although there are many exceptions, watch for these three clues as starters. One, if you see the word *business* in the course title, it is probably an undergraduate course. "Business Communications" usually includes both writing and speaking; "Business Writing" and "Business Speaking" (and their variants, "Speaking in Business," "Writing for the World of Business," and so forth) focus on only one skill. The title "Business English" is very rarely used anymore. If, on the other hand, you see the word *management* or *managerial* in the title, it is probably a graduate level course. "Management Communication" and "Communication for Managers" are typical titles. Finally, if you see the word *organizational* in the title, the course — taught at either the graduate or undergraduate levels — will emphasize the effects of the organization on communication: communication networks, information flow and direction, hierarchies, motivation, and so on. The communication skills, if any, tend to be interpersonal and small group communication, rather than writing and speaking.

Within any one of those courses, however, you may find any combination of the following eight areas[10] in addition to, or instead of, writing.

Broadcasting and Journalism

Some courses are about public communication — teaching students to become television, radio, or print journalists. Usually you will find this kind of course in a school of communication or journalism, not in a school of business or management.[11] But the shared word *communication* adds to the confusion.

Public Relations and Media Relations

Unlike courses in which students learn to become journalists, course work in public relations teaches students how to become business people who must deal with journalists. Many business communication courses include exercises in dealing with the press. Other courses include information not just on how *people* communicate in business, but also on how *corporations* communicate with their various audiences, such as shareholders, employees, and the general public. Corporate communication can include both what business people would call "reactive" communication, such as dealing with a crisis, and "proactive" communication, such as corporate advocacy. Finally, some courses include modules that overlap into the marketing curriculum: on corporate image and corporate advertising, for instance.[12]

Technology and History

Developments in electronic communication have drastically changed how and what we teach. Computers have changed how we teach: for instance, students can revise their papers differently or have quantifiable aspects of their writing analyzed. Computers have also changed how our students will communicate in business; some courses therefore include teaching students how to use technology, such as word processing and electronic mail.[13] Finally, some courses include historical perspectives on technology, for example, drawing parallels between the impact of today's innovations with yesterday's innovations, such as horizontal filing systems in the nineteenth century and telephones in the early twentieth century.[14]

Communication Theory

Many courses include some background in communication theory — whether the models be electronic or mathematical, social, rhetorical, or interpersonal. Some colleagues would argue that all communication theory is bunk, especially the "Dixie cup model" of sender and receiver. Others argue passionately on behalf of the need for a theoretical base.[15] Most would agree, however, that business communication courses should not teach only about theory, but that they should teach how to apply that theory.

Organizational Theory

As I said before, most courses titled "Organizational Communication" deal only with organizational issues such as hierarchies and networks. Their content may overlap with courses in "Organizational Behavior" or "Interpersonal Communication." Such courses do not cover writing and speaking skills. If they do include them, the skills are interpersonal (that is, one person talking to another person) or small group communication (that is, working in teams, as opposed to giving an oral presentation).

Business or management communication courses must take into account the organization, or environment, in which the writing or speaking takes place. Therefore, some organizational theory wends its way into most courses, but it might be part of audience analysis, such as considering the implications of writing upward or downward on the organizational hierarchy.

Strategy

What many composition instructors might call *rhetoric*, business communication instructors tend to call *strategy*. Thus *ethos, pathos,* and *logos* become *credibility, audience analysis,* and *message structure*. Increased awareness of and emphasis on strategy is one of the most important trends and developments in the field in the last twenty years. Older versions of the course tended to be more formulaic: students virtually copied, for instance, a series of "good news" and "bad news" letters. Now, the course tends to be more strategic: students are taught to make decisions — about their own credibility, their audience's needs, persuasive structures — rather than to copy formulas.

Interpersonal Skills

Some courses include training in interpersonal skills. The term *interpersonal* usually refers to communicating one-to-one, as a business person might do during a performance appraisal, a job interview, or a negotiation. In many schools, however, interpersonal skills are taught in organizational behavior courses, rather than in communication courses. Although some overlap occurs between one aspect of interpersonal skills and presentation skills — that is, delivery — students who are good at one are often not good at the other.

Speaking Skills

Interpersonal skills involve speaking, but when most people refer to *speaking skills,* they mean speaking to a group of people — presentation skills. The growth in this area over the last decade has been tremendous. Before then, most courses included writing skills only. Now, many include speaking skills. I predict that most programs will eventually be 50 percent writing and 50 percent speaking, as an increasing number are today.

One reason speaking is growing is that it is more useful for our students: business people in many jobs actually spend more time speaking than they do writing. Another reason is that students are generally more receptive to learning speaking skills than to learning writing skills. Instructors have learned that they can increase enthusiasm and motivation by including speaking in their course.

Speaking skills usually include three areas. First, structuring an oral presentation means teaching about openings, previews (or agendas) of main ideas, a limited number of main ideas with very explicit transitions and internal summaries, and closings. Second, choosing visual aids means teaching about when they are appropriate and necessary, what they can say, how to make them clear and readable, and what kind of equipment to use. Unlike teaching structure, which is basically the same as it was in Aristotle's day, teaching visual aids has changed dramatically recently. Computer graphics capabilities and document design research have had a tremendous impact on teaching visual aids. Finally, delivering an oral presentation includes teaching students to improve their poise, gestures, facial expression, eye contact, pitch, rate, filler words, and enunciation. A decade ago, many schools did not have access to video equipment to teach delivery skills. Now, many schools do, and video will undoubtedly continue to be a tremendously effective tool for teaching delivery.

Writing Curriculum

Now, finally, we come to writing, one of the many subjects taught in business and management communication courses. In some ways, teaching business writing is no different from teaching any other kind of writing. Good writing, in other words, is good writing. It is unified, emphatic, organized, coherent, and clear.

There are, however, some major differences between the business writing we teach in a business writing course and the academic writing we teach in an expository writing course. I will use the term *business writing* to refer to the kind of writing we see in business: letters, memos, and reports written to audiences within the company (such as a boss or a subordinate) or outside the company (such as a customer or a vendor). I will use the term *academic writing* to refer to the kind of writing we see in colleges and universities: essays written to evaluators (such as a professor or a teaching assistant) or to peers (such as professional colleagues or other students). In some sense, teaching business writing is a matter of translating academic prose into business prose.[16] Students have been reinforced for writing in an academic style most of their lives; no wonder they find it hard to switch. What, then, are we asking them to do differently?

Different Genres

Certainly the most obvious differences between business and academic writing have to do with genres. Teachers in composition departments generally teach students to write essays; teachers in business writing courses generally teach students to write memos, letters, and reports. Many courses focus on one genre, such as report writing or letter writing.

Overemphasis on the letter-writing genre seems to be decreasing. One reason is the trend away from the formulaic approach. The underlying strategy behind the formulaic "good news" or "bad news" letter applies equally to memos and presentations. Another reason is the recognition that our students will actually be spending more time at work writing memos than letters.[17]

Giving students the chance to write in business genres is helpful, but should not be the only focus of business writing courses. Why? Because such courses should emphasize the following additional differences between business and academic writing.

Different Audiences

A more important difference between business and academic writing has to do with the nature of the audience. Typical readers of an essay might be a professor, professional colleagues, or perhaps other students. These readers are interested in the analysis and thought process. On the other hand, typical readers of business writing — a boss, a subordinate, a customer — are interested in the results, the conclusion, the famous "bottom line." For example, a business writer should know that many managers routinely read the summary and conclusions section of a report, often skimming or skipping the body and the appendixes. An academic writer would not expect this kind of reading.

Teaching students the concept of audience analysis is crucial in any writing class. Methods of increasing audience motivation and interest are especially important in business writing. Furthermore, in business writing, audience analysis influences decisions about the next five areas I shall discuss: approach, highlighting, sentence structure, jargon, and word choice.

More Direct Approach

Given their readers, business writers cannot afford to be elegantly roundabout. Comparing the introduction to a work of literary criticism and the introduction to a memo provides a good contrast. Literary criticism — and, indeed, good freshman essays — will often have the thesis statement as the last sentence of the first paragraph. A memo, on the other hand, most often has the main idea stated first. The "bottom line," in fact, becomes the "top line." A paragraph provides another example. An academic paragraph may have its topic sentence first, last, or even in the middle. A business paragraph virtually always has its topic sentence first.

All good writing, in other words, is unified and emphatic. But business writing tends to be more direct, to use the beginning for emphasis rather than the ending.

Much More Highlighting

An academic essay looks different from a piece of business writing not only because of the genre, but also because of highlighting. The term *highlighting* refers to the use of headings and subheadings, page layout, typography (capital letters, underlining, bold face, italics), and lists to show both major organizational sections and main ideas. Once again, given readers who are likely to skim, it behooves a business writer to use highlighting techniques.

Teaching highlighting is not as easy as it may appear. For one thing, highlighting is not a mere matter of cosmetics. The underlying organization and structure must be sound. Therefore, mistakes in highlighting are often actually problems with organization. Similarly, the underlying coherence must be sound; mistakes in highlighting (especially use of lists) are often actually problems with transitions. Third, highlighting is not a matter of slapping on meaningless "category labels" such as "Background" or "Procedure." Instead, highlighting should actually show the main ideas, such as "Procedure for New Inventory System." Finally, highlighting involves tough choices about what the writer wants to emphasize, to differentiate visually from the rest of the document.

All good writing, in other words, is organized and coherent. But business writing tends to use highlighting to make that organization and coherence unmistakably obvious.

Different Sentence Structure Decisions

At the sentence level, all good writing should be clear — avoiding, for instance, overused noun chains, weak verbs, and inappropriate passive verbs. Let us take the passive as an example. Writing to busy readers means that business writers must be especially careful to avoid all of the familiar problems inherent in the passive: slowing down readers, adding unnecessary words, being pompous, making their meaning unclear, and coming off as a weak and indirect person. On the other hand, business writers are working within a business environment. You can imagine situations in which they might more appropriately tell their boss "time is being wasted at meetings" than "you are wasting time at meetings" or tell a committee "several objections might be raised" instead of "I have several objections." Use of the passive, then, should become a strategic choice for business writers.[17] I have my students write "passive" in the margin and turn in an explanation to prove they are making a conscious, strategic choice rather than falling into an unconscious habit.

Different Jargon Choices

All good writers eschew pompous words and unnecessary jargon. We find a special kind of pomposity in business writing — words like *optimal* for *best, fiscal expenditure* for *cost, parameter* for *limit, the undersigned* for *me,* and *locality* for *place,* and phrases such as *pursuant to your request* for *as you requested* and *attached hereto please find* for *here is.*

The matter of professional jargon, however, is more difficult for many writing instructors to deal with. Every profession has its own jargon; sometimes jargon can be a useful, appropriate, and efficient means of communication. I have seen writing instructors' credibility completely undermined because they insist that a business writer can *never* use terms such as *CEO, LIFO,* or *ROI* (meaning, by the way, Chief Executive Officer; Last In, First Out; and Return on Investment). The business writing instructor's job is to get students to save jargon for audiences for whom it furthers communication, rather than blocks it.

Different Proper Word Choices

Misuse of words like *anxious* to mean *eager, enthuse* to mean *be enthusiastic, impact* to mean *affect, interface* to mean *discuss, mandate* to mean *require, via* to mean *by means of,* and *viable* to mean *workable* — that is, not using words precisely as the dictionary defines them — is typically more important to writing instructors than it is to business students. Some business writing teachers waste what seems to me too much time and energy rigidly prescribing correct usage and attempting to obliterate incorrect usage. Others are remiss, spending no time at all on this issue — perhaps influenced by descriptive linguistics, but more likely out of laziness or weariness.

The challenge for business writing teachers is to get their students to maintain a sensible middle ground.[18] Business writers become sensitive to both the traditions and the changes in language: they should uphold tradition without being too rigid, be open-minded without being too permissive.

Summary

A large number of relatively motivated students are taking business communication from instructors with various backgrounds. The curriculum varies tremendously, often including public relations, media relations, technology, communication theory, organizational theory, strategy, interpersonal skills, and — most often — speaking skills in addition to writing. The writing curriculum itself differs from academic writing courses by nature of differences in genres, audience, approach, highlighting, sentence choices, jargon choices, and proper word choices. Finally, I cannot resist noting that if this article were a business memo, this paragraph — or "executive summary" — would have come first.

Notes

1. American Assembly of Collegiate Schools of Business, *Newsline* (Oct. 1985).

2. For more information on these and other programs, see the *Journal of Business Communication* and the *ABC Bulletin* (University of Illinois, English Building, 608 South Wright Street, Urbana, Ill. 61801). See especially C. D. Porterfield's "Toward the Integration of Communication and Management" in the Winter 1980 *Journal* and M. Munter's "Trends in Management Communication" in the Winter 1982 *Journal;* and R. Gieselman, "Megatrends" in the December 1985 *Bulletin.* Also, *IEEE Transactions on Professional Communication* (445 Hoes Lane, Piscataway, N.J. 08854) ran a special issue on management communication in September 1985. Finally, the AACSB publishes a compilation of course syllabi from various undergraduate and graduate schools, titled *New Directions for Business Communication* (available from Chuck Hickman, AACSB, Suite 220, 605 Old Ballas Road, St. Louis, Mo. 63141).

3. B. Bowman, "What Helps or Harms Promotability?" *Harvard Business Review* (Jan./Feb. 1964).

4. A. Edge and R. Greenwood, "How Managers Rank Knowledge, Skills and Attributes Possessed by Business Administration Graduates," *AACSB Bulletin* (Oct. 1974).

5. H. Hildebrandt, F. A. Bond, E. L. Miller, and A. W. Swinyard, "An Executive Appraisal of Courses Which Best Prepare One for General Management," the *Journal of Business Communication* (Winter 1983). For further citations regarding the importance of communication in business, see footnote #1 to the Hildebrandt article.

6. P. Drucker, *The Practice of Management* (New York: Harper & Row, 1954); H. Mintzberg, *The Nature of Managerial Work* (New York: Harper & Row, 1973); L. Sayles, *Managerial Behavior* (New York: McGraw-Hill, 1964); J. Kotter, "What Effective General Managers Really Do," *Harvard Business Review* (Nov./Dec. 1982).

7. W. Ouchi, *Theory Z: How American Business Can Meet the Japanese Challenge* (Reading, Mass.: Addison-Wesley, 1981); R. T. Pascale, *The Art of Japanese Management* (New York: Simon and Schuster, 1981); and T. Peters and R. Waterman, In Search of Excellence (New York: Harper & Row, 1982).

8. For more on remediation, see C. Daniel, "Communication Course First, Remedial English Afterward," *ABCA Bulletin* (Dec. 1983).

9. AACSB, *Newsline* (Oct. 1985).

10. This list was inspired, in part, by remarks of Professor Carter Daniel at Rutgers Graduate School of Management. Although I disagree with parts of his article, I highly recommend "Remembering Our Charter: Business Communication at the Crossroads" in the *Journal of Business Communication* (Summer 1983).

11. Usually. But not always. See "Journalism and Business Writing: A Roundtable" in the *ABCA Bulletin* (Sept. 1983).

12. See, for example, A. Shelby, "A Teaching Module: Corporate Advocacy" in the *ABCA Bulletin* (June 1984); M. Munter, "How to Conduct a Media Interview," *California Management Review* (Summer 1983); and P. Argenti, "Advanced Management Communication," *Journal of Business Communication* (Fall 1986): 69–73.

13. For more on computers in business communication courses, see M. Munter, "Using Computers in Business Communication Courses," *Journal of Business Communication* (Winter 1986).

14. See, for example, J. Yates, "Graphs as a Managerial Tool: A Case Study of DuPont's Use of Graphs in the Early Twentieth Century," *Journal of Business Communication* (Winter 1985).

15. See, for example, C. Kelly and W. Page, "Theoretical Model for Teaching Oral and Written Communication" (New York: New York University Communication Program, unpublished manuscript).

16. For more on the concept of "translation," see J. Forman, "Designing Writing Instruction of Planned Change," *The Writing Instructor* (Dec. 1985). For more on the distinctions between academic writing and other kinds of writing, see P. Elbow, *Writing with Power: Techniques for Mastering the Writing Process* (New York: Oxford University Press, 1981).

17. J. Fielden, "What Do You Mean You Don't Like My Style?" *Harvard Business Review* (May/June 1982).

18. For more on the concept of the "sensible middle ground," see G. Nunberg, "The Decline of Grammar," *The Atlantic Monthly* (Dec. 1983).

14 The Professional Writing Program and the English Department

John Brereton
University of Massachusetts at Boston

As the earlier chapters in this volume make abundantly clear, a rich variety of excellent research is currently being done in professional writing. Given the existence of this new work and the promise of much more to come, how will its influence be felt in teaching and learning? To ask that question is to recognize that most of the teaching and research will be carried on in English departments, places that have been reluctant to grant adequate recognition to the more practical, nonliterary sides of their subject. To what extent will the good research being done in professional writing find continued support in English departments? Will faculty be encouraged to develop additional courses and, ultimately, professional writing programs? Most important of all, what will it take to allow professional writing to prosper within traditional departments of English?

Predecessors of Professional Writing

As we think about the future, it becomes instructive to recall how professional writing's predecessors, particularly business and technical writing, fared during their long associations with English programs. Courses in technical writing, which came along early in this century, were offered in response to an obvious need: engineers required to write technical reports needed to learn the appropriate style and format. Most technical writing courses assumed that the significant questions (what to teach, how to judge success) would be determined by the subject specialists, engineering faculty; the writing teacher's role was merely to show students "the writing side": grammar, spelling, punctuation, style, and formatting devices.

Built in from the outset, in addition to the rather limited practical aim, was the notion that the English teacher was to carry out the wishes of experts in other fields. It was also understood that, for the English department, technical writing was purely a matter of instruction; basic research was not required, even if it treated crucial professional issues such as the nature of communication among engineers or how rhetorical analysis can help determine why certain formats work better than others. Consequently, technical writing research was primarily pedagogical. Teachers described how they organized their lessons or how they got their students interested in one part of the subject. Specialists also involved themselves in endless discussions of what technical writing really is.[1] As Carolyn Miller has noted, technical writing textbooks remained unsophisticated, embodying a naïve, positivist view of rhetoric and continually emphasizing form and style at the expense of invention.[2]

Not surprisingly, few English faculty members regarded technical writing as a worthy field of inquiry, a body of real knowledge. The subject, confined to meeting demands that other disciplines had set, represented a kind of outer-directedness (to borrow David Riesman's term) that has never led to prosperity in a college of arts and sciences. As a result, rarely were there more than two technical writing courses on any campus, and rarely were nonengineering students encouraged to take them. Often, liberal arts students were not permitted to fulfill their humanities requirement with technical writing, a way of making it plain to all that the courses were for the convenience of engineers and that the English department left to its own devices would not have taught them. Indeed, in some elite colleges, technical writing when taught at all was the province of the engineering school; the English department bypassed the subject altogether, thus avoiding the onus of having to hire (and perhaps give tenure to) specialists in the field.

Business writing, like technical writing, was created to fill a marginal, supplementary role and thus shared an equally low status. Pressure from business faculty (who emphasized the importance of communication but often had an overly simple notion of the process) often forced English faculty (who were more interested in literature than communication) to take on the task of teaching business students how to write sales proposals, memos, and corporate correspondence. Success or failure was measured by business people's standards, not professors'. If anything, business writing was held in even lower esteem than technical writing.

For most colleges most of this century, then, technical writing and business writing were considered dully practical stuff, barely connected in practice to the liberal arts, disdained by English teachers as beneath the notice of a humanist.[3] At the same time, the old-fashioned courses, with their limited horizons and naïve faith in formats, were hardly worthy of great respect. If such courses today represented the best of professional writing, I think English departments would be entirely right to stay away from them. But as this volume helps show, professional writing, after many years in the academic wilderness, is rapidly moving somewhere very different indeed.

The lowly state of professional writing persisted until very recently; even a decade ago signs of change were only just becoming visible. In 1975, *Options for the Teaching of English*,[4] based on the Modern Language Association's survey of the undergraduate curriculum at twenty-three colleges, described what was to be the start of a significant trend: increasing numbers of students, majors and nonmajors alike, were signing up for advanced writing courses of all types: technical, business, journalistic, legal, and scientific. English departments responded by adding a variety of upper-level writing courses. But *Options* reveals that there was no uniform pattern to the change; some colleges added whole arrays of courses, while others added a single course in journalism here, one in business writing there.

Only one department in the *Options* survey, Carnegie–Mellon's, reacted to new enrollments by dramatically changing the major and creating new sequences of courses to provide advanced instruction in professional writing. That is, Carnegie–Mellon's department had created a genuine professional writing program.[5] Since the *Options* 1975 survey, demand for advanced writing has grown dramatically, and professional writing has emerged even more as a field of its own. Many colleges have followed Carnegie–Mellon's lead and increased their offerings of advanced writing courses. Nonetheless, relatively few colleges have offered genuine *programs*, coherent sequences of course work and advising that supply students with real expertise as professional communicators. To this day, I suspect that few departments considering professional writing have a clear idea of what a program should look like or how it might affect the other departmental programs.

The Role of English Departments Today

With this bit of history behind us, we can move to the present and ask the key question: How can English departments offering professional writing provide the most effective teaching and learning environment for students and faculty alike? What most departments have done in the past — simply add new courses — is not necessarily the best thing to try, and certainly not the first. Instead, I maintain that faculty members must engage in some longer range thinking: to understand what current courses are accomplishing; to rethink their sense of the department and its programs to see where professional writing would best fit in; and to determine how well the existing programs are meeting student needs. In other words, professional writing should not be seen as an add-on; rather, it will require determining how the department's whole array of programs and policies might be affected. And I would suggest that professional writing, viewed not as some alien technology but as a special type of rhetoric, a genuinely liberal art, will fit very comfortably within most English departments.

Any professional writing program, no matter how constituted, must address itself to many different audiences: engineers and business majors required to take additional writing courses; students seeking careers as professional communicators (in journalism, publishing, public relations, and so forth); English majors who want courses to make them more employable upon graduation; and students who want to take an elective or two in specialized writing. It is conventional to distinguish two distinct groups among these students: the very small group who will become professional writers and the much larger group who will become professionals whose jobs require them to write. Neither group will be helped very much by the simple availability of one or two courses, but both will benefit from the presence of a coherent professional writing program, even if they take only a part of it. The program I will be suggesting, a strand of courses and a carefully structured internship, will provide an excellent liberal arts background that will also enable students to prepare for careers as professional communicators. At the same time, the successful operation of such a program will influence the way the English department trains professionals who write. In addition, all advanced composition and technical and business writing courses will be invigorated by the presence of additional course work, new faculty, and a more central place in the department's structure.[6] So before attempting to meet every possible type of student need in an isolated, ad hoc fashion (as has been the past practice), departments would do best to determine how much of a professional writing program they are capable of maintaining, or what parts of a full program best suit their needs.

The prime question in shaping an appropriate program is, what kinds of knowledge do students need? Everyone can agree on the simplest answer, a high degree of skill in writing. A good program should aim at nothing less than the mastery of many different styles, conventions, and formats, from the interview to the proposal to the précis to the narrative.[7] These should be taught so well and practiced so often that they become almost second nature, as they do, say, with newspaper reporters. The columnist Bob Greene claimed that the really difficult part of his job was coming up with the idea, the point. After that, he said, "The piece often writes itself." What he meant, I suspect, is that he knew how to place his writing process at the service of an idea or perception; his years as a writer had enabled him to turn out good prose routinely, as long as he had a good idea to start with (radio interview on the Larry King Show, aired on WEEI, Boston, February 1986). Such a skill operates productively across all disciplines and is by no means the province of journalism. Indeed, many business people write a good deal more than Greene's three columns a week; how much more productive they could be if they shared the conscious knowledge of the writing process Greene brings to his work. A good writing program ought to provide such good stylistic and editorial abilities (and the confidence that goes with them) that writers can immediately focus on larger and more important rhetorical concerns. And that part of writing, the development of a serviceable style that can be produced upon demand, certainly can be taught to a wide variety of students.

Beyond mastery of writing styles and formats comes skill in handling writing situations and settings: judging what really matters in a writing assignment; planning the work in order to meet deadlines; working in a group when the credit will go to someone else; asking an editor or supervisor the right questions about the assignment. These abilities are second nature to good speechwriters, managers, copywriters, or legislative assistants. Building them into more courses (and not just writing courses) will provide students with valuable experience for every subject, not just for careers as professional writers.

Next comes subject knowledge of a particular field. Here a program cannot realistically claim to provide anything approaching an in-depth understanding. For students coming from business and technical programs it can rely on a year or two of exposure to the profession. For others, however, the program can arrange to give students a working knowledge of a field's concepts and patterns of thought by means of internships and fieldwork experiences, which can then be discussed further in the classroom to provide a richer understanding of the field.

Finally, beyond writing style, settings, and subject knowledge comes something much less easy to define, which goes by the name of analytical ability or critical thinking and represents the kind of intelligence that should infuse all good writing. It is definitely not Aristotelian logic or a head for complex calculations, nor is it simple common sense. It's there when newspaper reporters and editors, working under tight deadlines, can get to the heart of the story in a single sentence, the lead. It's present in a sales conference, when someone can state exactly why this product is better than the competition. It's there when the footnotes in a company's annual report are explicit about the accounting measures employed.[8] It appears when a critic describes how the language of a certain passage of prose or poetry produces its effect in readers. It's a question of focusing immediately on the issues that matter. It is tempting to call this ability *problem solving*, but such a term limits it too much. It has to do with the *imagination* necessary to grasp an issue, to see connections between the present and the future, to ask "what if." Sometimes it's even needed to recognize that a problem exists. Although analytical ability does not fit in neatly with any curriculum — and we should not pretend that a program can teach it upon demand — it grows from a traditional liberal arts education. Here the ability to research a problem, to combine fact, inference, and speculation, seems especially useful. If liberal arts courses are not focused on exercising the imagination, on making connections, on seeing issues in a new light, then they are not preparing students to develop their analytical ability.

Elements of an Effective Program

Successful mastery of writing style, setting, subject knowledge, and analytical ability can lead to a superbly prepared student. The question is, how do they get implemented within the course and staffing structure of a typical English department? I believe successful preparation will stem from five distinct areas: composition courses, literature courses, new courses, programs (major, minor, certificates), and personnel.

Composition Courses

Composition courses, often the major part of a department's instruction, would seem to be the logical starting place for a good grounding in professional writing, especially since instructors have recently begun to concentrate on writing as more than simply the accurate transmission of a message. They have come to understand that the terms they once confidently used — clarity, revision, planning, audience — are highly problematical. Some of the best contemporary thinkers — Donald Murray, Janet Emig, Peter Elbow, among others — emphasize writing as a way of thinking and learning, a way of making sense of the world and of one's experiences. This process approach has inevitably involved a diminution of interest in the written product. Instead of getting it right (as if *right* had ever been so simple), students are encouraged to explore, to free-write, to engage in multiple drafts, to revise as a way of discovering their thoughts.

This extraordinarily rich and productive work, a necessary reaction to the overly prescriptive, exclusively product-oriented instruction that dominated until the 1960s, is having significant impact. What remains to be done, I think, is to build on the process approach, to extend it to incorporate more about the transaction between writer and reader. How, for instance, is the written message situated in the spectrum of communication? In different settings, a piece of writing takes on different roles: as something to think with; as a trial balloon; as a working draft; as response (genuine or feigned); as part of a paper trail; as finished piece of work. Often, indeed, the requirements of the text and situation determine the kind of approach a writer will take. We all know this, of course; rhetoricians have preached it for centuries. Yet little of it is embodied in composition courses, even when they are infused with the best contemporary thinking.

A single example will make my point: Emig and Elbow vigorously condemn the outline, yet professional writers (for example, those who write software manuals) must always submit an outline before getting approval to begin a piece of writing. Such a hierarchical writing structure is hardly process oriented (it may, in fact, help explain why those software manuals are so hard to read), but short of changing industry attitudes, submitting a formal outline will remain part of many professionals' job descriptions. Thus professional writing programs, no matter how influenced by the process approach, need to teach outlining, both the informal kind that aids thinking early in the composing process and the more elaborate kind that professionals submit.[9]

If the new thinking about the composing process needs to include the roles played by task and format in professional settings, the traditional composition course requires thorough revision. Freshman English has changed greatly in the past generation, but in many places it still remains a bastion of belletristic prose. Though explicitly literary texts have often been jettisoned, their place has been taken by a pantheon of essayists, a new canon of composition that begins with Swift's *A Modest Proposal* and jumps to twentieth century essayists such as Orwell, White, Baldwin, Didion, Angelou, McPhee, Wolfe, Gould, and Thomas. I submit that these writers are frequently taught and studied for their aesthetic qualities and that composition courses concentrating on them are often literature courses in disguise. It's not that they are not superb writers or that the issues they choose to write about are not important. It's just that by themselves they represent a very narrow range of stylistic options available to the beginning writer.

The model provided by so many of our best essayists is of an individual writing alone, with all the time in the world, about some subject he or she has freely chosen and is enthralled by. It's Montaigne in his tower, not the writer in the world facing deadlines, editors, collaborators, and demands for precise, highly focused prose of predetermined scope and format. In the traditional composition course, students are rarely introduced to the kind of top down writing required by news articles, for instance, or the summary and précis writing so common in the workplace. They never try their hand at a lead or a heading or an advertising slogan, or experiment with formatting devices such as numerical outlines or the manipulation of white space. These are not arcane skills far removed from an English department's purview; they are essential parts of the communication process that dramatically affect readers' perceptions. Without exposure to these professional tools, students will miss the chance to analyze and practice a significant part of human discourse. And need it be said that advocating a wider range of discourse does not mean confining composition solely to mundane, utilitarian, applied tasks? On the contrary, students who try out advertising slogans or headlines — in addition to traditional essays — often learn some nice lessons in how a reader's attention gets manipulated.[10]

Fortunately, the last decade has seen the appearance of some excellent texts that combine intellectual rigor with explorations of the rich variety of styles and formats available to writers: McQuade and Atwan, *Popular Writing in America*; Bazerman, *The Informed Writer*; and Behrens and Rosen, *Writing and Reading Across the Curriculum* all go beyond the traditional fare found in most composition readers and rhetorics, yet encourage a kind of analysis that is thoroughly in keeping with the liberal arts at their best.[11] The fact that all three enjoy good sales is an encouraging sign that many composition instructors are expanding the permissible range of material they cover.

Composition courses can also teach students how to apply analytical and rhetorical techniques to a wider range of formats. One kind of critical analysis that seems especially fruitful is illustrated by a section of Richard Ohmann's *English in America*,[12] in which the executive memos included in the *Pentagon Papers* demonstrate how the constraints of the memo form itself prevented anyone's using it to raise serious questions about the government's ultimate purposes. This kind of close analysis reveals how the format exerts a manipulative force on the writer. Ohmann's technique, brought to bear on the internal communications of bureaucracy, demonstrates one way that English departments can combine literary criticism with rhetoric to bring a richer understanding of writing in professional settings. Why is so little of it available in composition readers or rhetorics?

Literature Courses

It should not be amiss to suggest that literature courses can constitute an important part of any writer's training. This is particularly true if the course work is aimed at strengthening imagination and conceptualization, thus fulfilling one of the promises of a liberal arts education — that graduates will be able to analyze issues and write about them well, much better than their peers in other programs. If English majors do not learn to do so through their traditional literature courses, it is unrealistic to expect that some advanced writing courses added on will result in superior writing. And the technical or business writing teacher who wants to place high demands on students needs to rely on good preparation in the department's core courses.

In addition to introducing students to reading strategies and the range of literary accomplishment, literature courses foster conceptualization, analysis, structure — in short, thinking. Departments require students to read great works of literature for many good reasons, but simply to read them for the exposure, the experience, is hardly sufficient. If literature does not help students think and imagine better, to think about their thinking, then it is not doing enough. My colleague Ann E. Berthoff tells of one well-read student who suddenly realized, in a flash of insight, that elements of a poem — tone, meter, images, vocabulary, and so forth — could be regarded like the words of the U.S. Constitution, as *something to think with*. What had seemed so obvious to her other students was not at all apparent to him, despite his having taken a good number of literature courses. What were those courses doing? If students do not learn interpretation and rhetoric and poetics in literature courses — where those are the ostensible subject matter — then it is hard to see how they will learn them anywhere else.

Internships

Relatively few English departments have invested much energy in an internship program, probably because this sort of thing is not considered fully respectable. Where the internship exists, it often was set up quickly in response to demands from above. Its coordinator, rarely a senior professor at the center of things, is frequently overburdened with students and paper work. Placements are somewhat haphazard, with the match between intern and job done at the last minute. Monitoring always remains a problem, and it is often impossible to get all of the interns together for a meeting. For the internship to become a real part of the English program, a department must be willing to supply the care, structure, and commitment needed. When that happens, a strong internship will become the centerpiece of the entire professional writing sequence.

A department's role begins with providing adequate preparation so that students entering internships are not starting from scratch or failing to live up to the employer's expectations. This training can be very brief; in some cases a few hours are frequently enough. I recall a student, an excellent writer, who began a newspaper internship without knowing precisely what was meant by a lead or a sidebar. She spent two frustrating weeks catching up, when a brief exposure to terminology and two hours of practice would have saved her endless trouble. In other settings, more elaborate preparation could take the form of carefully planned course work linked to good advising. For instance, anyone contemplating doing writing for or about business should take the first two courses in accounting before embarking on an internship. Someone headed for technical writing would benefit from advanced work in mathematics and computer science. Similarly, an English major planning to enter advertising would be smart to take a first-rate course in graphic design before the internship. The right preparation will make for a better internship; not only will the best prepared student get the most attractive job, but what will be learned will be integrated into an already existing framework. Although many internships are unattractive because they pay too little, good preparation can be used to justify a satisfactory salary.

Missing from most internships is good follow-up, which serves to reintegrate the learning into the curriculum. Ideal follow-up is an internship seminar — during or after the term in which the internship is completed — which allows interns to continue or expand on the research undertaken on the job. My present professional writing seminar contains students who recently held internships at newspapers, in state and local government, TV, magazines, and corporations. They are able to apply their firsthand knowledge of the different writing tasks in those settings to larger questions of the communications process. Their presence makes for a richer class, one in which the relationships between theory and practice are visible at all times. Too often, I fear, the internship has been viewed solely as a means of career preparation, completely separate from the curriculum. Often it has become an early goodbye to college. It makes more sense to put it earlier, in junior year, and then to view it as a chance to get practical experience, which can *then* be connected to more classroom learning.

One practical way to build in adequate preparation and good follow-up is to establish an advisory board that meets formally a few times a year but whose members are willing to be available for informal contacts whenever necessary. The board needs a diverse membership: friends of the department who know the job market; recent graduates who want to see the department remain up to date; business people and professionals with long experience in their fields. The board's role includes keeping the department current on the fit between its programs and the job market; supplying ideas for new courses and programs; making connections for internships and job placements; helping shape and support department curriculum initiatives and grant proposals. Sometimes it is extraordinarily helpful to run an idea by someone in touch with the daily life of a professional; a board makes it possible to get advice by picking up the phone. The idea of a board might give rise to worries. Some will fear that a board will be far too practical minded and job oriented and will want to turn a college into a vocational school. No doubt that is possible; much depends on how the board is selected. But my experience has been just the opposite; advisory boards I have worked with want colleges to remain colleges, but are quite willing to advise on matters of fit between college programs and what happens to students after graduation.

New Courses

Only after a department has strengthened the core of its program should new courses be considered. In many cases, rethinking composition and literature courses and adding or revamping an internship will be enough to provide students the training they need. For instance, existing business or technical writing courses will benefit immediately from the general improvement of all writing course work, since students will be enrolling in them with much stronger preparation.[13] When the time comes to add a series of advanced writing courses that go beyond current offerings, a department ought to ask some probing questions: What specific knowledge will a new course offer beyond a new format and some additional practice? What kinds of thinking will it encourage? What is its intellectual content? Will the knowledge be general enough to enable students to adapt to new settings? That is, a professional writing course that merely aims to train students for entry level positions does not belong in a liberal arts department. If GM or the Pentagon or Legal Aid have a highly specialized way of writing, it is a mistake for colleges simply to devote themselves to teaching it. (Besides, GM is quite capable of teaching its format on its own.) English departments ought to offer rigorous writing courses that prepare students to assimilate any style, to adapt to any format, that of GM or of *PMLA*. If specialized courses do not provide the ability to adapt, to be critical, to analyze diverse approaches to different kinds of writing, to employ the imagination and intellect to their fullest capacity, then they are giving students an education that is neither liberal nor practical.

One essential priority of any new or revised professional writing course must be to connect writing and speaking more closely. By skimping on oral communication or relegating it to speech programs, English has too often failed to prepare students to become effective communicators and denied them one of the traditional benefits of a liberal arts education. One virtue of the old-fashioned technical and business writing course that still survives in its modern counterpart is its concentration on oral reporting skills, no matter how rudimentary. There, success or failure is public, and students quickly learn how well they meet their audience's expectations. (At some colleges, student presentations are given in a large auditorium, with the Dean of engineering in the audience.) Some may believe that a course or two in speech communication may solve the problem of oral communications; far better would be the reintegration of oral reporting assignments into the full range of English courses, not just those in composition. (Students can also be introduced to the proper use of technical aids, from overhead projectors to the new "smart" message boards.)

Similarly, students can get more understanding of the context in which communication operates by gaining technical knowledge of the production side: printing, graphics, paste-ups and mechanicals, professional copyediting, layout, and design. Many colleges once offered a course in printing books by hand, an introduction to the craft of publishing that was especially attractive to creative writers who could see their work go from conception to finished product in one term. An up-to-date alternative would be a workshop or an internship in computer-based printing, either with a mainframe or desktop publishing. Donald Knuth, author of *The Art of Computer Programming*, reports that his Stanford students respond enthusiastically to computer typesetting:

> I would say that about 60 percent of our students get infected with the idea that they can do beautiful typesetting. Therefore,

they are writing better term papers. They are thinking more about the problem of communication, and, since they are in control of it and don't have to explain a notation to some intermediary, then they are coming up with better notations. They will now consider a part of their own job description to be communicating in type, which they never would have thought if they had only a typewriter. My own experience is mainly with computer science students, but other parts of the community are affected too. You find a lot of chemists and a lot of physicists, and musicians to a great extent.[14]

The success of Knuth's computer science course depends on building in the aesthetic element, leaving space for imagination and technology and knowledge to combine.

Besides hands-on graphics, printing, or typesetting experience, today's students simply must possess facility with word processing. An entire course in the subject is hardly necessary; many good microcomputer and mainframe word-processing programs require only an active mind and a few hours' practice to enable an intelligent beginner to start in. Even the truly powerful microcomputer programs professionals use, for example, XyWrite (a relative of the ATEX system used in many newsrooms), Microsoft Word, or Word Perfect, can be running in a week if tutoring is available. The obvious place for requiring that all work be done on computer is in an intermediate or advanced course, where classes are smaller and instructors can count on a greater degree of computer literacy. A related skill is using computer graphics capabilities successfully. Too little is known of how graphics work *rhetorically*; yet without a feel for what graphics can do, a report writer finds them a burden rather than an opportunity.[15]

Programs

What will a professional writing sequence look like? Though the answer will of course vary according to a department's outlook and capabilities, it will probably begin as a small, high quality program leading to a minor, a certificate, or a concentration within the major. A typical program might offer a five- or six-course sequence such as the following:

> *Intermediate Composition.* Stress on style as a function of information being conveyed to different audiences; group work; introduction to different formats; word processing; preparation for internship. Since this course admits students to the professional writing sequence, a low grade ought to deter future work in the field. This course will also be the first part of a sequence required of business and engineering students.

Advanced Composition. Different sections aimed at specific disciplines such as engineering, science, management, and journalism. Students can take the course twice, each time with a different emphasis. Stress is on the formats and approaches required of specific job situations (for example, report assignments are determined in consultation with faculty of different disciplines). Oral presentations with visual aids required where appropriate. Case method especially effective here. Second part of sequence taken by engineers and business majors.

Internship. Open only to those who have completed Intermediate Composition. Requires demanding writing project, successful completion of job assignment, and regular meetings with faculty advisor. Can be done twice in different settings.

Internship Seminar. A senior-level course in professional communications, building upon experience of students who have had on-the-job training. Emphasis upon analyzing the role of communications in their settings, including readership analysis, criteria for success, and structure for decision making.

Electives (for example, sociolinguistics, communication, creative writing, nonfiction prose, English prose style). The precise nature of these electives will depend upon the quality and interests of the participating faculty members. Any of these subjects could be appropriate, but better none of these electives than weak ones. That is, the right kind of sociolinguistics course (say, one based on Hymes, Labov, Goffman, or Geertz) would be superb; a weak one would actually detract from the program. Similarly, some creative writing courses can build confidence and facility with the written word, while others that focus entirely on literary expression and aesthetics might not be as suitable.

Whether professional writing is a certificate or a minor or a track within the major does not matter. It is more important that the courses form a coherent sequence and are tied together by good faculty, a common goal, and full department commitment.[16] Many students will take only one or two courses rather than the whole sequence; the effect of an excellent small program, whatever its configuration, can be expected to spread well beyond its boundaries and thus lead to changes in unlikely places. For instance, a professional writing program will inevitably lead to a new emphasis on good advising and to a closer, more productive relationship with the college placement office. This can have only good effects on the department as a whole as students discover that the English department offers high quality, interesting learning *and* careers.

Personnel

Beyond curriculum decisions comes the issue of personnel. Faculty members appointed to teach professional writing should be carrying on research in the subject. In hiring them on tenure track lines, the department is in effect sponsoring their research as well as their teaching. Thus, the decision to hire someone who studies how professional documents get written signifies more than filling some empty classrooms; it indicates that such research is the sort of thing the department wants to be doing. And the initial hiring carries with it the responsibility of imposing reasonable criteria for tenure and promotion. For instance, it is unrealistic to expect a literary book from someone concentrating on professional writing. Since scholars in the field of professional writing tend to write texts and do consulting and collaborative work, the department's attitude toward such endeavors must be very clear. A faculty member's high daily fees, common in engineering or the sciences, will raise a few eyebrows in a department unused to consulting. Yet in some cases, faculty members who are not consulting are in danger of falling behind, since it is one of the best ways to keep in touch with new developments in the field.

Tenure and promotion standards are ultimately more than a question of fairness or morale; they become indices of the department's real commitment to the subject. Is the department willing enough to hire first-rate writing people that it will rethink its criteria? (This is not an issue of *lowering* standards, of course; professional writing teachers should display the same quality in publication, teaching, and service as anyone else; it is more a matter of how departments interpret their existing standards.)

What can a vigorous, professional writing program contribute to an English department? The obvious answers begin with more student enrollment, either as majors or minors. Students from other disciplines will sign up for advanced work in technical or business writing as well as for other English courses. English majors will see that it is possible to combine a humanities major with genuine preprofessional training. Then there is the satisfying of deans' and administrators' natural desires to provide a better fit between instruction and student needs. These are perfectly sensible reasons, yet they should not impress a faculty committed to the liberal arts. No, professional writing has to contribute more, and I think it can. It can, for one thing, enable students to become better communicators and thus gain more control over their lives as well as their career options. And the research that accompanies such a program can shed light on the writing process itself by asking questions that include all forms of writing: How do professionals compose? What characterizes different genres of writing (the essay, technical writing, legal writing, scientific communication, to name prominent examples)? How is success measured in specialist writing? To what extent does format determine a writer's process? What precise role do the exigencies of publication play in the production and reception of prose? As such a list and the contributions to this volume show, there really is a subject here, a genuine field of intellectual inquiry worthy of the best liberal arts tradition.

Furthermore, close study of professional writing as artifact, as object, can sharpen the way even the most thoughtful critics tend to read cultural history. Raymond Williams, hardly a belletrist, has blandly stated that "the most important development in English prose since 1780 is the emergence of the novel as the major literary form" (*Writing in Society*, p. 73).[17] Such an unqualified statement depends on one's purview. I would argue that during the nineteenth century the dramatic growth of bureaucratic and business reports and the rise of technical writing had a much more significant impact upon English prose than the novel did. Such an impact may not appear obvious in Arnold, Carlyle, Ruskin, Eliot, Mill, or Trollope, despite the long years they spent as professionals writing nonfiction. But it shows up more plainly in thousands of unknown writers doing the world's work. My point is not to debate Williams but to suggest that serious research into professional writing can do more than garner students and provide practical avenues to careers. By establishing a professional writing program, an English department may find an unexpected dividend: some new, richer ways of regarding traditional literary studies as well.

Notes

1. One can easily discern the parallels with regular composition courses, which in the past, with a few notable exceptions, dutifully devoted themselves to many of the same tasks.
2. Carolyn R. Miller, "A Humanistic Rationale for Technical Writing," *College English* 40, 6 (Feb. 1979): 610, 614.
3. What good research went on occurred at universities where separate departments were established (such as at Michigan), or at places where the liberal arts never assumed a dominant position (such as at Rensselaer

Polytechnic Institute). Business and technical writing professors at such institutions well understood how to conduct research in professional communications.

4. Elizabeth Cowan, ed., *Options for the Teaching of English* (New York: Modern Language Association, 1975).

5. I doubt the wisdom of aiming all students toward such neat categories, particularly while they are still deciding upon their majors.

6. At present, many business and engineering faculty warn that English departments are not the best places to teach professional writing. In one recent article, for instance, engineering programs were told that when they send "students to English departments to learn technical communication, they risk having their students taught principles that are in conflict with engineering principles." See J. C. Mathes, Dwight Stevenson, and Peter Klaver, "Technical Communication: The Engineering Educator's Responsibility," *Engineering Education* 69 (Jan. 1979): 332. One has to agree; most English departments at present lack sufficient staff who understand the nature of communication in business or engineering. My argument here is that since those English departments are now teaching advanced writing and will be doing more of it in the future, they had better start hiring and promoting the right people. In this case, the right people not only understand engineering and business principles, but are able to help articulate and clarify those principles to their professional colleagues through their research.

7. For an excellent bibliography of surveys covering the communication needs of different disciplines, see Elizabeth Tebeaux, "Redesigning Professional, Writing Courses to Meet the Communication Needs of Writers in Business and Industry," *College Composition and Communication* 36, 4 (Dec. 1985): 427–28.

8. In reading annual reports, experts claim they usually ignore the glossy pictures and rosy prose and instead head directly to the bottom line and the footnotes. George H. Sorter, professor of accounting at New York University, relies on the *style* of the footnotes as well: "Footnotes that are detailed and clear often go hand in hand with a company that is doing well and whose management is confident. Abridged, confusing footnotes often are a warning sign. . . . Most notes are written not to disclose but to hide." Eric N. Berg, "Plumbing a Company's Biography," in *New York Times*, Sunday, 1 June 1986 (sec. 12: *Personal Investing*: 46).

9. Linda Flower's description of the issue tree in *Problem Solving Strategies for Writers*, 2d ed. (San Diego: Harcourt Brace Jovanovich, 1985, 95–107) provides an outlining technique halfway between the informal and the elaborate. Janet Emig and Peter Elbow attack the teaching process that requires a complete outline before any writing is committed to paper. This richly deserved condemnation of teaching with outlines spills over in Emig to an attack on all outlines. For instance, Emig was delighted to discover that, in the group of professionals she surveyed about their writing practice, only half used outlines (among them, not surprisingly, was B. F. Skinner). See Emig, *The Composing Process of Twelfth Graders* (Urbana, Ill.: National Council of Teachers of English, 1971); and Elbow, *Writing without Teachers* (New York: Oxford University

Press, 1973). In contrast to Emig and Elbow, Donald Murray, whose background includes a career as a journalist, seems much more aware of the constraints facing professionals when writing. See especially Murray, *Writing for Your Readers* (Chester, Conn.: Globe Pequot Press, 1983).

10. My students were shocked when I assigned a one-sentence blurb and planned to count it the same as a two-page analytical essay. But when I explained how much billboards and television time cost, and how much effort goes into promotional campaigns or the search for an appropriate title, they understood instantly that quality and length are not synonymous.

11. Bazerman and Behrens and Rosen would benefit from sections specifically targeted at students heading for business; perhaps units on economics or business ethics would be most useful. See Charles Bazerman, *The Informed Writer,* 2d ed. (Boston: Houghton Mifflin, 1985); and Laurence Behrens and Leonard J. Rosen, *Writing and Reading across the Curriculum* (Glenview, Ill.: Scott Foresman/Little, Brown, 1988). See also Donald McQuade and Robert Atwan, *Popular Writing in America,* 4th ed. (New York: Oxford University Press, 1988).

12. Richard Ohmann, *English in America* (New York: Oxford University Press, 1975).

13. Elizabeth Tebeaux makes a strong argument against separate courses for disciplines such as business and engineering. She encourages heterogeneous grouping in writing courses, arguing that such grouping is what happens on the job (*CCC* 36 [Dec. 1985]: 422). I agree entirely that heterogeneous grouping works best *in the first course*. The second course can build on the first and focus on specific disciplines. Thus I see a three-course technical or business writing sequence: freshman composition, intermediate composition (Tebeaux's "heterogeneous grouping"), and advanced composition (offered as "Writing for Engineering" or "Writing for Business," though of course open to all students who can keep up with the work). Some might fear that many students will not survive such a sequence. I disagree, after having seen it in operation in a variety of settings, from open admissions to highly selective colleges.

14. Donald Knuth, "Computer Science Considerations," an interview conducted by G. Michael Vose and Gregg Williams. *Byte* 11, 2 (Feb. 1986): 172.

15. At present, "computerizing" freshman composition is just a budget-minded administrator's dream. From a faculty member's viewpoint, it makes much more sense to start with the smaller, more manageable enrollments in upper-level programs and then, in due time, to apply what has been learned to introductory courses.

16. Of course it does matter if all the department's other programs have the status of majors or minors and professional writing does not. Professional writing needs to be on a par with other, similar programs.

17. Raymond Williams, *Writing in Society* (Oxford: Oxford University Press, 1976).

Contributors

Virginia A. Book is professor of agricultural communications at the University of Nebraska–Lincoln, where she has served as coordinator of the technical communication teaching division. She is a past president of the Council for Programs in Technical and Scientific Communication, a fellow of the Association of Teachers of Technical Writing, and a fellow of the National Association of Colleges and Teachers of Agriculture. She serves on several editorial boards and is a consultant to businesses and government agencies. Among her publications are numerous articles on technical communication, including an annual bibliography.

John Brereton is associate professor of English at the University of Massachusetts at Boston. At Wayne State University, he directed the writing program and was codirector of the professional writing project on a grant from the Fund for the Improvement of Postsecondary Education. He has published articles on composition instruction, is the author of a rhetoric text, *A Plan for Writing*, and a reader, *Themes for College Writing*, and has edited *Traditions of Inquiry*, a collection of articles on the history of composition.

Edward P. J. Corbett is professor of English and director of advanced composition at The Ohio State University. Editor of *College Composition and Communication* (1974–79), he has also served on the editorial board of such journals as *Philosophy and Rhetoric, Style*, and *Quarterly Journal of Speech*. His numerous books include *Classical Rhetoric for the Modern Student, Rhetorical Analysis of Literary Works*, and *The Little English Handbook*.

Barbara Couture is associate professor in the English Department at Wayne State University, where she directs the composition program and has coordinated the technical writing program. Her publications include *Functional Approaches to Writing: Research Perspectives, Cases for Technical and Professional Writing* (coauthor, Jone Rymer), and several articles on the case method and linguistic approaches to technical and expository writing.

Donald H. Cunningham is professor of English and director of technical communication at Texas Tech University. He is a fellow of the Association of Teachers of Technical Writing and an associate fellow of the Society for Technical Communication. He was editor of *The Technical Writing Teacher* for ten years. Three of his recent textbooks are the third edition of *How to Write for the World of Work* (with Thomas E. Pearsall), *Creating Technical Manuals* (with Gerald Cohen), and *Fundamentals of Good Writing* (with Thomas E. Pearsall).

297

Dan Dieterich is professor of English at the University of Wisconsin-Stevens Point and founder of its administrative writing program. One-time chair of the CCCC Committee on Business Communication, he is a cofounder and current president of the Association of Professional Writing Consultants.

John L. DiGaetani is associate professor of English at Hofstra University in Hempstead, New York, and has taught business and technical communication at the Harvard Business School, Long Island University, and the University of New Orleans, in addition to Hofstra. He is the author of several books on business communication, including *Writing Out Loud: A Self-Help Guide to Clear Business Writing* and *Writing for Action: A Guide for the Health Care Professional.* He is also editor of *The Handbook of Executive Communication,* and his essays have appeared in many books and journals.

Linda Driskill is associate professor of administrative science and English at the Jesse H. Jones Graduate School of Administration of Rice University. A coauthor of *Decisive Writing* with Margaret Simpson, Dr. Driskill has written articles on trends in product liability and the writing of warnings, organizational communication theory, and corporate culture. She also serves as a corporate communications consultant for companies in the financial services and chemical industries.

Linda Flower is professor of English at Carnegie-Mellon University and codirector of the Center for the Study of Writing at Berkeley and Carnegie-Mellon; she was previously director of the business and professional writing program, Graduate School of Industrial Administration. Her work includes articles on writing research and a textbook, *Problem-Solving Strategies for Writing.*

Brian Gallagher is professor of English at LaGuardia Community College, CUNY, and adjunct professor of English at the Graduate Center, CUNY. A former director of composition, at present he directs a special program of computer-based intensive writing courses. He has written articles and books on literature (American, Afro-American, Irish), language, film, the teaching of writing, and the use of computers in higher education. Most recently, he has completed a biography of the American illustrator, Neysa McMein.

Robert D. Gieselman is associate professor of English and director of business and technical writing at the University of Illinois at Urbana-Champaign. He is the author of numerous books, articles, and reviews in business communication and an active consultant for business and publishing houses. Editor of the *Journal of Business Communication,* he is also the executive director of the Association for Business Communication.

George D. Gopen is director of writing programs, teacher of legal writing, and associate professor of English at Duke University, as well as lecturer on law at the Harvard Law School. As a consultant, he specializes in legal writing and is a partner in the firm of Clearlines, Inc. His publications include works on pedagogy, composition theory, and rhetorical analysis of literature.

C. H. Knoblauch is associate professor of English and director of writing at SUNY at Albany. He has served as a communication consultant in both business and government and has authored books and articles on rhetorical theory and composition.

Myra Kogen has taught professional writing at Hofstra University and LaGuardia Community College, CUNY, and was in charge of corporate training in writing at Chase Manhattan. She has published articles on business and technical writing and on literature and composition, and is currently a member of the CCCC Committee on Technical Communication. She directed an NEH-funded writing-across-the-curriculum program at Hofstra and now directs the Writing Center at Brooklyn College, CUNY.

David Lauerman is associate professor of English and assistant to the dean for academic development at Canisius College of Buffalo, New York, where he teaches developmental and professional writing courses and directs the Western New York Writing Project. He directed the Canisius writing-across-the-curriculum research project, reported in Odell and Goswami's *Writing in Nonacademic Settings,* and carries on research and consultation for local businesses.

Mary Munter is adjunct associate professor of management communication, The Amos Tuck School of Business Administration, Dartmouth College. She previously founded and directed the communication skills program at the Stanford Graduate School of Business. Her work includes various articles; a short guidebook, now in its second edition, *Guide to Managerial Communication;* and a new textbook, *Business Communication: Strategy and Skill.*

Nell Ann Pickett is professor of English at the Raymond Campus of Hinds Community College in Mississippi. She is past chair of the NCTE Committee on Technical and Scientific Communication and is editor of the journal *Teaching English in the Two-Year College.* Her works include five books on writing and numerous articles on technical writing. She founded the Institute in Technical Communication, held each summer in Mississippi.

Janice Redish is vice president and director of the Document Design Center at the American Institutes for Research in Washington, D.C. A linguist by training, she works with business and government agencies to improve the writing and design of all sorts of documents. She is the author of numerous articles on document design and the writing process.

Jone Rymer is associate professor of business communication in the School of Business Administration, Wayne State University. Her work includes *Cases for Technical and Professional Writing* (coauthored with Barbara Couture), which received an NCTE Scientific and Technical Communication Award. Among her other publications are articles on professional composing processes and the application of such research to teaching; one of these papers won the Best Article Award from the Society for Technical Communication.

Jack Selzer is associate professor of English and director of composition programs at Penn State University. Educated at Xavier University and Miami University, he teaches both introductory and advanced courses in composition, literature, and business and technical writing. His essays on composition, professional writing (and baseball) have appeared in many books and journals.